LUTHERAN
PRAYER BOOK,
FOR THE USE OF
FAMILIES AND INDIVIDUALS

PARTLY ORIGINAL, BUT CHIEFLY COMPILED
WITH
INTRODUCTORY REMARKS ON FAMILY PRAYER

BY

BENJAMIN KURTZ, D.D., LL.D.,

ORIGINAL PUBLISHING INFO:

BALTIMORE:
PUBLISHED BY T. NEWTON KURTZ,
NO. 151 WEST PRATT STREET
1860

LUTHERAN PRAYER BOOK, FOR THE USE OF **FAMILIES AND INDIVIDUALS** PARTLY ORIGINAL, BUT CHIEFLY COMPILED WITH **INTRODUCTORY REMARKS ON FAMILY PRAYER** By Benjamin Kurtz

Just & Sinner
425 East Lincoln Ave.
Watseka, IL 60970

www.JustandSinner.com

ISBN 10: 069261267X
ISBN 13: 9780692612675

PREFACE

TO THE FIRST EDITION

THOUGH it is believed that nothing will be found in this Prayer-book to prevent its free use in any Protestant Christian family, yet it has been prepared mainly with a view to the Lutheran Church. In the German language we are abundantly supplied with such helps; but in English, a general and complete Prayer-book, adapted to daily devotion, to special occasions, and to every emergency, has thus far remained a desideratum, which it has been our aim to supply. It is therefore hoped that the Lutheran Church especially will encourage this enterprise.

We greatly prefer that both ministers and laymen should pray *extempore*. Prompted and guided by the Holy Spirit, the prayers that come forth fresh from our own heart, couched in our own language, even though homely and defective, will be more likely to express our peculiar wants and to prove edifying to those who join in the solemn and delightful exercise. But there are seasons when even those who are accustomed to pray extempore would prefer the aid of a Prayer-book; heads of families, whose duty it is to lead in family-prayer twice a day for a long time, are in danger of falling into tautology, sameness, and consequent coldness and formality; and there are, moreover, many who are deterred altogether from attending to this important duty by diffidence or by supposed want of ability. The latter persuade themselves that to lead in social or family prayer is a *gift* which they do not possess, and cannot attain; and under this plea they neglect it entirely. To meet all these cases, so far as lay in our power, has been our great design.

A considerable number of "Occasional Prayers," suited to almost every supposable condition, will be found. These are designed to be incorporated in the daily morning and evening prayers, as circumstances may require. The precise point at which they are to be introduced is sufficiently indicated. They may, however, also be used separately or apart from the stated daily devotions.

A selection of Prayers for *Children* has also been appended, which, we trust, will not prove unacceptable to mothers and others, to whom the care of training up the "little ones" of our church has been assigned.

As the singing of God's praise is a delightful part of family devotion, a collection of HYMNS and TUNES has been added. The Hymns have been culled from various authors, but principally from the General Synod's Lutheran Hymn-book; and in the selection of the Music we have been aided by a gentleman of science as well as refined taste, in whose judgment in such matters we repose entire confidence.

With these remarks, we commend the book to God's blessing, hoping the church may find cause to approve of it, and earnestly praying that it may become one of the aids by which the great ends of the family organization shall be secured, and a means whereby the worship of God shall be extended and perpetuated among the families of this land, and especially of the Lutheran Church.

B. K.

BALTIMORE, April 1, 1852.

PREFACE

TO THE SECOND EDITION

THE first edition of this Book of Prayer, though amounting to nearly *four thousand copies*, was soon exhausted; which seems to indicate that the author did not form a wrong judgment, when he deemed a work of this kind in the English language, a desideratum in the Lutheran Church. The demand, since it has been sold out, has not only continued, but has been constantly increasing; and Latterly orders have also arrived from foreign countries, which has induced the publisher to have it stereotyped, so that he is now enabled to furnish it by tens of thousands at short notice and on more favorable terms.

In order to render it still more useful, the author has given it a thorough revision, made many improvements, and considerably enlarged it. The first edition contained a regular series of prayers for six successive weeks; prayers for two more weeks have been added in the present edition, so that it now furnishes, in one unbroken chain, *one hundred and twelve*, instead of *eighty-four*, morning and evening devotions, independently of the numerous festival, occasional, special, and other prayers. Every prayer has been carefully re-examined, and many of them abridged by the omission of what appeared to be tautological; many words of classical derivation have been stricken out and others of Anglo-Saxon origin substituted; and various other emendations have been introduced.

A valuable TABLE has been prefixed for the regular perusal of the Holy Scriptures. By this plan, the Psalms and New Testament will be read *twice*, and the Old Testament *once* in *each year*. Also, a list of REFERENCES TO SELECT *portions* of *the sacred Scriptures*, which will be found exceedingly convenient.

A *Form* has also been prepared for commencing with prayer those Sunday-schools in which none of the teachers have as yet acquired ability to offer up extempore prayer in public. We indeed think that all teachers should be practical Christians, and should find no difficulty in praying in public, and therefore require no such help. But as this is, unfortunately, not always the case, and much embarrassment has been experienced in this very respect, and as we judge that the use of a form on such occasions is less objectionable than the omission of prayer altogether, we presume the service in question will not be unacceptable. We would not, however, recommend it to schools in which the teachers are capable, as they ought all to be, of offering up their own prayers in public. To meet the wishes of those who think that the introductory exercises are rendered more interesting and edifying by the use of responses on the part of the pupils, we have prepared a few; though we cannot say that we think favorably of them, especially in view of their tendency to formality and abuse. Those who, like ourselves, have no predilections for such exercises, will not use them, while all are bound to be tolerant toward others who differ in their views and practices in matters not essential.

The Morning and Evening Prayers for the additional two weeks have been prepared with great care, and will be found to be deeply spiritual, and characterized by great simplicity and a truly evangelic spirit. The peculiarity of those for the *eighth* week is, their adaptation to the experience of the sinner, in his progress from conviction of sin and humiliation, through the several stages of the process of conversion, until he reaches the period of the dedication of his heart to God, of his anxiety for the advancement of true religion, and his joyful thanksgiving for mercies received. We cannot restrain the hope that this portion of the book will be found particularly acceptable, and receive the sanction of every practical Christian.—May God's blessing attend our humble labors.

B. K.

BALTIMORE, Jan. 1, 1856.

CONTENTS

INTRODUCTION

MORNING AND EVENING PRAYERS

PARTICULAR DAYS AND SEASONS

OCCASIONAL PRAYERS AND THANKSGIVINGS

PRAYERS AT TABLE

PRAYERS FOR CHILDREN

INTRODUCTION

PRAYER IN GENERAL

1. *What is Prayer?*

Prayer is the converse of the heart with God, or an appeal to him to bestow blessings, or to avert evils. In the Lord's prayer we call on him, first, to confer some good, and second, to turn away some evil. David represents it as "the words of his month and the meditation of his heart." Ps. 19:14. It may be more fully defined as a heartfelt address to the Supreme Being, consisting of adoration, confession of sin, supplication for pardon, and blessings in conformity to the divine will, intercession, and thanksgiving. It may, however, consist of a single petition, be extemporaneous, written, or printed.

2. *To whom must prayer be addressed?*

To the triune God only: he himself says, "Thou shalt have no other gods before me." Ex. 20:3. And when Satan tempted Christ to fall down and pray to him, he indignantly replied, "Get thee hence, Satan: for it is written, Thou shalt worship the Lord thy God, and him only shalt thou serve." Matt. 4:10. We may, however, call on either of the persons of the Holy Trinity. John 5:23; Phil. 2:9–10; Heb. 1:6; Acts 7:59. But we have no scriptural authority to pray to angels, nor to saints, such as the apostles, the Virgin Mary, or the departed spirits of other holy persons. Angels may indeed convey the sufferings or necessities of the righteous on earth to God; and so, likewise, glorified spirits in heaven may intercede for those living on earth, as they did while in the flesh; but it would be in vain, as well as contrary to the teaching of the Bible, to ask them do so, because, being neither omnipresent nor omniscient, it is impossible for them to hear us. The Most High says, "I am God, and there is none else." It is his prerogative to search the heart, to understand the secret breathings of the soul, and to hear the multitudes of suppliants who are simultaneously sending forth their requests from ten thousand different locations of his vast empire. Moreover, he alone can pardon sin and fulfill all our desires. What supreme folly, then, to offer up prayer to the creature instead of the Creator; to present our petitions to those who can neither hear nor answer, while there is a God who both heareth and answereth, and is more willing to give than we are to receive!

3. *What is meant by praying in Christ's name?*

To do a thing in the name of another, often means to do it by his authority; thus, to pray in Christ's name is to pray because he requires it, or in obedience to his command. But this is not all. It also implies that in approaching and addressing a throne of grace, we rely entirely on the blood and righteousness of Christ, or the vicarious sacrifice of himself on the cross, trusting confidently in his precious promises, and looking for a gracious answer wholly on account of his infinite merits. The mere uttering of his name in our supplications is by no means sufficient; for to pray in Christ's name, presupposes that we are convinced of our total want of merit before God, and that all our hope of a hearing is based upon the perfect righteousness which he wrought out for us by his passion and death. This is an essential feature of acceptable prayer. Christ says, *"No man cometh unto the Father, but by me."*

4. *What is implied by praying "in spirit and in truth?"*

In *spirit* signifies with feeling and fervor; not merely with the lips or by empty forms, but from the heart and through the influence of the Holy Ghost.

In *truth* means in sincerity, in opposition to outward pretense. Thus, a man prays in *spirit* when, by the assistance of the Holy Ghost, he brings all his affections and desires to the throne of God; and he prays in *truth*, when every purpose and passion of his heart, and every part of his prayer, are sincere and regulated by the Word of God. *He* is most devout who exercises the fullest faith in Christ, and whose soul is most fully possessed of his spirit.

5. *You have spoken of the Holy Ghost in connection with prayer: is his assistance necessary in order to pray effectually?*

Yes; the apostle teaches us (Rom. 8:26) that "we know not what to pray for as we ought; but the Spirit itself maketh intercession for us with groanings that cannot be uttered." We are by nature averse to pray, and unless moved by the Spirit, we should have no inclination; nor have we ability to pray aright unless aided by the Spirit. But, blessed be God! the Spirit knocks at the door of our heart and offers his aid, even before we ask or seek it. Let us rejoice that the Spirit of prayer is promised to all. Zech. 12:10: "And I will pour on the house of David, and upon the inhabitants of Jerusalem, the spirit of grace and supplications;" see also Matt. 7:11.

Holy Spirit, breathe a spirit of prayer on our families, our churches, and our nation! May the Holy Ghost teach us to pray with the understanding, the heart, and with fervor! Then shall we pray acceptably and effectually, both for ourselves and for others.

6. *How shall we know whether our prayers are answered?*

In many cases the answer is so clear and manifest, that we need no special proof. Every praying man can bear testimony to this truth. The *manner* and *time* in which mercies are received often afford evidence on this subject. The *manner.*—If the mercy is granted speedily and unexpectedly, (Isa. 65:24,) and if we receive not only what we sought, but other blessings in addition, (1 Kings 3:12–14,) then we may be sure God has answered. The *time:*—If we receive blessings at the very juncture we most need them, or when we are most earnestly and importunately supplicating them, we may also be satisfied that God has hearkened to our cry. See a remarkable instance in Acts 12:6, 7, 12.

God may, however, and not unfrequently does, delay answering prayer for wise and merciful purposes. Perhaps he withholds the desired blessing in order to teach us to be more earnest and constant in our supplications; perhaps to prepare us to value it more highly, and to be more thankful when we receive it; perhaps because he designs ultimately to bestow some different and more precious good than that which we pray for, and for its proper reception we require a prolonged course of discipline and preparation. Thus, the apostle besought the Lord repeatedly and for a length of time before he responded, "My grace is sufficient for thee; for my strength is made perfect in weakness."

7. *For what blessings ought we to pray?*

For "blessings in conformity to God's will." In that perfect model of prayer bequeathed to the church by its Great Head, we are taught to pray, "Thy will be done." And the same lesson is impressed upon us by his own example. With the deepest fervor and pathos, he prayed that he might be delivered from the awful agony he was suffering—"O my Father, if it be possible, let this cup pass from me." But he added, "nevertheless, not as I will, but as thou wilt." All our prayers, therefore, should be offered in unreserved submission to the Divine will, and we should desire nothing it is not his good pleasure to confer.

8. *But how shall we know what is in conformity to God's will?*

By diligently reading the sacred Scriptures, and especially acquainting ourselves with the many precious promises which abound on almost every page of the inspired volume. In numerous instances we are expressly instructed what to pray for; and in the countless promises we plainly see what is in accordance with his will, and what he therefore will bestow, if we call on him in the name of Christ. God has promised "exceeding abundantly above all that we can ask or think," (Eph. 3:20;) and in these promises we find an exhaustless mine of blessings to seek for in prayer. From them we learn that it is agreeable to God's will to bestow *temporal* blessings. Isa. 33:16; Ps. 34:10. But as his promises of *spiritual* good are far more abundant and glorious, and as the blessings which concern the soul and immortality exceed those which have respect only to the body and to time, as much as the heavens are above the earth, we are bound to make spiritual and eternal blessings the principal burden of our supplications. How emphatically our Lord inculcates this truth when he admonishes us, "Seek ye FIRST the kingdom of God and his righteousness, and all these things shall be added unto you!" Matt. 6:33.

Oh, let us seek the grace of God in our own soul and the pure robe of Christ's righteousness; let us search for them as for hidden treasures; and finding them, as we certainly may, we shall possess what is infinitely more valuable than rubies, and compared with which everything else on earth is utterly worthless!

9. *For whom ought we to pray?*

Paul exhorts us to "make supplications for *all men*" We have no right, therefore, to exclude any rational being on earth from our prayers. The *church*, especially, and her *ministry*, should share in our sympathy. We should pray for her unity and prosperity, for the healing of divisions and the removal of useless distinctions; that fraternal affection may animate her members, and that all may learn to feel, that while "one is their Master, even Christ, they all are brethren." The *ministers* of the church in particular should be made the subjects of our appeals at the mercy-seat, that they may not shun to declare the whole counsel of God, and may watch for souls as those who must give an account. A faithful minister is one of the most estimable blessings with which an individual church can be favored; and if God would curse a people, he can scarcely do it more effectually than by letting them have unconverted and faithless men to minister to them.

That we should pray for *ourselves*, is self-evident. For we have eternal interests pending as well as others; and it is plain that if we are indifferent about our own souls, we can feel no concern for salvation for our neighbors. The *civil government, magistrates, cabinet officers*, or *ministers of state*, our *brethren*, our *enemies*, and *all sorts* of men, both those that are living and those that shall live hereafter, should be remembered in our supplications. *Judson*, the distinguished missionary, felt it to be his especial duty to pray for his posterity, that his children and children's children, to the latest generation, might be a godly seed and useful subjects of Immanuel's kingdom, whom the Lord would delight to bless, and whom he, the pious progenitor, might meet and rejoice with in heaven.

Our personal enemies and the enemies of God's church are appropriate subjects of intercession. We should entreat God to change and convert them, to correct and sanctify their tempers, and incline them to peace and love; and that they may become the friends of God and of his kingdom, and be exalted with us to eternal glory. The gospel expressly teaches us "to love our enemies, bless them that curse us, do good to them that hate us, and pray for them that despitefully use us and persecute us." Matt. 5:44. Hatred, wrath, and revenge are accordingly forbidden, and the exercise of love and good-will toward all is required. In this the religion of Christ rises high above every other system, and most gloriously proclaims its heaven-born origin. Never, before the despised Galilean appeared, who however was at the same time the God of the universe, had the world heard such a teacher nor such doctrine!

In one word, we must make *the whole family of man* the subject of our prayers.

10. *Is it right to pray for the dead?*

No; God has not commanded this, either directly or indirectly; either by general principle or specific precept. To pray for departed spirits, would therefore not be "in conformity to his will." We have, moreover, no example on record in the Bible, of a pious man's praying for the deceased. And if we had, it would possess no binding force, since the teaching of God is higher authority than example even of the pious. Independently of all this, we learn from the Scriptures that the present life is the only state of probation; that while here we may repent and be saved; but that death decides and fixes unalterably and forever the character and condition of every one.

11. *What is the design of prayer?*

It is briefly and simply to obtain from God, in his own appointed way, the blessings we need. The awakened sinner is sensible that he is spiritually "miserable, poor, blind, and naked," and accordingly needs many blessings which none but God can confer. Prayer is the instrumentality instituted by God to obtain these blessings. We therefore pray because God has commanded it, and because it is his pleasure to impart blessings in answer to it. He might supply all our spiritual wants without our prayers, just as he might furnish food and raiment without a single effort on our part; but it is very certain that this is not his accustomed mode of procedure. A wealthy and benevolent man said to one of his humble dependents: "I am kindly disposed toward you and always ready to relieve your necessities; but for reasons satisfactory to myself, and which would also satisfy you if you could understand them, it is my fixed determination to afford you no relief unless you ask me, and that too in a becoming manner." Thus God acts. In his wise counsels, as well as in the moral fitness of things, there is an inseparable connection between appropriate prayer and the blessings bestowed upon the suppliant. "I will yet for this be inquired of by the house of Israel, to do it for them." Ezek. 36:37.

> "Gott will gebeten seyn, wenn er was soll geben,
> Er verlanget unser Schrei'n, wenn wir wollen leben."

Let it not, therefore, be inferred that prayer is an arbitrary arrangement, and exhibits God as a despot rather than as a kind and merciful Father. On the contrary, there is the highest wisdom and propriety in ordaining prayer as the medium of obtaining blessings. The man who prays is by this very act taught to feel his wants and dependence on God, and prepared to receive the blessings he needs with a spirit of gratitude, reverence, and obedience. It is not despotic, but reasonable and proper, for infinite wisdom to bestow on an humble suppliant that which it would very properly withhold from him who refuses to pray. One man feels that he is unspeakably poor and helpless, while God is infinitely rich and merciful; another thinks he is increased in goods and has need of nothing, and proudly asks in his conduct: "What is the Almighty, that I should serve him, and what profit shall I have if I pray unto him?" The one prostrates himself before God in profound self-abasement, and, in humble reliance on Christ's atonement, pleads for mercy; the other is too self-sufficient, too indolent, too indifferent, or too worldly-minded, to seek for mercy, or ever to bow his knees before the Majesty of the universe, or to receive a single favor at the hands of God, with due appreciation and grateful reverence. Is there not a moral fitness in communicating to the one, and withholding from the other? Reason declares that there is, and revelation places it beyond a cavil or a doubt. In the Scriptures we are taught expressly that such is absolutely the system of infinite wisdom and goodness; and that blessings actually descend only as answers to prayer. It is "the hungry (the praying penitent) that is filled with good things, while the rich (the self-sufficient) are sent empty away." Luke 1:53. "This is the confidence that we have in him, that if we ask anything according to his will, he heareth us." 1 John 5:14.

In this view of the design of prayer, the objections based on God's *omniscience, immutability* and *benevolence*, accordingly, all fall to the ground. The intention is not to make him acquainted with our wants; for he knows them better than we do ourselves. Nor to alter his mind or bring about a change in his counsels; for with him there is no variableness nor shadow of turning. Nor to incline him to kindness; for he is infinitely disposed to exercise compassion toward all who look to him for it, without any moving argument from us. He does not say: "Ask," that I may know what you want; or "ask," and I will change my mind; or "ask," and you will persuade me to give; but simply and unconditionally: "Ask, and ye shall receive; seek, and ye shall find; knock, and it shall be opened unto you." The design, then, is to comply with God's command; to obtain mercy in his own appointed way, and to awaken and cultivate that frame of mind and condition of heart which will prepare us for the proper reception and due appreciation and application of his blessings.

Let everyone, therefore, attend to this duty, confident that if he pray faithfully he will not pray in vain. Let him remember that prayer was instituted by God, and that he cannot but honor his own institution, and be pleased with those who comply with it. Prayer makes us better, wiser, and lovelier in his sight, cherishing in us those views and emotions which constitute the character of a Christian. It soothes every tumult of the bosom; allays our fears; comforts our sorrows; invigorates our hopes; gives us peace now and the hope of glory to come. It restrains from sin; fortifies against temptation; recalls from wandering; gives tenderness and serenity to conscience; enlightens on the subject of duty and danger; and inspires with ardor, confidence and delight in the Christian course.

12. *Is it the duty of all men to pray?*

Yes; God commands all men everywhere to pray; and everyone is bound to obey. It has been said that the unconverted have no right to pray, and that they only bring upon them God's displeasure if they attempt it. This does not appear to be a fair representation of Scripture doctrine. If unregenerate men offend God, it is not because of an humble attempt to pray, but because they persist in their impenitence and refuse to be converted. John 9:31 is quoted to prove that God will not regard the supplications of the impenitent: "Now we know that God heareth not sinners; but if," &c. But this is not decisive, because this was merely the declaration of a man who had been blind and who was not inspired; it alludes, moreover, only to the prayer of an impostor who prays for the gift of miracles. Solomon represents God as saying to the wicked: "They shall call upon me, but I will not answer; they shall seek me early, but they shall not find me." Prov. 1:28. But this refers to the hopeless cries of the wicked, after their day of probation has ended. There are, however, inspired passages which teach that presumptuous sinners will not be heard, such as Prov. 15:8; Isa. 1:15; Amos 5:22, 23. But why will God not hear them? Because they do not pray aright. Let them humble themselves in penitence before God, and call upon him in all their deep moral degradation, in the name of Christ, and their prayers will be acceptable, and bring down pardon and salvation, though they were ten thousand times more vile and hell-deserving than they are.

But still it is their duty to pray, though while clinging to their sins they cannot pray acceptably. God commands all men to pray, and suspends the bestowal of his blessings upon the performance of this duty. To plead exemption on account of impenitence and consequent inability, would be nothing less than seeking to excuse one delinquency by pleading guilty to another, or to justify one violation of God's law by committing another. Jehovah can make no allowance for our persistence in willful iniquity; and as theft does not extenuate falsehood, so unbelief cannot palliate prayerlessness.

But even to the unregenerate, prayer is not wholly useless. They universally believe that they *can* pray with their present disposition, so as at least to satisfy themselves; and, not improbably, God also. Now, there is perhaps no way in which they so effectually unlearn this doctrine as by their own attempts at prayer. They soon learn to see their own prayers in a light and with a distinctness and certainty never, perhaps, experienced in any other case. Amid the anxiety and earnestness with which awakened sinners pray, they come, without an exception, first to doubt their own ability to pray as they ought, and then, without a doubt, to believe that their prayers are wholly destitute of evangelical worth. This important part of self-knowledge is acquired in no other way so readily as by attempts to pray. By such means, thousands of sinners have been brought to a state of absolute humiliation, and a full conviction of their entire dependence on Christ for holiness and salvation. Not to be able to pray, so as to be in some degree satisfied and comforted by our prayer, is to be poor indeed. This humbled, dependent state of mind is that in which the grace of the gospel is usually bestowed on men.

13. *How must we pray in order to insure an answer?*

This question has already been incidentally answered; but for the sake of plainness we will recapitulate. We must pray—

1. In *faith.* "What things soever ye desire when ye pray, believe that ye receive them, and ye shall have them." Matt. 11:2–4. This faith implies, at least, some knowledge of, and full confidence in, God's promises, in which he engages to hear us and to bestow all needful blessings.

2. In *Christ's name.* See answer to question 3.

3. In *spirit and in truth.* See answer to question 4.

4. In unqualified *submission to the divine will.* See answer to question 8.

5. With perseverance. 1 Thess. 5:17: "Pray without ceasing." Eph. 6:18: "Praying always with all prayer and supplication in the Spirit, and watching thereunto with all *perseverance.*" Though we meet with the greatest difficulties; though an answer be long delayed, and our

spiritual enemies tempt us a thousand times to abandon the duty, yet must we hold on despite of all discouragement. Job 13:15: "Though he slay me, yet will I trust in him." The parable of the importunate widow was expressly designed to teach this very important lesson: "that men ought always to pray, and not to faint;" Luke 18:1; and in Matt. 15:21–29, we have a striking example of earnest, persevering, and finally successful prayer.

If we pray thus, we may rest assured that God will answer; if not in the way that we desire, yet in some other way, more conducive to his glory and to our own welfare; as in the case of Moses, who prayed that he might be permitted to enter the earthly Canaan, and God transported him to the heavenly Canaan, which was infinitely better. This assurance is based upon,—

1. God's promises, Ps. 50:15, and 10:17; Matt. 7:7, 8; John 16:23; 1 John 3:22; Isa. 45:19; James 5:6.

2. Numerous examples recorded in Scripture, viz.: Elias, David, Abimelech and Abraham, Moses, Hezekiah, Daniel, Cornelius, Canaanitish woman, the ten lepers, &c.

3. The testimony of multitudes of Christians in all ages and Christian countries; and of numerous living witnesses, who know from their own experience that God heareth prayer.

It must not, however, be supposed that prayer is answered because there is anything meritorious in it; for all blessings are the gifts of God's rich grace on account of the infinite merits of Christ. Nor that a change is effected in the mind of God; for he is immutable. But it is because it is God's established plan to give in answer to prayer, and because there is a peculiar propriety, becoming his character, so to act. Prayer is, therefore, as necessary a prerequisite to a blessing, as ploughing and sowing, rain and sunshine, are to a harvest; in fact, there is even a more regular connection between the former than the latter. For there are blessings which never are given to men who do not pray, such as peace of conscience, joy in the Holy Ghost, increase of grace, final perseverance in piety, &c. These are the test of all blessings; they are never found by prayerless men; but they are, without fail, imparted to all who pray in faith, and are evidently given in answer to prayer.

As prayer, then, is the only communication between mankind and their Maker, and the only means of obtaining blessings from him, does it not follow, that the man who refuses or neglects to pray voluntarily cuts himself off from all hope of good? The easiest, least expensive, and least burdensome mode of acquiring good, is to ask for it; and he who refuses cannot rationally hope for any blessing. "To renounce all good," said a distinguished man, "when it is attainable by any means, however difficult, is the conduct of a *fool.* To renounce it when the means are the easiest possible, is the conduct of a *madman.*" Such a fool and such a madman is he who will not pray. To pray costs neither money, pains, nor time. Why then do multitudes neglect to pray? "The true explanation," says the same writer, "of this mysterious, sottish violation of every dictate of reason, conscience, and revelation, is that all these persons hate their duty. *They sin against God, and wrong their own souls; they hate him, and love death.*" See Dwight's Theology.

LORD, TEACH US TO PRAY.

FAMILY PRAYER

14. *What is meant by Family worship?*

The collecting together of the members of a family, at stated periods, for divine worship.

15. *In what does it consist?*

Usually in singing God's praise, reading the Scriptures, and calling upon the Lord in Christ's name.

16. *Is family prayer expressly enjoined in Scripture?*

It is not; and this has often been urged as an apology for its neglect. But none but the ignorant, and those who are averse to the duty in question, will attempt to justify the omission under so groundless a plea. If no duties were obligatory except those which are *expressly* commanded in the Scriptures, the number of our moral and religious obligations would be greatly diminished. We find no direct injunction to observe the first day of the week as the Christian Sabbath, to love our children, to build churches, to attend public worship, pray in secret, baptize infants, administer the Eucharist to females, or to do a thousand other things which everyone knows to be his duty. And to claim exemption from them on account of the absence of an express command, would be justly regarded as an evidence of the grossest misapprehension. How could it be expected that God would *explicitly* enjoin every duty incumbent upon us? Why, this would have swelled the Bible to a size which must have defeated its very object.

17. *What is God's usual plan in prescribing moral duty?*

It is evidently not in accordance with his plan to legislate in regard to each and every particular, but to lay down universal principles, easily understood, and applicable to every state, condition, or occurrence in life. One such principle or general statute may embody ten thousand special duties, or apply to an indefinite number of specific cases. No one can doubt that it is our duty to relieve our neighbor when sick, or protect his property when in danger, or succor his wife and child when assailed. But where is the *express* command to this effect? There is, however, one golden rule which meets each of these cases, and any number of similar ones: "Therefore, all things whatsoever ye would that men should do unto you, do ye even so to them." This general principle, while it is of easy comprehension and may be readily applied, supersedes special legislation on every point to which it appertains. Thus there are general precepts in God's Word, which imply the necessity of family prayer as clearly and forcibly as if it were directly and literally commanded.

It is also inconsistent with God's accustomed mode of dealing, explicitly to prescribe a duty which is already in active practice. Thus, when Christ commenced his ministry among the Jews, the practice of baptizing proselytes and their children was already in vogue. Hence there was no necessity for an express injunction to baptize infants; the general command to baptize all necessarily included them as distinctly as it did adults, and would undoubtedly be so understood unless accompanied by an express prohibition of infants. In like manner, there was no necessity to prescribe a law requiring parents to love their children and to provide for them, because the very organization of the family relation involved this; and it was, moreover, already secured by the law of nature—a more ancient statute than any on record. This remark applies with great force to the subject of prayer. Dr. Dwight tells us that the world was three thousand years old, and that eight hundred years had elapsed after the call of Abraham, before any command at all to pray is found in the Scriptures. Ps. 122:6; Jer. 29:7. And yet, it is well known, that during this time prayer is frequently mentioned, and that men *actually did pray.* Gen. 24:63; Job 15:4; 16:17; 23:16. Are we authorized, and is it reasonable, in view of this fact, to demand an express command for family prayer?

18. *Is there no express injunction whatever in the Bible for any particular kind of prayer?*

No; both secret and public prayer are referred to, but not in the form of a command. They are spoken of as duties already in force, and which would continue to be practiced; and all that was deemed requisite, was to regulate the manner of their performance. Matt. 6:5, 6. The duty of prayer *in general* is indeed plainly and repeatedly inculcated; we are also instructed as to the manner in which it should be discharged; and we know certainly that God's people did pray. How inconsistent then, how absurd, to attempt to excuse our neglect of family prayer under the wretched subterfuge that there is no express command for it!

We find many passages in the Scriptures which imply the duty under consideration, as plainly as any duty can be implied; "Praying always (at all times) with *all prayer.*" Eph. 6:18. "I will that men pray *everywhere:*" 1 Tim. 2:8. "*In everything* by prayer and supplication, with thanksgiving, let your requests be made known before God:" Phil. 4:6. "Be ye therefore sober, and *watch unto prayer.*" 1 Peter 4:7. If it be objected that *family prayer* is not explicitly mentioned in any of these passages, we would ask, is it not plainly included? Can we pray *at all times, with all prayer, everywhere, in everything, watching unto prayer*—without praying in our own *house,* with our own *children,* at the head of our own *family,* and around our own *domestic altar?* If anyone deny that family prayer forms any part of the precept, because it is not *expressly specified,* another may deny that *secret* prayer is intended, because that is not *specified*; and a third may object, on the same ground, that *social* and *public* is not meant; thus, all and every kind of prayer may, on the principle of the caviler, be set aside. By this kind of evasion and equivocation, nominal Christians and ungodly, men may delude their own conscience, but they cannot deceive their Maker. They are, in fact, trifling with the sacred Scriptures; destroying their true import, and inviting the vengeance of a jealous and a holy God!

19. *How is the Lord's Prayer to be regarded in relation to this subject?*

This model of prayer was evidently designed to teach us *when* and *where,* as well as *for what,* to pray. That it was intended as a *family prayer,* or a model of one, is clear from the general phraseology. It is not worded, *my* Father, but *our* Father who art in heaven—not give *me,* but give *us*—not forgive *me,* but forgive *us*—not lead *me,* but lead *us* not into temptation, &c.

20. *Is family prayer alluded to in the Scriptures?*

Yes; frequently, and always as something with which God is pleased, while the neglect of it has provoked the expression of his abhorrence. In proof of this we refer the reader to the following: "I know that he (Abraham) will command his children and his household after him, and they shall keep the way of the Lord, to do justice and judgment." Gen. 17:19. Joshua carried out the following noble resolution: "As for me and my house, we will serve the Lord;" Josh. 24:15. And it is said of Job, that "he rose up early in the morning and offered burnt-offerings. Thus did Job *continually,*"—Job 1:5—*i. e.,* every day, or it was his daily practice. These facts are all recorded to the praise of the individuals named, and in every instance God manifested his approbation. We have reason also to believe that Christ and his apostles, when together, united in daily devotion, pouring out their common wants and commending themselves to the paternal guidance and mercy of God; and they might well be regarded as a *family*. But God's indignation at the neglect of this duty is as strongly declared as his approval of its performance. "Pour out thy fury upon the heathen that know thee not, and *upon the families that call not on thy name.*" Jer. 10:25. It is a solemn and a fearful fact, that those families that call not on God are here numbered among the heathen who know not God!

21. *Is it not unreasonable to ask for an explicit enactment on this subject?*

We think it is; because the law of our nature—the inherent affection implanted by our God in the human bosom—prompts us to do all we can for our children's welfare. What sacrifice will not a mother or a father make for their good? When a beloved child is sick, do we ask for an iron statute to learn whether we shall send for a physician? When the storm howls, the flood roars, or the flame rages, do we demand an express law before we can venture to stretch forth a helping arm? If, then, God has kindly furnished to us the means of establishing them in virtue, arming them against temptation and sin, and preparing them for usefulness to others and comfort to themselves, for a life of peace and honor and happiness on earth, and of glory and joy eternal in heaven, why should we hesitate and cavil, and demand an express statute enforcing the use of those means? Can such an individual be found in a Christian land and among the friends of God? If such an one read this essay, we address you as a Christian father, as a dying man and an accountable agent, and "beseech you that this night the God of heaven may be invoked in your family, and that your abode become consecrated as the dwelling-place of the Most High!" If we live in the neglect of family worship, the opinion of Hesiod, a heathen poet of Greece, may condemn us at the judgment day. He says: "Bring your best burnt-offering, holy and pure, and with all thy might, before thou liest down, and when thou risest up, present it before the immortal God; then he will look upon thee with an heart filled with delight; he will bless thee in thy temporal concerns; and while others for their contempt of God are obliged to part with their temporal property, you shall be able to purchase rich estates."

22. *What are the considerations that should induce us to observe family prayer?*

They are numerous; we can now direct attention only to a few. We should practice this duty because—

1. *God requires it.* It has already been conceded that family prayer, as distinct from other modes of worship, is not *explicitly* enjoined in

the Bible. But if any one plead this as an excuse for neglecting it, he is deluding his own soul. Prayer was undoubtedly instituted by divine appointment from the creation of man, and was traditionarily spread through all nations, as a duty evident to common sense, and acknowledged by the universal voice of mankind. Hence we find that both Patriarchs and Gentiles, Jews and Christians, practiced it in the earliest ages. It was therefore not the intention of the Scriptures to institute it anew, in any of its forms, and we have no more right to look for an *express* command for *family* prayer, than for *secret* or *public* prayer; neither of which is enjoined in the Bible as an original duty, and all which are treated as existing, and regulated as duties already acknowledged and practiced. But that God requires us to observe family prayer, just as he does any other kind of prayer, has been abundantly proven in the answer to Questions 16–21. We will only again revert to Eph. 6:18, where we are commanded to "pray always with all prayer," which unquestionably includes family prayer. To "pray always," means *at every season*; and "with all prayer," signifies *with prayer of every kind.* By this precept, then, we are required to pray on every occasion suited to the performance of the duty; and with such prayer as becomes the circumstances, wants, and character of those by whom the duty is to be performed. That family prayer is one kind of prayer especially suited to the wants and circumstances of the family, will not be disputed by those who are sincerely in search of truth.

2. *The relation in which families stand toward God constitutes a strong appeal in favor of this duty.* God is the Author of the family organization; he not only called man into existence, but also instituted matrimony, thereby creating the family relation, on which depend all the comforts of social life and civilized society. Gen. 2:18–24. Does not this great fact furnish a strong argument in support of family prayer? Do we not as a family owe homage and service to Him who is the founder of the family relation and the great proprietor of all families?

As he is the Founder, so also is he the Governor and Benefactor, of this interesting relation. As *Governor*, he has prescribed the very best laws for the regulation of the family. Eph. 5:25–33, and 6:1–18; Col. 3:10–25, and 4:1, 2. As *Benefactor*, he preserves the family, supplies its wants, wards off danger, comforts in sickness and trial, sanctifies affliction, and is the rich source of countless social and other blessings. How powerfully do these considerations address us in favor of a family altar! God's government of the family relation is wise and gracious; all his rules and regulations are based in love and adapted to multiply its comforts and promote its truest interests. The blessings that are constantly flowing in upon the domestic circle from the Father of mercies, are so numerous and varied, and so kindly suited to its necessities, that language is too feeble to set them forth. Now, if it be the duty of an individual in his individual capacity to acknowledge God and to render homage and service to him, because God is his Maker, Ruler, and Benefactor, is not a family much more under obligations, on the same ground, to worship and serve him in its family capacity? It is admitted by Christians, that an individual church, or nation, is bound to worship and serve God in its capacity as church or nation, because God is its Founder, Governor, and Benefactor; why then is it not the duty of a family, founded, governed and blessed by the same God, to bow down before him in its family character, and unite in prayer and thanksgiving? Personal mercies should be gratefully acknowledged, and personal blessings prayerfully sought, in a personal capacity, national in a national capacity, and family in a family capacity.

3. A third and most cogent consideration in favor of family prayer, is found in the fact that *the great ends of the family organization cannot be accomplished without it*. One of these ends is, the training up of children for usefulness and happiness in this life and for eternal salvation in the world to come. In order to attain this great end, the family must be governed by sound principles. "There are," says a distinguished writer, "two ways of governing a family. One is with the rod of a tyrant, and the rage of the furies; by cold, unfeeling statutes, and never-ending reproof; by passion, and fire, and wrath. The other is by love, and tenderness, and discipline administered with calmness, and yet with a faithful hand; by calling into exercise all that is tender in the social affections—all the budding and blossoming ingenuousness of the child; by the aid of the conscience and of reason; and by severity only when other means fail; and then suffering the feelings of the *father* to be seen, at the same time that the firmness of the *ruler* shows itself to the child." It will be readily perceived that the former mode is that which tyrants choose, while the latter is the plan of God. The one is despotic, the other parental. The first shuts God out of view; the second borrows its features from his moral government. One may be regarded as the product of human weakness and depravity; while the other is an actual bringing down of the great principles on which our *heavenly Father* acts in his moral administration, to bear on the smaller community over which an *earthly father* presides. This premised, we remark—

(*a*) That the true principles of domestic government cannot be fully carried into effect without prayer. If we would observe them, we must be acquainted with them and embody them in our spirit and daily practice. To this end we must not only search the Scriptures and study God's plan of governing men, but also be *instant in prayer.* It is by earnest converse with God in solemn devotion, that we maintain familiarity with him, keep his plan of governing constantly before us, and are enabled in some good degree to imitate it in our families.

The restraints also which family prayer throws around us greatly favor sound domestic discipline. How can he who has just been engaged in the solemn act of presenting himself and family to the God of love, indulge in fits of ill-nature, and outbursts of temper?—and if he know that soon the period will again arrive when he and all the members of his little community shall bow before the Lord at one common altar, must not anger, passion, and wrath be forced to flee away? Even in this first view of the subject, family prayer seems to be so important, that we doubt whether any father has ever succeeded or ever will succeed in fully carrying out gospel principles in the government of his family, while living in the neglect of his duty.

(*b*) The administration of family government requires that the *father should be held in high regard.* But what is there in the wide world that renders the paternal character so venerable, and so embalms it in the warm affections of the family, as the habitual connection of the image of the father with the sacredness of religion? It is impossible to treat such a man with disrespect, or to esteem lightly the principles by which he is endeavoring to govern his family. Let the father then be to his family what the pastor is to the flock; let him add to the paternal character the venerableness of the priest of his family; let him daily unite with them in prayer, and he will enjoy their confidence; his laws and opinions will be invested with authority; and thus governing by gospel principles, his children will grow up in the nurture and admonition of the Lord.

(*c*) Family prayer is necessary in order to impart the greatest efficacy to the religious instruction of the family. All admit that a family should receive religious instruction in order to answer the great end of its organization. But can such instruction prove effectual in the absence of prayer? Let us illustrate. *Prayer* is an essential duty of religion; there can be no true religion without it. Of course, then, the parent attempts to inculcate this duty. But while he is giving lessons in relation to it, he himself never once unites with them around the family altar! His precepts and his example are at open variance. What is the consequence? Why, his *precepts* remain unheeded, and his *example* proves all-powerful. Children, even little children, are exceedingly observant. They will say: If prayer is of so much moment, then, why does not our father pray with us and for us? Why does he not set us the example? He teaches *us* to pray, but we never see *him* pray; therefore, prayer is not of much account. Let it not be said that children do not reason so logically. It is well known that they do, and thousands of instances might be adduced.

23. *Are there other inducements to family prayer?*

Yes, many. Under the last question we referred only to three, viz.: the requirement of God; the relation subsisting between him and families; and its importance in order to attain the great ends of the family organization, the principal of which is the proper education of children. Under Question 21 we cited several examples of family prayer from the Scriptures; this list might easily be enlarged. For instance, Adam, immediately after his fall, was taught by God to offer sacrifice to the Most High. He taught his children the same duty, as is evident from the account we have of Cain and Abel, though the worship of the former was hypocritical and not accepted. Noah, so soon as he left the ark, presented sacrifices to God, Gen. 8:20, 21, and, no doubt, being a preacher of righteousness, prayed with his family while in the ark. Abraham practiced domestic worship. Gen. 18:19. Isaac and Jacob, even when they went abroad, were careful to erect temporary altars for the worship of God. And though Joshua was a military man, and burdened with the cares of government, yet he found time to worship the Lord with his family. Josh. 14:15. Job, David, and Cornelius also maintained this practice. Job 1:5; Ps. 101:1, 2; Acts 10:1, 2.

We might yet further appeal to the importance of the family trust, as an inducement to domestic worship. The immortal souls of those composing our families are, in a manner, committed to our hands. How awful the thought, that any of these blood-bought souls should at the last day be laid to our charge!—if our children or servants should accuse us, in the face of an assembled world, for withholding those means of grace which, if they had been observed, might have issued in their salvation! Some of our family may precede us to the bar of God; and how would it harrow up our souls, should we, in viewing the final resting-place of a departed child, be forced to say: "There lies one of my children with whom and for whom I never prayed!" Should we be called hence before them, would it not be equally agonizing to leave them with the bitter reflection that we never once invited them to bow their knees with us around a family altar? We seek their comfort in this life; why not make an effort to secure to them an inheritance beyond the grave? Is it wise, is it rational, to limit our love to the body that turns to dust, and to time that soon fades away, while they have a soul that never dies, and are destined to an eternity that will know no end? If there be no religion in a family, it is daily making progress in sin.

If we love our country, we should pray with our families. Religion begins with individuals; then extends to families and small communities; then to towns and cities, and finally spreads itself over the length and breadth of the land. If then there be no family religion, there can be no national religion, and the country becomes a moral wilderness—a spectacle dreadful to behold, and deeply to be deplored by the patriot as well as the Christian. The blessing of the Lord abideth on the praying family: Prov. 3:23; Ps. 118:15, and 128:1, 2. His curse on the home of the irreligious: Jer. 10:25; Prov. 3:33; Jer. 10:16; and who can tell what that curse is!—But it is unnecessary to press this subject further. If the foregoing does not convince, neither would additional arguments. We shall conclude with a remark of one of the wisest and best men† that our country has produced: "How great the privilege to hold a daily intercourse with God in our dwellings; to have our houses converted into temples for that adorable Deity whom the heaven of heavens cannot contain; to mention our domestic wants before him, with the encouraging hope of supply; to vent the overflowings of gratitude; to spread the savor of his knowledge; to have our families devoted to him, while others live estranged from the God of their lives, and to talk of him whom angels celebrate on their golden harps in anthems of praise!"

24. *How often should family prayer be attended to?* There is a difference of opinion on this subject. Some teach that a family ought to be assembled for prayer three times a day; others twice, and yet others only once. Many of those who adopt the last view lay great stress on *secret* prayer, and think that more frequent attendance to this form of prayer should be inculcated. As the Bible furnishes no specific directions on this point, Christians are bound conscientiously to consider the subject, and to act according to the best knowledge they can obtain. While we would not censure the father who calls his family around the altar but once a day, whether in the morning or the evening, we feel bound to recommend the performance of the duty twice each day;—in other words, we plead for both the "*morning and the evening* sacrifice."

The family has been defended and preserved during the night; health, life, and numerous other mercies have been continued to them; refreshed by repose, cheered by the smiles of the opening day, and the affectionate greetings of all around; is there in all this no cause for united thanks? But this little community have their constantly recurring wants; they need their daily food, raiment, grace, &c. They have their employments, and require the daily blessing of God upon them, or all their efforts will prove in vain. Does not this furnish suitable matter for renewed petition? They are exposed to temptations and trials; the great adversary is awake as soon as they are, and ever upon the watch for an opportunity to lead them captive. They are surrounded with dangers; disease and death often lurk in the food they eat and the atmosphere they inhale. Anacreon lost his life by being choked with a raisin; Fabius, a Roman Senator, was strangled by a hair, while taking a draught of milk; and Absalom suddenly lost his life by being caught by his long, beautiful hair in the branches of a tree! "Thou knowest not what a day may bring forth." Now, in view of all this, is there no cause for morning supplication as well as early praise? Is there not a propriety, to which no one can shut his eyes, in entering on the day with thanksgiving and prayer?

And when the day is gone and night has come, what a vast collection of mercies have been showered upon us! how many dangers, seen and unseen, have been averted! and are our hearts not touched with a sense of gratitude? We have not during the day loved God supremely, and our neighbor as ourselves; unholy thoughts, desires, and tempers—probably, also, words and actions inconsistent with our Christian calling—are chargeable against us. Have we no cause for humiliation, no need of appealing to a throne of grace for pardon and mercy? The family are again about to separate for the night; sleep is the image of death;—"so very much like it," said a good man, "that I cannot close my eyes without first commending my soul to God." Unconscious of existence; as utterly defenseless in our slumbers as a babe; wholly dependent on the mercy of God for life, protection, and a renewal of our strength, and ignorant whether we shall open our eyes upon the light of another day—is there no just ground, no moral fitness, in once more assembling around the family altars and uniting in prayer, praise, and reading the Scriptures?

25. *How should family prayer be conducted?*

So far as concerns the *spirit* and *frame of mind* requisite to acceptable prayer, this question is already answered. See Question 14. But in regard to the *manner* in which it should be conducted, we remark—

(*a*) That family prayer should be *regular*. It should so enter into the domestic arrangement as to form one of its essential constituents.

(*b*) It should be *solemn and impressive*. If he who leads in prayer manifest a light and volatile spirit, or a want of deep interest in the exercise, not only will the object be defeated, but serious injury will result. The family should plainly perceive, and be made to feel by our example, that we are in the presence of the Majesty of the universe, holding communion with an immaculate and sin-hating God, and earnestly seeking blessings of paramount importance both for time and eternity. But all mock solemnity and affectation in tone and manner should be carefully eschewed. The language should be plain and simple, the utterance distinct and intelligible, and the expressions chaste and suitable. High-sounding words, elaborately turned periods, and attempts at eloquence, are especially out of place; they savor of pride, offend God, and are destructive of solemnity. Austerity, gloominess of appearance, cold formality, forbidding reserve, and magisterial airs, are equally incompatible. Few audiences are more ready to observe these and similar defects in prayer, than a family; and none will sooner grow tired and turn away with disgust, in view of them. Coldness and spiritual death become any occasion better than a meeting around the family altar. "Let the snows of Greenland and the ice of the northern seas be in any place of devotion, rather than on that where you plead with God for the guidance and salvation of your sons and daughters."

(c) Family prayer should be conducted under *the influence of affectionate regard.* The apostle requires us to "be kindly affectioned one to another with brotherly love; in honor preferring one another; fervent in spirit, serving the Lord." Rom. 12:10, 11. This beautiful admonition is worthy of constant observance in all our domestic intercourse; but when we come together to sing, and pray, and bow before the family altar, we should especially feel the tenderest emotions toward each other, and *delight* to feel them. Our tempers should be chastened, and never be permitted to affect our prayers; and offensive and mortifying personalities should on no occasion be indulged. We may, and indeed ought to, make a prudent and affectionate use of the knowledge we possess of the circumstances of the various individuals present; but at the same time we must remember, that we are not to pray *at*, but *for* them.

(d) It should be *short.* Tediousness, repetition, and monotony are the bane of family devotion. Their tendency is to disgust and weary the family, and to instil into the children a dread and hatred of the whole system. The Lord's prayer, which was evidently intended to be used in the family, is a model, as well in relation to its brevity as its unsurpassed simplicity and plainness. A child soon learns to understand this prayer, and is never wearied by its *length.* Some seem to make it a rule to pray for everybody, and everything, in every prayer. Frequently they begin with the creation, and trace its history down to the millennium, and these *historical* prayers are easily spun out to a quarter or half an hour's length. If we really desire to disgust a family, and are ambitious to destroy all the effects of devotion, then this is precisely the course we should pursue.

(e) It should be *pointed and to the purpose.* When we kneel down, we should endeavor to have a few topics before the mind, and aim at presenting those topics in all possible simplicity. "Till men learn to concentrate their feelings, and have really some *object* for which they wish to pray—an object in which they feel *some* interest—the business of praying will be dull, monotonous, disgusting."

(f) *The whole family should be present.* If our children are permitted to be irregular in their attendance, it will not be difficult to foresee the future character of such sons and daughters. Those parents are pointing thorns for their dying pillow who suffer their children, under light pretexts, to neglect family prayer.

But it should not be forgotten that our servants are a part of the family as well as our children. They are under our care, and their religious intruction and improvement are, for the time being, committed to our charge. Their attachment to our persons and interests, and their fidelity and good conduct, can in no way be more effectually secured, than by inviting, and if reluctant, by encouraging them to join us in our devotions. If our domestics are Romanists, and *will not* consent to hear the Bible read and join us in prayer, then we must aim at so living out our religion before them, as to constrain them to admit that ours is a holy and sanctifying religion. In some cases this has proven an effectual means of causing the scales to fall from their eyes, and begetting even a desire to share in our religious privileges.

26. *Does the Bible prescribe the posture to be observed in prayer?*

It does not. As we have no express precept regulating the attitude to be assumed in preaching and hearing the gospel, receiving the Holy Supper, &c., so we are not directed as to *posture* when we offer up our prayers. These are non-essentials, which God has submitted to the sense of propriety of his people. The efficacy of prayer depends not upon the situation of the body or the grammatical fitness of our language, but on the condition of the heart and the exercise of faith in Christ. Men may pray *standing* or *kneeling*, or they may *prostrate* themselves before God. We have examples on record in the Scriptures of all these postures; but it is worthy of remark, that there is not a single case referred to of prayer in a *sitting* position. On one occasion "Solomon *stood* before the altar of the Lord in the presence of all the congregation of Israel, and spread forth his hands toward heaven." 1 Kings 8:22. On another, he ascended a scaffold prepared for the purpose, and "he *kneeled* down upon his knees before all the congregation," &c. 2 Chron. 6:13. The apostle Paul "*kneeled down*, and prayed with them all." Acts 20:36; see also Psalms 95:6; Luke 22:41. "The publican *standing* afar off," &c. Luke 18:13. Christ says: "When ye *stand* praying," &c. Mark 11:25. Christ "*fell on his face*, and prayed,"

&c. Matt. 26:39. See also Num. 16:22; Josh. 5:14; 1 Chron. 21:16. Our Lord also "*kneeled* down and prayed," &c. Luke 22:41.

Prostration is indicative of a very deep and uncommon sense of sin, and may be most suitably used in secret prayer. Dr. Clarke says, "this was the ordinary posture of the suppliant when the favor was great which was asked, and deep humiliation required." See his comment on Matt. 26:39. In the Greek Church we observed the worshippers praying with uncommon rapidity while *standing*, but occasionally they *prostrated* themselves, and touched the floor with the forehead, and immediately rose again.

The *standing* and *kneeling* posture is most frequently mentioned in Scripture. Where there is no convenient space for kneeling, we should think standing would be preferred. *Kneeling* has some advantages; it is naturally an expression of humility, and is calculated to lead to this feeling and to a sense of our wants and our dependence upon God. "But *sitting*," says a distinguished writer, "or other postures of rest and laziness, ought not to be indulged, unless persons are aged or infirm." When prayer is drawn out to such an unreasonable and unscriptural length (unfortunately too often the case) as to render it fatiguing to mind and body to maintain a prayerful frame and a standing position, we think a sitting posture is excusable, while at the same time we are compelled to censure the error that leads to this apparent impropriety. The *lifting up* or *spreading out of the hands*, on the part of the individual leading in prayer, was a very common practice among the saints of old; and is a very natural expression of our seeking help from God. The countenance should be composed to gravity and solemnity; the eyes should not be allowed to rove—we think it best to keep them closed. Sighs and groans, and responses of "amen," during prayer, are offensive to some; but if they are the sincere expression of religious emotion and do not interfere with the devotions of others, we can take no exception to them; and we are free to confess that there are occasions when we feel greatly inclined to indulge them, and should regard it as an arbitrary restraint upon our Christian liberty to be prevented. But noise made by the hands, or feet, or knees, violent motions of the head, &c., are not only unmeaning, but have always appeared to us to be irreverent, and inconsistent with the solemnity of the exercise.

It would seem, then, that we have nothing more authoritative, to guide us in regard to posture in prayer, than example; and this is not binding any further than as it accords with the plain principles laid down in the gospel, or with the general direction: "Let all things be done decently and in order." 1 Cor. 14:40. A vast majority of Protestant Christians are in the habit of standing during public prayer, and of kneeling in family worship, on days of public humiliation and prayer, and on some special occasions. The Methodists, Episcopalians, and Roman Catholics kneel; in the Greek Church they stand and prostrate themselves alternately. In the Lutheran Church standing is generally practiced in public worship; but in their more retired meetings, such as prayer-meetings, the "weekly lecture," family worship, and when they meet for services preparatory to the Lord's Supper, they most generally kneel. The Scriptures give Christians liberty to consult their own inclinations and sense of propriety in this matter, and no ecclesiastical or other body have a right to deprive them of this liberty. Whatever posture we choose to observe, we should be careful not to condemn or even to find fault with others who dissent from us, and prefer a different position.

27. Is it the duty of a mother to conduct family prayer in the absence of the father, or in case he refuses to attend to it when at home?

If the father is decidedly opposed to family worship, and forbids it to be observed, it is the duty of the mother, "in patience possessing her soul," to submit. But this need not prevent her from retiring at stated periods with her children, and thus in secret supplicating the blessing of God on them and him. But if the husband, while he refuses to conduct the devotions, is nevertheless willing that his wife should do so, the case is a plain one. It is her duty to establish and maintain domestic worship, and there is no principle in the Bible nor rule of propriety in well-organized society which she violates.

If the mother be a widow, the obligation to observe the duty in question presses even more peremptorily than in the case just supposed. No mother more needs the aid and comfort of family devotion, than she who, in the providence of God, has been deprived of her husband and the father of her children. She feels more than ever her own insufficiency and her dependence on God. In her bereavement she is sensible that she requires peculiar aid and special grace in the great business of rearing, governing, and directing her children. More than half the human assistance, counsel, and encouragement she enjoyed, is taken away, and it is often amid sighs and tears that she contemplates her responsible relation, her own weakness, and her utter inability, apart from divine instruction and assistance. Oh, with what overwhelming force does the appeal in favor of family worship come home to her timid and desolate heart! Nor is it easy for children to treat with disrespect a praying, widowed mother. We speak the language of the Rev. A. Barnes, with slight alterations: "This is the very time and occasion for seeking the God of grace; and his ear will not be heavy to hear, nor his arm short to help her, that comes and pleads, day and night before his throne, his own oft-repeated promise to the widow and the fatherless. There is no scene on earth, it seems to me, so lovely as that of a bereaved family thus pouring its sorrows into the ears of God, and seeking repose on his bosom. And in that family—that widowed and fatherless family— where this is wanting, there is a chasm which no adorning, no amiableness, no intelligence, can fill. God should be acknowledged there. It is the very place where there should be an altar. And if all places of worship should be broken up; if all our assemblies should be dissolved; if the fires of devotion everywhere else should grow dim, or expire, yet they should be seen to shed their pure beams on the abode of the widow, and to diffuse light and joy in the otherwise sad dwelling-place of the fatherless. The plea of want of ability should not be urged there. It is proper to use forms of prayer; and the widow comes to her duty under the advantage of more cheering promises made to her in the Scriptures, than are made to any other class of the human family."

28. *Is not the want of ability to lead profitably in family prayer a justification of its omission?*

No; God requires all men to pray; therefore all are bound to pray; and all may become *able* to pray to edification if they will. It is not learning or talent that enables men to conduct in prayer, but a humble and contrite heart. If the heart is not in this condition, it is our own fault. But even believers sometimes plead *inability*. In their case the excuse arises from pride. These same persons can converse, and often with fluency, with their families and their neighbors; they are at no loss for words when they would speak on politics, trade, the price of produce, &c.; if they are sick, they can pour out their complaints; if in need of any comfort, they know how to ask for it; if favored with some turn of good fortune, they can give expression to their gratification. In all these cases we hear of no want of ability. But when urged to express their wants and the wants of the family to God, then they seek to justify themselves behind the plea of inability. What marvelous inconsistency and self-delusion! The publican, in all his poverty and wretchedness, could exclaim: "God be merciful to me a sinner!" Was it eloquence, intellectual power, or fluency, that taught him thus to pray, and secured to him the commendation of the Son of God? no, it was his brokenness of heart and contrition of spirit, wrought in him by the power of the Holy Ghost.

When alone in their closets, men can pray; there is then no want of language, and they are never known to urge the plea of inability. But in the presence of their fellow-sinners they are suddenly deprived of speech! What does this prove but *pride* of heart, and that they have more respect for sinners than for God, and are more afraid of worms of the dust than of the Lord God of Hosts? If they were not so proud, they *could* pray in their families. When an objection can be reduced to this pitiful extremity, we are willing to leave it there.

But may not this inability be remedied by the sinner, even without the aid of forms? Undoubtedly it may. Study to become acquainted with, and more and more to realize, your fallen and perishing condition. Look at the loathsomeness of sin; contemplate the immaculate holiness of God; consider the dreadful curse of the law and the awful miseries of hell; seek to be impressed with a humble sense of your sinfulness, unworthiness, guilt, and helplessness; and then it will be no difficult task to plead with God in prayer. It is as natural for the penitent to call upon God, as it is for the babe, when applied to the breast, to imbibe its nourishment. How readily the man pinched with hunger seeks for food! how eloquently the condemned criminal pleads for life, or the drowning man for help! Learn to feel your spiritual wants, and simultaneously you will learn to pray that they may be supplied. Realize that beneath a heavy load of sin you are sinking into perdition, and you will need no other prompting than that of the Spirit who has revealed your guilt, to constrain you to cry out: "Lord, save, or I perish!"

Read the Scriptures, particularly the Psalms, and you will find abundance of matter for thanksgiving and prayer, clothed in the most suitable language.

Plead with God to pour out upon you the spirit of supplication. Fletcher says: "To seek the Spirit is prayer. While you are asking the Spirit to teach you to pray, you are receiving the first lesson in prayer—you have begun already to pray."

29. *Will not an unusual degree of constitutional diffidence justify the neglect of family worship?*

We admit that some men are naturally more timid than others, and find great difficulty in expressing themselves with clearness on any subject. But still this is no just ground for the omission of family worship. Cannot such men speak to their children, or in the presence of their children, on other topics? why not then converse with God in their presence? Is it creditable to any father to be so afraid of his children, as to neglect one of his most important religious duties? How can a man maintain sound discipline in his family, if he be afraid of it? how be a Christian if he tremble more from fear of his children than from the displeasure of God? The apostles and martyrs trembled not before a threatening world; they quailed not in the presence of bloody tyrants, and would rather face the rack and the stake than depart from God's will. When Luther deemed it his duty to go to

Worms to answer before the Diet, he would do so though he had to encounter as many devils as there were tiles on the houses. The timid should bear these things in mind. They should remember that fearful declaration of Christ: "He that is ashamed of me and my words before men, of him shall the Son of man be ashamed before his Father, and the holy angels." He who would do his duty as a Christian must be prepared to take up the cross and to practice self-denial; he must be willing to suffer opposition, derision, and even persecution. His duty is imperious, and if reproach, ridicule, and contempt lie in his way, he must cheerfully meet and bear them. We say not that timidity is a sin; but if we allow it to gain the ascendency and to prevent us from the discharge of duty, then it becomes a snare, is undoubtedly offensive to God, and may prove ruinous to the soul.

30. *May not a man's efforts be so constantly taxed, in order to provide things temporal for his family, as to leave him no time for family prayer?*

Those who think they have no time for family prayer are men who have no taste for it; and if they would closely examine their own hearts, they would find that the true cause of the neglect is not want of time, but want of inclination, or rather downright opposition to the duty. Such have just ground to suspect their religion; and a rigid scrutiny would probably result in a conviction that they are wholly unconverted, and on the broad road that leads down to darkness and death.

If the Bible demanded long and laborious services, the apology would wear the semblance of plausibility; but such is not the case. It pleads only for the duty, and leaves the time to be employed in it to our own conscience. And surely, a few minutes in the morning and evening, which might even be redeemed from sleep, from the toilet, or from unprofitable reading and remark, would not injuriously interfere with secular business or worldly enjoyment.

Why is it that those who love to be engaged in family worship are never heard to urge a want of time? They also have families to provide for, a worldly calling to attend to, and a large and pressing business to look after. But who ever heard them complain that family prayer led them to neglect their secular duties, or that the time so occupied was the cause of the failure of their business? "An investigation on this subject might show, that all conscience is not on the side of the objector; that the acknowledgment of God interferes with no man's welfare; and that there may be a conscientious appropriation of time, even among those who practice family devotion."

But suppose a man is so deeply immersed in business that he really cannot maintain prayer in his family and attend to his business too—what then? Can anyone hesitate for a moment as to the path of duty? Must the claims of the soul yield to those of the body, and the interests of eternity to those of time?

But the truth is, though none of us have too much time, yet all have sufficient for all the duties that God requires. "There is," says the pious Fletcher, "sufficient time both for the objects of the present life, and for the life which is to come. Pious heads of well-regulated families, who have the management of extensive and important business, find time to serve God, and to call their families around the domestic altar. They find that such time, so occupied, never interferes with their temporal interest, but rather brings down from heaven a rich blessing upon their calling and their comforts. Oh, follow the example of these holy characters! then you will enter upon a new era of your existence, even an era of blessedness and happiness. It is an old proverb, 'Prayer and provender hinder no man.' Provender to the horse does not hinder the journey of the traveller; and the prayer of the believer does not hinder the advancement of his temporal prosperity."

All time—every minute and moment of it—is God's time. He commits it to our trust, and will call us to account for its application. Is it not amazing, that we cannot consecrate a few minutes of it, every morning and evening, to his special service? Is it not astounding that we can find so much time every day to provide for the body, which is soon to be laid in the grave and to feed worms, and not one transient quarter of an hour to provide for the soul, which is destined to appear in judgment before God, and to exist forever in heaven or in hell! Oh, the infatuation, the stupidity, the folly and madness of poor, self-deluded man!

We add, in the language of Barrow, "Do we take devotion itself to be no business, or a business of no consideration? Do we conceit, when we pay God his debts, or discharge our duty toward him, when we crave his mercy, when we solicit the main concernments of our souls, that we are idle, or misemployed? that we lavish our time, and lose our pains? What other affairs can we have of greater moment, or necessity, than this? Can there be any interest more close and weighty than this of promoting our own soul's eternal health and happiness? Is not this indeed the great work—*the only necessary matter*—in comparison with which all other occupations are trifling? What are the great businesses of this world? What but scraping for pelf, compassing designs of ambition, courting the respect and favor of men, gratifying sinful curiosity and carnal humor? Shall these

images, these shadows of business, suppress or crowd out devotion?—
that which procureth wealth inestimable, pleasure infinitely
satisfactory, and honor incomparably noble above all that this earth
can afford? Is it not, beside, no such indispensable business, but rather
some base dotage on lucre, some inveigling bait of pleasure, that
crosseth our devotion? Is it not often a complimental visit, an
appointment to tattle, a wild ramble in vice or folly, that so deeply
urgeth us to put off our duty? Nay, is it not commonly sloth, rather
than inclination to any other employment, which diverts us from our
prayers? Is it not the true reason why we pray so seldom, not because
we are very busy, *but because we are extremely idle*; so idle that we
cannot willingly take the pains to withdraw our affections from
sensible things, to reduce our wandering thoughts, to compose our
hearts to right frames, to bend our untoward inclinations to a
compliance with our duty? Do we not betake ourselves to other
conversations and commerces, merely for *refuge, shunning* this
intercourse with God and with ourselves."

CONCLUSION

In conclusion, we would congratulate all those families in which
the worship of God is regularly maintained. They doubtless know,
from happy experience, that it is good to draw nigh to the Most High,
and in proportion as they worship and serve Him in spirit and in
truth, is the measure of their consolations and spiritual enjoyments.
As the house of Obededom was blessed because the ark was in it, so
you are blessed because a reconciled God in Christ dwells among you.
God's presence accompanied the ark; so he is in the midst of those
who meet in Christ's name to worship him. You are now living with
God; you have daily communion with him; the arms of his love
constantly encircle you, and his mercy will abide upon you. He will
not leave nor forsake you. As you are his, and delight in his worship
now, you shall be his in death; he will own you in judgment, and be
your everlasting portion in heaven. And if you find so much comfort
while you worship him in weakness on earth, how much greater will
be your enjoyment, when, made perfect through grace, you shall be
assembled before the throne of God and the Lamb in heaven and join
in his worship in the company of angels and the spirits of the just
made perfect!

Would that we could persuade every reader to enter on a course
of personal and family piety! If you could appreciate the rich
consolations and glorious prospects secured to all its possessors by
vital religion; you would require no other argument. If you are living

without God in the world, then you know something of the barrenness of irreligion; you feel, at least in your retired and reflective moments, how utterly insufficient the world, with all its advantages, is, to meet the wants of an immortal mind, and how exceedingly desirable it is to be prepared to leave this world in peace and hope. Oh, should not this consideration alone be sufficient to determine you to make the resolution individually: "I will arise and go to my father," and, as the head of a family, "As for me and my house, we will serve the Lord?" We beseech you to consecrate your dwellings to the worship and service of God; let every returning day witness the incense of your devotions, sprinkled by faith with the blood of atonement, ascending with acceptance to the throne of grace. Or, will you exclude God from your dwellings? Shall his presence and his grace be cast out from your families, and his Spirit have no place in your hearts nor in the hearts of your children? Oh, we beseech you to relent, to yield, and consent to have the God of Zion to dwell among you. Invite him into your house, press him to abide with you, to live in you and reign over you, and he will hear your prayers, and mercifully respond: "This is my rest; here will I dwell, for I have desired it."

OUR LORD'S PRAYER

Our Father, who art in heaven; hallowed be Thy Name; Thy kingdom come; Thy will be done in earth, as it is in heaven: give us this day our daily bread; and forgive us our trespasses, as we forgive them that trespass against us; and lead us not into temptation, but deliver us from evil; for Thine is the kingdom, and the power, and the glory, forever and ever. Amen.

NEW TESTAMENT BENEDICTION

The grace of our Lord Jesus Christ, and the love of God, and the fellowship of the Holy Ghost, be with us all evermore. Amen.

OLD TESTAMENT BENEDICTION

The Lord bless us, and keep us; the Lord make his face to shine upon us, and be gracious unto us; the Lord lift up the light of his countenance upon us, and give us peace now and forevermore. Amen.

FAMILY PRAYERS

FIRST WEEK

LORDSDAY MORNING

Scripture Lesson

AND God spoke all these words, saying, I am the Lord thy God, which have brought thee out of the land of Egypt, out of the house of bondage. Thou shalt have no other gods before me. Thou shalt not make unto thee any graven image, or any likeness of anything that is in heaven above, or that is in the earth beneath, or that is in the water under the earth: thou shalt not bow down thyself to them, nor serve them: for I the Lord thy God am a jealous God, visiting the iniquity of the fathers upon the children unto the third and fourth generation of them that hate me; and showing mercy unto thousands of them that love me, and keep my commandments. Thou shalt not take the name of the Lord thy God in vain; for the Lord will not hold him guiltless that taketh his name in vain. Remember the Sabbath-day, to keep it holy. Six days shalt thou labor, and do all thy work: but the seventh day is the Sabbath of the Lord thy God: in it thou shalt not do any work, thou, nor thy son, nor thy daughter, thy man-servant, nor thy maid-servant, nor thy cattle, nor thy stranger that is within thy gates: for in six days the Lord made heaven and earth, the sea, and all that in them is, and rested the seventh day: wherefore the Lord blessed the Sabbath-day, and hallowed it. Honor thy father and thy mother; that thy days may be long upon the land which the Lord thy God giveth thee. Thou shalt not kill. Thou shalt not commit adultery. Thou shalt not steal. Thou shalt not bear false witness against thy neighbor. Thou shalt not covet thy neighbor's house, thou shalt not covet thy neighbor's wife, nor his man-servant, nor his maid-servant, nor his ox, nor his ass, nor anything that is thy neighbor's. And all the people saw the thunderings, and the lightnings, and the noise of the trumpet, and the mountain smoking: and when the people saw it, they removed, and stood afar off. And they said unto Moses, Speak thou with us, and we will hear: but let not God speak with us, lest we die. And Moses said unto the people, Fear not: for God is come to prove you, and that his fear may be before your faces, that ye sin not.— *Exodus* 20:1–20.

Prayer

O THOU who art the Author and Preserver of our lives, unto thee we would lift up our hearts. Teach us to approach thee with that reverence which becometh all thy creatures; and draw near to us, as a God of pity, of mercy, and of grace.

As disciples of Jesus Christ, who hope for acceptance only through his merits and mediation, we would now offer up our morning sacrifice to the God, and Father, and fountain of all good. This is the day upon which thy Son rose from the dead, finishing the work of our redemption; the happy day when the love of God, the grace of Jesus Christ, and the fellowship of the Holy Ghost, may be humbly expected wherever two or three are met together in the name of the adorable Trinity. Wilt thou then, O most high and incomprehensible Jehovah! accept of the dedication which we now make thee of our bodies and souls?

We are sensible that we have rendered ourselves unworthy of thy notice, having lost thy image, and broken thy commandments. But, God of all grace, thou art in Christ again reconciling a guilty world unto thyself, not imputing unto men their trespasses; and, therefore, we would now believingly, yet humbly, ask and hope everything for his sake. Let all the sins we have committed be blotted out of the book of thy remembrance. Let these worthless souls of ours be clothed with the wedding garments of a Redeemer's righteousness. O thou Giver of every good and perfect gift, create in us clean hearts, and renew right spirits within us, that we may love thee—that we may fear thee—that it may be as our meat and our drink at all times to do thy holy will. We thank thee, O God, for that providential care and goodness which thou hast exercised toward us during the past week, and the past night. Prepare us for all the duties in which we are this day to be engaged. When we are allowed to enter into thine earthly temple, let all worldly wishes, worldly cares, and worldly thoughts, be banished from our minds. Let thy word preached enlighten our understandings, spiritualize our hopes, confirm our faith, rekindle our love, and inspire us with new resolutions to live more becoming the professions we have made, and the privileges we enjoy.

And when we return from thy house, forbid, O God, that we should spend any part of thy day in thinking our own thoughts, speaking our own words, or minding our own pleasures; but let it be an entire Sabbath of rest unto our souls.

O Lord, we would intercede in behalf of all mankind! Thou hast promised, by the blood of thy covenant, to speak peace unto the heathen. Soon, O God, give them to thy Son as his inheritance, with the utmost parts of the earth for his possession. Where the gospel is preached and professed, may multitudes be converted, and made a willing people in the day of thy power. Pour out, O God, a double portion of thy Holy Spirit upon all the ministers of the everlasting gospel; and may they be enabled to discharge the important trust committed to them with fidelity and diligence, and with abundant success. Let the churches with which we are more immediately connected have rest; and, walking together in the fear of the Lord, and comforts of the Holy Ghost, may they be edified and multiplied.

(Occasional Prayers.)

May our relatives and friends, wherever they are, be the objects of thy providential care, and the subjects of thy saving grace. Such as may now be more immediately under thy afflicting hand, O God, console, support, and in thy due time deliver; and may we all have an interest in that sure promise, that all things at last shall work together for good.

Now, unto the King eternal, immortal, and invisible, the only wise God, be honor and glory, forever and ever. *Amen.*

LORDSDAY EVENING

Scripture Lesson

IN the end of the Sabbath, as it began to dawn toward the first day of the week, came Mary Magdalene, and the other Mary, to see the sepulchre. And, behold, there was a great earthquake: for the angel of the Lord descended from heaven, and came and rolled back the stone from the door and sat upon it. His countenance was like lightning, and his raiment white as snow: and for fear of him the keepers did shake, and became as dead men. And the angel answered and said unto the woman, Fear not ye: for I know that ye seek Jesus, which was crucified. He is not here; for he is risen, as he said. Come, see the place where the Lord lay: and go quickly, and tell his disciples that he is risen from the dead; and, behold, he goeth before you into Galilee; there shall ye see him: lo, I have told you. And they departed quickly from the sepulchre with fear and great joy, and did run to bring his disciples word. And as they went to tell his disciples, behold, Jesus met them, saying, All hail. And they came and held him by the feet, and worshipped him. Then said Jesus unto them, Be not afraid: go, tell thy brethren that they go into Galilee, and there shall they see me. Now, when they were going, behold, some of the watch came into the city, and showed unto the chief priests all the things that were done. And when they were assembled with the elders, and had taken counsel, they gave large money unto the soldiers, saying, Say ye; His disciples came by night, and stole him away while we slept. And if this come to the governor's ears, we will persuade him, and secure you. So they took the money, and did as they were taught; and this saying is commonly reported among the Jews until this day. Then the eleven disciples went away into Galilee, into a mountain where Jesus had appointed them. And when they saw him, they worshipped him: but some doubted. And Jesus came and spoke unto them, saying, All power is given unto me in heaven and in earth. Go ye, therefore, and teach all nations, baptizing them in the name of the Father, and of the Son, and of the Holy Ghost; teaching them to observe all things whatsoever I have commanded you: and, lo, I am with you always, *even* unto the end of the world. Amen.—*Matthew* 28.

Prayer

IT is a good thing to give thanks unto the Lord, and to sing praises unto thy name, O Most High, to show forth thy loving-kindness in the morning, and thy faithfulness every night.

We this evening acknowledge the blessings of another Lords Day. Thus thou art affording us opportunities to retire and to learn, among all the cares of life, that one thing is needful; and to hear the inquiry, What is a man profited, if he should gain the whole world and lose his own soul?

We thank thee that the lines are fallen to us in pleasant places, and that we have a goodly heritage: so that we can add to private meditation and devotion the public ordinances of religion; and can sit under our own vine and fig-tree, none daring to make us afraid. We bless thee, that we have not only the Scriptures, but the ministry of the gospel; and have this day not only read, but heard, the words of eternal life.

But, O God, the effects we experience while waiting upon thee often prove like the morning cloud, and early dew. Render, we beseech thee, the impressions made upon us deep and durable: keep these things forever in the hearts of thy people; and let thy word *dwell* in us richly, in all *wisdom.*

May the instructions we receive attend us in every part of our life, and regulate, and excite us in the discharge of all our duties, so that, whether we are husbands or wives, parents or children, masters or servants, we may adorn the doctrine of God our Savior in all things. May we be satisfied with no knowledge, no belief, no professions, no feelings, in religion—while our hearts are void of thy love, and we are strangers to that grace which bringeth salvation, and teacheth us to deny ungodliness and worldly lusts, and to live soberly, righteously, and godly in the present world.

We take shame to ourselves, not only for our open violations of thy law, but for our secret faults, our omissions of duty, our unprofitable attendance on the means of grace, and all the sins of our holy things. Our iniquities are increased over our head, and our trespass is gone up into the very heavens—and there he is gone also, who is our Advocate with the Father, and the Propitiation for our sins. Behold his hands and his feet: and hear, O hear, the voice of the blood of sprinkling, that speaketh better things than that of Abel.

Remember the millions who were never favored with the advantages we enjoy, and would be grateful for the crumbs that fall from our table. They never smiled when a Lordsday appeared. They never heard the name of Jesus. O, send out thy light and thy truth. Let thy way be known on earth; thy saving health among all nations.

(Occasional Prayers.)

We now commit ourselves, with all our interests, friends, and relations, into thy hands. Guard us through the defenseless hours of sleep, from every evil to which we are exposed. If it should please thee to call us hence this night—may we awake in glory, and be forever with the Lord: or if thou shouldst continue us in being, may we rise in health and comfort, to pay thee the homage of a grateful heart, in a course of cheerful obedience.

Prepare us, we beseech thee, for the rest that remains for thy people; in which we shall join the general assembly and church of the first-born, in ascribing blessing and honor, and glory, and power, to him that sitteth upon the throne and to the Lamb, forever and ever. *Amen.*

MONDAY MORNING

Scripture Lesson

THEREFORE, being justified by faith, we have peace with God, through our Lord Jesus Christ; by whom also we have access by faith into this grace wherein we stand, and rejoice in hope of the glory of God. And not only so, but we glory in tribulation also: knowing that tribulation worketh patience; and patience, experience; and experience, hope: and hope maketh not ashamed; because the love of God is shed abroad in our hearts by the Holy Ghost which is given unto us. For when we were yet without strength, in due time Christ died for the ungodly. For scarcely for a righteous man will one die; yet peradventure for a good man some would even dare to die. But God commendeth his love toward us, in that, while we were yet sinners, Christ died for us. Much more then, being now justified by his blood, we shall be saved from wrath through him. For if, when we were enemies, we were reconciled to God by the death of his Son, much more, being reconciled, we shall be saved by his life. And not only so, but we also joy in God, through our Lord Jesus Christ, by whom we have now received the atonement. Wherefore, as by one man sin entered into the world, and death by sin; and so death passed upon all men, for that all have sinned: (for until the law, sin was in the world: but sin is not imputed when there is no law. Nevertheless, death reigned from Adam to Moses, even over them that had not sinned after the similitude of Adam's transgression, who is the figure of him that was to come. But not as the offence, so also is the free gift. For if through the offence of one many be dead, much more the grace of God, and the gift by grace, which is by one man, Jesus Christ, hath abounded unto many. And not as it was by one that sinned, so is the gift: for the judgment was by one to condemnation, but the free gift is of many offences unto justification. For if by one man's offence death reigned by one; much more they which receive abundance of grace, and of the gift of righteousness, shall reign in life by one, Jesus Christ:) therefore, as by the offence of one judgment came upon all men to condemnation, even so by the righteousness of one the free gift came upon all men unto justification of life. For as by one man's disobedience many were made sinners, so by the obedience of one shall many be made righteous. Moreover, the law entered, that the offence might abound: but where sin abounded, grace did much more abound; that as sin hath reigned unto death, even so might grace reign through righteousness unto eternal life, by Jesus Christ our Lord. *Romans* 5.

Prayer

ALMIGHTY and everlasting God, in whom we live and move and have our being, we acknowledge our daily dependence upon thee. We thank thee for thy goodness, in watching over us during the darkness of the night, in protecting us from evil, and in permitting us again to behold the morning light. Accept, heavenly Father, this our grateful sacrifice of praise and thanksgiving; and enable us to approach thy throne with humble reverence and godly fear; feeling our necessities; confessing our sins and unworthiness; and seeking pardon and forgiveness, through the merits of thy beloved Son, Jesus Christ, our Lord.

Give us grace, merciful God, to dedicate both our souls and bodies to thee and thy service, in a sober, righteous, and godly life; and, in pity to the weakness and corruption of our nature, we beseech thee to help our infirmities and strengthen our resolutions. As a father pitieth his own children, even so be thou merciful unto us. Grant us the constant assistance of thy Holy Spirit; that we may be effectually restrained from sin, and excited to our duty. Imprint upon our hearts such a dread of thy displeasure, and such a grateful sense of thy goodness, as may make us both afraid and ashamed to offend thee. Keep in our minds a lively remembrance of that great day in which every thought and word and deed will be judged in righteousness, when those that sleep in the dust of the earth shall awake—some to everlasting life, and some to shame and everlasting contempt. Purify our hearts, and direct us in all our ways. As we approach nearer and nearer to the eternal world, make us more diligent, and watchful, and circumspect. Keep us this day from all evil, and defend us from danger and adversity. Guard us in the hour of temptation, restrain our passions, regulate our desires, and preserve us especially from the sins which most easily beset us. Grant us patience and resignation, if thou shalt see fit to visit us with affliction or calamity; and, in whatsoever state or condition it may please thee to place us, grant us grace therewith to be content. Make us just and upright in all our dealings; kind and compassionate to our neighbors; quiet and peaceable in all the relations of life; faithful to every trust committed to us; and ready to do good to all men, according to our abilities and opportunities.

(Occasional Prayers.)

Heavenly Father, receive with favor this our morning offering, and grant our petitions, not for our own deservings, but for the sake, and through the merits of Jesus Christ thy Son our Lord. *Amen.*

MONDAY EVENING

Scripture Lesson

THERE is therefore now no condemnation to them which are in Christ Jesus, who walk not after the flesh, but after the Spirit. For the law of the Spirit of life in Christ Jesus hath made me free from the law of sin and death. For what the law could not do, in that it was weak through the flesh, God sending his own Son in the likeness of sinful flesh, and for sin, condemned sin in the flesh, that the righteousness of the law might be fulfilled in us, who walk not after the flesh, but after the Spirit. For they that are after the flesh, do mind the things of the flesh; but they that are after the Spirit, the things of the Spirit. For to be carnally minded is death; but to be spiritually minded is life and peace: because the carnal mind is enmity against God; for it is not subject to the law of God, neither indeed can be. So then they that are in the flesh cannot please God. But ye are not in the flesh, but in the Spirit, if so be that the Spirit of God dwell in you. Now, if any man have not the Spirit of Christ, he is none of his. And if Christ be in you, the body is dead because of sin; but the Spirit is life because of righteousness. But if the Spirit of him that raised up Jesus from the dead dwell in you, he that raised up Christ from the dead shall also quicken your mortal bodies by his Spirit that dwelleth in you. Therefore, brethren, we are debtors, not to the flesh, to live after the flesh. For if ye live after the flesh, ye shall die; but if ye through the Spirit do mortify the deeds of the body, ye shall live. For as many as are led by the Spirit of God, they are the sons of God. For ye have not received the spirit of bondage again to fear; but ye have received the Spirit of adoption, whereby we cry, Abba, Father. The Spirit itself beareth witness with our spirit, that we are the children of God: and if children, then heirs: heirs of God, and joint heirs with Christ: if so be that we suffer with him, that we may be also glorified together. For I reckon, that the sufferings of this present time are not worthy to be compared with the glory which shall be revealed in us. For the earnest expectation of the creature waiteth for the manifestation of the sons of God. For the creature was made subject to vanity, not willingly, but by reason of him who hath subjected the same in hope; because the creature itself also shall be delivered from the bondage of corruption into the glorious liberty of the children of God. *Romans* 8:1–21.

Prayer

ALMIGHTY and everlasting God, by whose merciful providence we are preserved from day to day, enable us to draw near to thee with reverence and godly fear. Turn thee unto us, in loving-kindness, and hearken unto our prayer. Pardon, we beseech thee, all the sins of this day. Thou hast not dealt with us according to our sins, nor rewarded us according to our iniquities. Hide not thy face from us when we cry unto thee, but refresh us with thy Spirit, and show us the light of thy countenance. By thy help alone we are enabled to will and to do those things which are good and acceptable unto thee. Grant us thy continual mercy and grace. Let thy fatherly hand be over us, to sustain and preserve us. Let thy holy Spirit be ever with us, to guide us in the knowledge and obedience of thy word, that so in the end we may obtain everlasting life.

To thy gracious care and protection, heavenly Father, we commit ourselves and all our friends and relatives this night. Guard us, we beseech thee, from every danger, and bring us in peace and safety to the beginning of another day. Enable us, by thy grace, to walk worthy of the vocation wherewith we are called; with lowliness and meekness; with long-suffering, forbearing one another in love; endeavoring to keep the unity of the Spirit in the bond of peace; till we all come, in the unity of the faith and of the knowledge of the Son of God, unto a perfect man, unto the measure of the stature of the fullness of Christ.

Give us grace to put off the old man, which is corrupt according to the deceitful lusts; that we may be renewed in the spirit of our mind, and may put on the new man, which, after God, is created in righteousness and true holiness.

Grant us, O God, according to the riches of thy grace, to be strengthened with might by thy Spirit in the inner man; that Christ may dwell in our hearts by faith; that we, being rooted and grounded in him, may know the love of Christ, which passeth knowledge, and be filled with all the fullness of thee our God.

(Occasional Prayers.)

Now unto Him that is able to do exceeding abundantly above all that we ask or think, according to the power that worketh in us—unto him be glory in the church by Christ Jesus, throughout all ages, world without end. *Amen.*

TUESDAY MORNING

Scripture Lesson

AND seeing the multitude, he went up into a mountain; and when he was set, his disciples came unto him: and he opened his mouth, and taught them, saying, Blessed are the poor in spirit: for theirs is the kingdom of heaven. Blessed are they that mourn: for they shall be comforted. Blessed are the meek: for they shall inherit the earth. Blessed are they which do hunger and thirst after righteousness: for they shall be filled. Blessed are the merciful: for they shall obtain mercy. Blessed are the pure in heart: for they shall see God. Blessed are the peace-makers: for they shall be called the children of God. Blessed are they which are persecuted for righteousness' sake: for theirs is the kingdom of heaven. Blessed are ye when men shall revile you, and persecute you, and shall say all manner of evil against you falsely, for my sake. Rejoice, and be exceeding glad; for great is your reward in heaven: for so persecuted they the prophets which were before you. Ye are the salt of the earth: but if the salt have lost his savor, wherewith shall it be salted? it is thenceforth good for nothing, but to be cast out, and to be trodden under foot of men. Ye are the light of the world. A city that is set on a hill cannot be hid. Neither do men light a candle, and put it under a bushel, but on a candlestick; and it giveth light unto all that are in the house. Let your light so shine before men that they may see your good works, and glorify your Father which is in heaven. Think not that I am come to destroy the law or the prophets: I am not come to destroy, but to fulfill. For verily I say unto you, Till heaven and earth pass, one jot or one tittle shall in no wise pass from the law, till all be fulfilled. Whosoever, therefore, shall break one of these least commandments, and shall teach men so, he shall be called the least in the kingdom of heaven: but whosoever shall do and teach them, the same shall be called great in the kingdom of heaven. For I say unto you, That except your righteousness shall exceed the righteousness of the Scribes and Pharisees, ye shall in no case enter into the kingdom of heaven. *Matthew* 5:1–20.

Prayer

O THOU King eternal, immortal, and invisible, we would adore thee, and take shame to ourselves; and, though allowed to approach thy divine Majesty, we would never forget the humiliation and contrition which become such creatures as we are. Father! we have sinned against heaven and in thy sight, and are not worthy to be called thy children; we are unworthy of the least of all thy mercies.

Oh, for hearts of flesh! Lord, help us to feel our vileness, to deplore our guilt, and to cast ourselves at thy feet, abhorring ourselves and repenting in dust and ashes. And impart to us that faith which will enable us to hope in thy word, and derive strong consolation from the invitations and promises of the gospel. We have come to implore the greatest blessings the God of love can give: we have come to call thee Abba, Father, to lean on thy arm. It is thy commandment that we should believe on the name of thy Son, Jesus Christ. Lord, we assent, we submit. Since he came into the world to save sinners, we take him as *our* Savior; and glory in him, as made to us wisdom and righteousness, sanctification and redemption.

And oh, may our minds be fixed and filled with admiring thoughts of his person and offices; may our hearts be inflamed with a sense of his boundless compassion and love. By the new and living way, which he has not only revealed but consecrated for us, may we come to thee, and enjoy all the advantages of a state of reconciliation and friendship with God. To thee may we commit our way and our works; and in everything by prayer and supplication make known our requests unto God; and be thou always near, to guide us and to defend, to relieve us in trouble, and to help us in duty.

(Occasional Prayers.)

Again thy goodness hath preserved our spirits. Through the dark and silent watches of the night, thou hast suffered no evil to befall us, nor any plague to come nigh our dwelling. Oh that we were truly thankful, and could show forth thy praise in our lives as well as with our lips!

Thou takest pleasure in the prosperity of thy servants: may we always take pleasure in the advancement of thy glory. Thou art never weary in doing us good: may we never grow weary in well-doing. Thy mercies are new every morning: every morning, by thy mercies, may we present our bodies a living sacrifice, holy and acceptable, which is our reasonable service.

And to the God of our salvation, the Father, the Son, and the Holy Spirit, be ascribed the kingdom, the power, and the glory, forever and ever. *Amen.*

TUESDAY EVENING

Scripture Lesson

YE have heard that it was said by them of old times, Thou shalt not kill; and whosoever shall kill shall be in danger of the judgment: but I say unto you, That whosoever is angry with his brother without a cause, shall be in danger of the judgment; and whosoever shall say to his brother, Raca, shall be in danger of the council; but whosoever shall say, Thou fool, shall be in danger of hell fire. Therefore, if thou bring thy gift to the altar, and there rememberest that thy brother hath aught against thee, leave there thy gift before the altar, and go thy way; first be reconciled to thy brother, and then come and offer thy gift. Agree with thine adversary quickly, while thou art in the way with him; lest at any time the adversary deliver thee to the judge, and the judge deliver thee to the officer, and thou be cast into prison. Verily, I say unto thee, Thou shalt by no means come out thence, till thou hast paid the uttermost farthing. Ye have heard that it was said by them of old time, Thou shalt not commit adultery: but I say unto you, That whosoever looketh on a woman to lust after her, hath committed adultery with her already in his heart. And if thy right eye offend thee, pluck it out, and cast it from thee: for it is profitable for thee that one of thy members should perish, and not that thy whole body should be cast into hell. And if thy right hand offend thee, cut it off, and cast it from thee; for it is profitable for thee that one of thy members should perish, and not that thy whole body should be cast into hell. It has been said, Whosoever shall put away his wife, let him give her a writing of divorcement; but I say unto you, That whosoever shall put away his wife, saving for the cause of fornication, causeth her to commit adultery: and whosoever shall marry her that is divorced committeth adultery. *Matthew* 5:21–32.

Prayer

O GOD, by thy mercies, we again surround this family altar and engage in the exercises of devotion. May we worship thee, a holy God, in the beauty of holiness; and thee, who art a Spirit, in spirit and in truth. Such worship alone thy word requires; but such worship thy grace alone can enable us to render. All our sufficiency is of thee: do thou work in us to will and to do of thy good pleasure.

We confess the number and offensiveness of our transgressions, and acknowledge that we deserve to perish. But we bless thee for the everlasting consolation and good hope, through grace, which the gospel affords; for the news of a Mediator between thee and us; of a

High-Priest, who has put away sin by the sacrifice of himself; of an Advocate with the Father, who ever lives to make intercession for us, and of a Savior, in whom it has pleased thee, that all fullness should dwell.

Produce in us true repentance unto life. Give us that faith by which we shall be justified from all things, and have peace with God, through our Lord Jesus Christ. To the Redeemer's cross may we retreat, and there find security and relief, refreshment and delight.

We bless thee for thy word. May it dwell in us richly in all wisdom. May we make it, not only the man of our counsel, but a light unto our feet, and a lamp unto our path. May we take it along with us into all the concerns of life; and whether we are rich or poor, whether we are parents or children, whether we are appointed to govern or serve, may we walk by this rule, that mercy and peace may be upon us.

Regard those who, under the pressure of affliction, are saying, Brethren, pray for us. Be with them in trouble. Thou knowest the anxieties of thy people, lest any by their temper or conduct should injure the religion they profess; let thy grace be sufficient for them: let faith and patience have their perfect work: let them glorify thee in all their trials.

Bless all in authority over us, and so rule their hearts and strengthen their hands, that they may punish wickedness and vice, and maintain true religion and virtue.

(Occasional Prayers.)

We now commit ourselves to thy merciful protection for this night. May we lie down to rest at peace with thee and with all the world. Forgive, we humbly pray thee, all the sins we may have committed this day. If, in our intercourse with our friends or foes, we have manifested a spirit unlike that of thy dear Son, do thou be graciously pleased to forgive it. If we have neglected our duty to the poor, or the needy; if we have failed in setting a holy example before each other; if we have had improper feelings toward thee or our fellow-men,—we pray thee to forgive us. Sprinkle upon us that blood which cleanseth from all sin; and take us into thy holy care and keeping. Let no plague come nigh our dwelling. Preserve us from sickness and sudden death; from alarm, and from the devouring elements; from the pestilence that walketh in darkness, as thou hast done from the destruction that wasteth at noonday. And raise us in the morning, fitted for all the duties and events of another day. These mercies, and whatever else we need, we humbly ask in the name of thy dear Son, our Savior Jesus Christ; to whom, with thee and the Holy Ghost, be all honor and praise, both now and forever. *Amen.*

WEDNESDAY MORNING

Scripture Lesson

AGAIN, ye have heard that it hath been said by them of old time, Thou shalt not forswear thyself, but shalt perform unto the Lord thine oaths: but I say unto you, Swear not at all: neither by heaven; for it is God's throne: nor by the earth; for it is his footstool: neither by Jerusalem; for it is the city of the great King: neither shalt thou swear by thy head; because thou canst not make one hair white or black. But let your communication be Yea, yea; Nay, nay: for whatsoever is more than these cometh of evil. Ye have heard that it hath been said, An eye for an eye, and a tooth for a tooth: but I say unto you, That ye resist not evil; but whosoever shall smite thee on thy right cheek, turn to him the other also. And if any man will sue thee at the law, and take away thy coat, let him have thy cloak also. And whosoever shall compel thee to go a mile, go with him twain. Give to him that asketh thee; and from him that would borrow of thee turn not thou away. Ye have heard that it hath been said, Thou shalt love thy neighbor, and hate thine enemy: but I say unto you, Love your enemies, bless them that curse you, do good to them that hate you, and pray for them which despitefully use you, and persecute you; that ye may be the children of your Father which is in heaven: for he maketh his sun to rise on the evil and on the good, and sendeth rain on the just and on the unjust. For if ye love them which love you, what reward have ye? do not even the publicans the same? And if ye salute your brethren only, what do ye more than others? do not even the publicans so? Be ye therefore perfect, even as your Father which is in heaven is perfect. *Matthew* 5:33–48.

Prayer

O LORD God Almighty, who art, and wast, and art to come, thy name is most holy, and thy glory reacheth above the heavens. We adore thee, that through thy beloved Son thou hast opened the way to the throne of grace, and hast declared thyself to be rich in mercy to all that call upon thee in truth.

Great and glorious God, we are bound to give thee our fervent thanks, because thy hands have made us, thy power preserves us, and thou givest us all things richly to enjoy. Thou hast lightened our eyes again, and hast caused the outgoings of the morning, as well as of the evening, to rejoice over us. We adore thee, O God, for thy goodness, wisdom, and power, displayed in our creation. We adore thee that in the time of danger thou hast been our defense against the multiplied evils and calamities in which many others have been involved. But in an especial manner we adore thee for thy unspeakable mercy and everlasting love, in sending thy beloved Son to be a propitiation for our sins, and that thou hast made peace through the blood of his cross, to reconcile sinners unto thyself.

Merciful Father, make us sensible that we are not worthy of the least of thy mercies, and grateful that thy loving-kindness is ever more and more toward us. Help us to own thy providence in all our concerns, and to bless the hand that smites us in all the afflictions and trials of this mortal life. May we trace up all our streams of earthly and spiritual comfort to the fountain of eternal love in Christ Jesus.

O thou Holy Spirit, whose office it is to take of the things of Christ, and show them with power to our souls, discover to us more and more of the all-sufficiency of the Lord Jesus, and of the endearing offices and relations which he sustains toward his people.

May we know him as our life and peace, our wisdom and righteousness, our sanctification and redemption, our refuge and the rock of our strength.

Blessed Lord, put thy fear into our hearts; give us understanding to know thy will in all things, and grace to perform the same. Enable us to gain the victory over our besetting sins. Wean our affections from the things of time and sense. Put the world, the flesh, and the devil under our feet. And enable us to glorify thee with our bodies, our souls, and our spirits, which are thine. Help us to reflect that we are not redeemed with corruptible things, such as silver and gold, but with the precious blood of Christ, as of a lamb without spot and blemish. May our walk and conduct prove that we are his true disciples; may we walk in his steps, and run with enlarged hearts in the way of his commandments.

(Occasional Prayers.)

O Lord, may all our dear relations and friends be dear to thee. Have mercy on those who are alienated from thee, through the ignorance that is in them, and who neither see nor feel the guilt and corruption of their nature. Enlighten their dark minds, and make them wise unto salvation through faith in Jesus Christ. Be gracious also to those who have received a good hope through thy grace; establish their faith, animate their hope, increase their love, and fix their affections surely there, where true joys are to be found. And while the door of mercy is yet open, cause sinners of every description to flee to Him who delivereth from the wrath to come. O Lord, let the word of thy truth have free course and be glorified; let the borders of thy church be enlarged; and let every tongue, and kindred, and people unite in praising the God of their salvation.

Hear us, O heavenly Father, for the sake of Him who hath loved and redeemed us, even the Lord our Righteousness; to whom, with thee and the Holy Spirit, our guide and comforter, be ascribed the kingdom, and the power, and the glory, now and for evermore. *Amen.*

WEDNESDAY EVENING

Scripture Lesson

TAKE heed that ye do not your alms before men, to be seen of them; otherwise ye have no reward of your Father which is in heaven. Therefore, when thou doest thine alms, do not sound a trumpet before thee, as the hypocrites do in the synagogues and in the streets, that they may have glory of men. Verily, I say unto you, They have their reward. But when thou doest alms, let not thy left hand know what thy right hand doeth; that thine alms may be in secret: and thy Father, which seeth in secret, himself shall reward thee openly. And when thou prayest, thou shalt not be as the hypocrites are: for they love to pray standing in the synagogues, and in the corners of the streets, that they may be seen of men. Verily I say unto you, They have their reward. But thou, when thou prayest, enter into thy closet; and when thou hast shut thy door, pray to thy Father which is in secret; and thy Father, which seeth in secret, shall reward thee openly. But when ye pray, use not vain repetitions, as the heathen do: for they think that they shall be heard for their much speaking. Be not ye therefore like unto them: for your Father knoweth what things ye have need of before ye ask him. After this manner therefore pray ye: Our Father which art in heaven, hallowed be thy name. Thy kingdom come. Thy will be done in earth, as it is in heaven. Give us this day our daily bread. And forgive us our debts, as we forgive our debtors. And lead us not into temptation; but deliver us from evil: for thine is the kingdom, and the power, and the glory, forever. Amen. For if ye forgive men their trespasses, your heavenly Father will also forgive you. But if ye forgive not men their trespasses, neither will your Father forgive your trespasses. *Matthew 6:1–15.*

Prayer

O THOU eternal and unchangeable God, thou art the same yesterday, to-day, and forever: by thine almighty power and providential care we have been preserved another day, and through thy grace we are permitted once more to approach thee in prayer. We are not our own, for we have been bought with a price. Help us to consecrate ourselves and all that we have and are to thee. Enable us to glorify thee in our bodies and spirits, which are thine.

We render thee thanks for the mercies which have followed us to the present hour. Bless the Lord, O our souls, and forget not all his benefits.

Enable us, by thy grace, to show forth thy praise in a holy and consistent walk and conversation. May we let our light so shine, that others, seeing our good works, may glorify our Father who is in heaven.

We would confess our multiplied offences against thee, our innumerable transgressions of thy holy law, and our aggravated sins of omission and commission. We are guilty in thy sight. We deserve thy wrath. But, O most merciful Father, for the sake of thy Son Jesus Christ, pardon our iniquities, justify us freely on account of his righteousness, and accept us graciously in thy beloved. Wash us in that fountain which was opened in the house of David for sin and uncleanness. Sprinkle us with atoning blood. Create within us clean hearts, and renew within us right spirits. Vouchsafe to us the grace of thy Spirit, that being enlightened, strengthened, and sanctified by the same, we may depart from all iniquity, and adorn the doctrine of God our Savior in all things.

Almighty God, visit in mercy and with salvation, the congregation of worshiping Christians with which we are connected. Make bare thine arm for the salvation of sinners, and give abundant success to the ministration of thy word and ordinances among us. To this end, revive thy work in the hearts of thine own children, and plenteously endue thy servant, our pastor, with wisdom and grace from on high, that he may rightly divide the word of life, and faithfully discharge the duties of his office. May the young be trained in the nurture and admonition of the Lord, that they may remember their Creator in the days of their youth.

Bless all thy ministering servants and thy church universal with an abundant outpouring of thy Holy Spirit, and with a time of refreshing from the presence of the Lord.

Regard in tender mercy and compassion, O Lord God, our absent relations and friends. Make them, by thy grace, the children of thine adoption and heirs of eternal life. Heal the sick and comfort the afflicted. Give strength to the weak, succor to the tempted, encouragement to the desponding, faith to the unbelieving, and needed grace to all.

To thy watchful care and kind protection, O thou Keeper of Israel, we commend our bodies and souls this night. Preserve us from all evil; grant us refreshing sleep; and, if consistent with thy divine will, permit us in health and comfort to behold and enjoy the light of another day.

(Occasional Prayers.)

Hear us, O Lord, in these our humble petitions. Accept our thanksgivings and praise, and graciously own and accept us, through Jesus Christ our Redeemer. *Amen.*

THURSDAY MORNING

Scripture Lesson

MOREOVER, when ye fast, be not as the hypocrites, of a sad countenance; for they disfigure their faces, that they may appear unto men to fast. Verily I say unto you, They have their reward. But thou, when thou fastest, anoint thy head, and wash thy face; that thou appear not unto men to fast, but unto thy Father which is in secret: and thy Father, which seeth in secret, shall reward thee openly. Lay not up for yourselves treasures upon earth, where moth and rust doth corrupt, and where thieves break through and steal: but lay up for yourselves treasures in heaven, where neither moth nor rust doth corrupt, and where thieves do not break through nor steal: for where your treasure is, there will your heart be also. The light of the body is the eye: if, therefore, thine eye be single, thy whole body shall be full of light. But if thine eye be evil, thy whole body shall be full of darkness. If, therefore, the light that is in thee be darkness, how great is that darkness! No man can serve two masters: for either he will hate the one, and love the other; or else he will hold to the one, and despise the other. Ye cannot serve God and mammon. Therefore I say unto you, Take no thought for your life, what ye shall eat, or what ye shall drink; nor yet for your body, what ye shall put on. Is not the life more than meat, and the body than raiment? Behold the fowls of the air: for they sow not, neither do they reap, nor gather into barns; yet your heavenly Father feedeth them. Are ye not much better than they? Which of you, by taking thought, can add one cubit unto his stature? and why take ye thought for raiment? Consider the lilies of the field, how they grow; they toil not, neither do they spin: and yet I say unto you, That even Solomon, in all his glory, was not arrayed like one of these. Wherefore, if God so clothe the grass of the field, which to-day is, and to-morrow is cast into the oven, shall he not much more clothe you, oh ye of little faith? Therefore take no thought, saying, What shall we eat? or, What shall we drink? or, Wherewithal shall we be clothed? (for after all these things do the Gentiles seek:) for your heavenly Father knoweth that ye have need of all these things. But seek ye first the kingdom of God, and his righteousness; and all these things shall be added unto you. Take therefore no thought for the morrow: for the morrow shall take thought for the things of itself. Sufficient unto the day is the evil thereof. *Matt.* 6:16–34.

Prayer

ALMIGHTY and merciful Father, thou art our hope and our stronghold: thou art our God, in whom we will trust. Thou hast kept us through the dangers of the past night: thou hast brought us in safety to the beginning of another day. For these, thy great mercies, we bless thee. Nay, we come before thee, under a deep and humiliating sense of our unworthiness. Helpless and miserable sinners, we ask nothing for our own merits or deservings. But we know, O Lord God, that thou art full of compassion and mercy, long-suffering, and plenteous in goodness and truth. Oh turn thee unto us, therefore, and have mercy upon us. For the sake of thy dear Son, Jesus Christ, pardon our transgressions, and receive us graciously, and hear the supplications which we present unto thee in his all-prevailing name.

And since we are by nature prone to evil, and unable of ourselves to purify our hearts, we pray thee, O God, to cleanse our thoughts by the powerful efficacy of thy grace, from all vain desires, and sinful imaginations. Grant unto us thy Holy Spirit. May he dwell within us, as a Spirit of purity and holiness, a Spirit of truth and of wisdom, of peace also, and love, and of holy joy and consolation. May we pass this day in humble consciousness of our dependence, in thankful remembrance of thy mercies, and in the diligent performance of thy commandments. May no evil thoughts, or angry passions, or distressing doubts or fears disturb us. May we serve thee, our God, with cheerfulness and fidelity, and live in peace and charity, and brotherly love with all men.

We pray thee, O Lord, so to animate our minds with the glorious hopes set before us in thy word, that all our present trials and sacrifices, and self-denials may be borne with cheerful resignation and submission. May we count the loss of all things as nothing, in comparison with the inward satisfaction and joy, which the gospel affords in the midst of worldly disappointments. But, O God, deliver us, we beseech thee, from every false or delusive hope. Let us remember, that other foundation can no man lay, than that which is laid, even Jesus Christ our Lord. On this foundation may we begin, and continue, and finish all our doings; until every evil habit is destroyed, every sinful inclination cast out, every temptation overcome, and every terror done away; and until thy Spirit shall bear witness with our spirit, that we are the children of God.

(Occasional Prayers.)

To the care and protection of thy good providence, heavenly Father, we now commend ourselves, and all our relatives, friends and brethren. Look with favor upon those who ask an interest in our prayers; and may our mutual and united supplications ascend to thy throne as acceptable incense, and receive an answer of peace, through the merits and intercession of Jesus Christ our Lord. *Amen.*

THURSDAY EVENING

Scripture Lesson

JUDGE not, that ye be not judged. For with what judgment ye judge, ye shall be judged: and with what measure ye mete, it shall be measured to you again. And why beholdest thou the mote that is in thy brother's eye, but considerest not the beam that is in thine own eye? or how wilt thou say to thy brother, Let me pull out the mote out of thine eye; and, behold, a beam is in thine own eye? Thou hypocrite, first cast out the beam out of thine own eye; and then shalt thou see clearly to cast out the mote out of thy brother's eye. Give not that which is holy unto the dogs, neither cast ye your pearls before swine, lest they trample them under their feet, and turn again and rend you. Ask, and it shall be given you; seek, and ye shall find; knock, and it shall be opened unto you: for every one that asketh, receiveth: and he that seeketh, findeth: and to him that knocketh, it shall be opened. Or what man is there of you, whom if his son ask bread, will he give him a stone? or if he ask a fish, will he give him a serpent? If ye, then, being evil, know how to give good gifts unto your children, how much more shall your Father, which is in heaven, give good things to them that ask him? Therefore all things whatsoever ye would that men should do to you, do ye even so to them: for this is the law and the prophets. Enter ye in at the straight gate, for wide is the gate, and broad is the way, that leadeth to destruction, and many there be which go in there-at: because straight is the gate, and narrow is the way, which leadeth unto life, and few there be that find it. *Matthew* 7:1–14.

Prayer

ALMIGHTY God, whose ears are ever open to the petitions of thy humble servants, and who hast graciously promised, that whatsoever we ask of thee in prayer, believing, we shall receive, mercifully look upon us at this time, and enable us to draw near to thee in humble reverence and godly fear. We lament the coldness of our hearts; we confess and bewail our daily iniquities. But we beseech thee, gracious God, unworthy as we are to approach thee, and bowed down as we are with infirmity, to accept our imperfect services through the intercession of thy dear Son. Grant that our supplications and thanksgivings may be sprinkled with his most precious blood, which cleanseth from all sin; and so may come up as a memorial before thee, acceptable, and well pleasing in thy sight. And pour down upon us a more abundant measure of grace and supplication, that we may hereafter approach thee in fervent prayer, and worship thee in spirit and in truth.

Hear our prayers, O God, for those whom it is our duty and our desire to remember at the throne of grace. Endue with a spirit of wisdom and faithfulness, those who are appointed to watch over the fold of Christ. Let none of them be as hirelings who care not for the sheep. But raise up pastors according to thy heart, who shall seek that which is lost, and bring again that which is driven away, and bind up that which is broken, and strengthen that which is weak. May they take heed to themselves, and to all the flock of which the Holy Ghost hath made them overseers, to feed thy church, which thy blessed Son has purchased with his blood.

And, O thou blessed Jesus, who didst come to seek and to save that which was lost, look with an eye of pity upon those who are still as sheep going astray, and especially on the lost sheep of the house of Israel. Bring them home, merciful Lord, to thy flock, that they may be saved with the remnant of the true Israelites: and grant that they and we, as one fold, under one Shepherd, may learn of thee, who art meek and lowly in heart, and thus find rest to our souls. Feed us in green pastures; and lead us forth beside the waters of comfort. Conduct us to the end of our life, in the paths of righteousness. And when we pass through the valley of the shadow of death, be thou with us, that thy rod and staff may sustain and support us, and bring us at last to thy heavenly fold.

(Occasional Prayers.)

Grant these and all our petitions, through the merits of Jesus Christ our Savior, who liveth and reigneth with thee, O Father, in the unity of the Holy Ghost, one God, world without end. *Amen.*

FRIDAY MORNING

Scripture Lesson

BEWARE of false prophets, which come to you in sheep's clothing, but inwardly they are ravening wolves. Ye shall know them by their fruits. Do men gather grapes of thorns, or figs of thistles? Even so every good tree bringeth forth good fruit; but a corrupt tree bringeth forth evil fruit. A good tree cannot bring forth evil fruit; neither can a corrupt tree bring forth good fruit. Every tree that bringeth not forth good fruit is hewn down, and cast into the fire. Wherefore by their fruits ye shall know them. Not everyone that saith unto me, Lord, Lord, shall enter into the kingdom of heaven; but he that doeth the will of my Father which is in heaven. Many will say to me in that day, Lord, Lord, have we not prophesied in thy name? and in thy name have cast out devils? and in thy name done many wonderful works? And then will I profess unto them, I never knew you; depart from me, ye that work iniquity. Therefore, whosoever heareth these sayings of mine, and doeth them, I will liken him unto a wise man, which built his house upon a rock: and the rain descended, and the floods came, and the winds blew, and beat upon that house; and it fell not: for it was founded upon a rock. And every one that heareth these sayings of mine, and doeth them not, shall be likened unto a foolish man, which built his house upon the sand: and the rain descended, and the floods came, and the winds blew, and beat upon that house; and it fell: and great was the fall of it. And it came to pass, when Jesus had ended these sayings, the people were astonished at his doctrine: for he taught them as one having authority, and not as the scribes. *Matthew* 7:15–29.

Prayer

O LORD our God! thy name is most excellent in all the earth: thou hast set thy glory above the heavens, and thou art worthy to be celebrated with everlasting praises of men and angels; for thou hast created all things, and for thy pleasure they are and were created. Thou hast formed us for thyself, that we should show forth thy praise, and live to thy glory, as we do continually live upon thy bounty.

But, O Lord our God! we have not honored thee as we should. We have rebelled against thee and transgressed thy laws. We have been ungrateful in the reception of thy blessings, and are justly exposed to thy displeasure.

For these things we desire to humble ourselves here before thee; entreating thy gracious favor, and thy mercy in Christ Jesus. Give us, we beseech thee, repentance and pardon for all that is past, wherein we have offended thee; whether in omitting our duty, or failing in it, or doing contrary to it.

And strengthen us, good Lord, with might, by thy Spirit in the inner man, to make us more watchful against the corruption of our nature, the temptations of the devil, and the distractions and allurements of this sinful world, wherein we live. Oh destroy in us every vicious inclination, every evil habit and rebellious notion. Increase and confirm in us still more and more thy true knowledge, and faith, and fear, and love; and every grace of thy Holy Spirit, which thou knowest to be most wanting in us and necessary for us. And however it goes with us, as to the concerns of this present time, oh that we may still be found in the way of our duty, fearing God, and working righteousness; that we may secure our interest in the great Savior of the world, so that when all here shall fail us, thou mayest take us up, and be the strength of our hearts, and our portion for evermore.

(Occasional Prayers.)

Day by day we magnify thee, O Lord, who makest every day of our lives still a further addition to thy mercies. We bless thee for our last night's preservation and protection, and for the rest and refreshment which thou hast given us therein. Oh cause us to hear thy loving-kindness in the morning, for in thee do we trust. Cast us not away from thy presence; take not thy Holy Spirit from us; but direct all our ways to please thee, our God, that thou mayest crown us with blessing and good success. And by all the comforts of creatures, oh draw our hearts still nearer to thyself, the blessed Creator of every comfort; and let our meditations of God be sweet as well as frequent, that, delighting ourselves in the Lord, thou mayest give unto us the desires of our hearts. Such mercy and grace we beg for ourselves, and all ours, and thine everywhere, for the sake of our great Mediator and Savior. *Amen.*

FRIDAY EVENING

Scripture Lesson

HEAR me when I call, O God of my righteousness: thou hast enlarged me when I was in distress; have mercy upon me, and hear my prayer. Oh ye sons of men, how long will ye turn my glory into shame? how long will ye love vanity, and seek after leasing? But know that the Lord hath set apart him that is godly for himself: the Lord will hear when I call unto him. Stand in awe, and sin not: commune with your own heart upon your bed, and be still. Offer the sacrifices of righteousness, and put your trust in the Lord. There be many that say, Who will show us any good? Lord, lift thou up the light of thy countenance upon us. Thou hast put gladness in my heart, more than in the time that their corn and their wine increased. I will both lay me down in peace, and sleep; for thou, Lord, only makest me dwell in safety.

Behold, bless ye the Lord, all ye servants of the Lord, which by night stand in the house of the Lord. Lift up your hands in the sanctuary, and bless the Lord. The Lord that made Leaven and earth bless thee out of Zion. *Psalm* 4 and 134.

Prayer

O LORD, our God, thou art most high and mighty, most wise, and holy, and good! Thou art, and forever wast, and forever shalt continue, unspeakably blessed and glorious, above all that we are able to express or to conceive. Oh how wonderful is thy condescension to look down upon us, poor sinful worms, that dwell here in houses of clay, whose foundation is in the dust! Lord, what is man that thou takest knowledge of him, and the son of man that thou makest account of him! Thou dost not at all need us, nor anything of ours, O blessed God; but we all stand in great and continual need of thee, our only sovereign good; in need of thy mercy and forgiveness, thy grace and guidance, thy blessing and assistance.

The desire of our souls, therefore, is to thy name, O Lord, and to the remembrance of thee. Oh remember not against us our former iniquities; enter not into judgment with us, according to the desert of our sins; but according to thy mercy remember thou us. For thy goodness' sake, O Lord, blot out our transgressions as a cloud; and justify us freely by thy grace, through the redemption that is in Jesus Christ. And bless us, holy God of our salvation, in turning us from all our iniquities, and giving us grace, to repent and amend our lives according to thy holy word.

To this end be thou pleased to enlighten our darkened minds, that we may not be unwise, but understand what the will of the Lord is; reform our depraved wills, inclining them to a cheerful and ready compliance with all the motions of thy good Spirit. Regulate our unruly passions; purify our corrupt affections; and convert all the faculties of our souls to be instruments of thy glory, as they have been of thy dishonor; and make our bodies fit temples for thy Holy Spirit to dwell in. Yea, sanctify us wholly, that we may, as we ought, sanctify thy blessed name.

(Occasional Prayers.)

The same things also we beg in behalf of all who ought to share in our prayers. Oh forgive the sins and relieve the miseries of thy poor creatures everywhere. Enlarge the borders of thy church, and make additions to it daily of such as shall be saved. Oh that all who are called Christians may be truly Christians, both in their right believing and their holy living. Advance the interest, and extend the limits of thy Son's kingdom, and may all nations flow into it, as to their rest. Bless our land, and endue our rulers with wisdom from on high. Give our judges the spirit of discernment, and aid and countenance our magistrates in the faithful execution of their office. Make them all men fearing God, and eschewing evil. And Oh that all who are called to serve at thy altar may be blessed with skilful understandings, and compassionate hearts, and exemplary lives. Make them wise to win souls, and faithful and successful in their sacred office, as workmen that need not be ashamed. Bless all the places of learning and education; and make all this people the Lord's people; that they may all know thee from the greatest to the least. Remember them all for good, who have been any way instruments of our good; and all that have, or would hurt us, O Lord, forgive. Give unto all that mourn in Zion, beauty for ashes, the oil of joy for mourning, and the garments of praise for the spirit of heaviness. O Lord! continue thy gracious favor to us, and thy Fatherly care over us this night. And so supply us still with thy grace, that we may finish our course with joy, and in the end of our lives be received into thy glory: which we beg for the all-sufficient merits of our only Redeemer; for whom, and to whom, with thee, O everlasting Father, and the Holy Ghost the Comforter, be all praise, and honor, and glory ascribed of us, and of all the Israel of God, now and for evermore. *Amen.*

SATURDAY MORNING

Scripture Lesson

I AM the true vine, and my Father is the husbandman. Every branch in me that beareth not fruit he taketh away; and every branch that beareth fruit he purgeth it, that it may bring forth more fruit. Now ye are clean through the word which I have spoken unto you. Abide in me, and I in you. As the branch cannot bear fruit of itself, except it abide in the vine; no more can ye, except ye abide in me. I am the vine, ye are the branches: he that abideth in me, and I in him, the same bringeth forth much fruit; for without me ye can do nothing. If a man abide not in me, he is cast forth as a branch, and is withered; and men gather them, and cast them into the fire, and they are burned. If ye abide in me, and my words abide in you, ye shall ask what ye will, and it shall be done unto you. Herein is my Father glorified, that ye bear much fruit; so shall ye be my disciples. As the Father hath loved me, so have I loved you: continue ye in my love. If ye keep my commandments, ye shall abide in my love; even as I have kept my Father's commandments, and abide in his love. These things have I spoken unto you, that my joy might remain in you, and that your joy might be full. This is my commandment, That ye love one another, as I have loved you. Greater love hath no man than this, that a man lay down his life for his friends. Ye are my friends, if ye do whatsoever I command you. Henceforth I call you not servants; for the servant knoweth not what his lord doeth: but I have called you friends; for all things that I have heard of my Father have I made known unto you. Ye have not chosen me, but I have chosen you, and ordained you, that ye should go and bring forth fruit, and that your fruit should remain; that whatsoever ye shall ask of the Father in my name, he may give it you. These things I command you, That ye love one another. *John* 15:1–17.

Prayer

ALMIGHTY and everlasting God, through whose merciful kindness we are preserved from day to day, we approach thy throne of grace this morning, in the name of thy beloved Son.

We humble ourselves in thy sight for all our iniquities, and particularly for those which we have committed during the past week. We are sorry and ashamed that we have had thy glory so little before our eyes; that we have sinned against thee, our neighbor, and ourselves. By leaving undone what thou hast commanded, and by doing that which thou hast forbidden, we have broken thy law, in thought, and word, and deed. Lay not, we pray thee, our sins to our charge; but wash them away in the fountain which thou hast opened for sin and for uncleanness. And, O thou God of holiness, give us grace and strength to subdue them. Renew us after thy likeness, in righteousness and true holiness. Make us holy as thou art holy, and pure as thou art pure. O God, make clean our hearts within us; and take not thy Holy Spirit from us.

And since life is short and uncertain, and every week brings us nearer to the end of all things, enable us to lay aside every weight, and the sin that doth so easily beset us, and to run with patience the race that is set before us, looking unto Jesus, the author and finisher of our faith. Preserve ever in our minds a lively remembrance of that day when the throne shall be set, and the books shall be opened; and every one of us shall give account of himself to thee.

We humbly beseech thee to receive the thank-offerings which we desire now to present on thy altar. Thou hast guarded us from numberless perils, and preserved us from desolating calamities. From thy hand we have been fed and clothed; in sorrow and temptation thou hast sustained us by thy Spirit; in our guilt thou hast redeemed us by the blood of thine own Son; and it is only through thy forbearance and tender mercies, that we have been spared to the morning of this day. Who can utter thy mighty acts, O Lord, or show forth all thy praise? Grant, that from the abundance of the heart, we may speak thy praise; and that, at the close of every week, we may be found growing in grace, in thankfulness, and in every fruit of the blessed Spirit.

Keep us, we beseech thee, O Lord, this day, under the protection of thy good providence, and prepare us, both in body and soul, for the holy duties of the approaching Sabbath. May no regard to the fashions or friendship of the world cause us to profane it; nor any weariness of the world tempt us to consume its sacred rest in slothful indulgence, in vain conversation, or unhallowed pleasure. Suffer us not to form frivolous excuses for absenting ourselves from thy sanctuary. But, if permitted in thy providence, may we go with the multitude to thy house of prayer, with the voice of joy and praise. There may we give thee the glory which is due unto thy name, and worship thee in the beauty of holiness. Grant that the Scriptures, which thou hast caused to be written for our learning, may be applied to our hearts in the demonstration of the Spirit and of power.

We pray thee, finally, O merciful Lord, to remember and to bless with thy choicest mercies, all our relations and friends. Keep them, we beseech thee, under the protection of thy good providence, and make them to have a perpetual fear and love for thy name. Let thy fatherly hand be ever over them: let thy Holy Spirit be ever with them, and so lead them in the knowledge and obedience of thy word, that, in the end, they may obtain everlasting life, through Jesus Christ our Lord. *Amen.*

SATURDAY EVENING

Scripture Lesson

THE Lord reigneth: let the earth rejoice; let the multitude of isles be glad thereof. Clouds and darkness are round about him: righteousness and judgment are the habitation of his throne. A fire goeth before him, and burneth up his enemies round about. His lightnings enlightened the world: the earth saw and trembled. The hills melted like wax at the presence of the Lord, at the presence of the Lord of the whole earth. The heavens declare his righteousness, and all the people see his glory. Confounded be all they that serve graven images, that boast themselves of idols: worship him, all ye gods. Zion heard, and was glad; and the daughters of Judah rejoiced because of thy judgments, O Lord. For thou, Lord, art high above all the earth: thou art exalted far above all gods. Ye that love the Lord, hate evil; he preserveth the souls of his saints; he delivereth them out of the hand of the wicked. Light is sown for the righteous, and gladness for the upright in heart. Rejoice in the Lord, ye righteous; and give thanks at the remembrance of his holiness. *Psalm* 97.

Prayer

O GOD, thou hast made, and thou upholdest all things by the word of thy power. One generation passeth away, and another cometh; and we are hastening back to the dust whence we were taken. The heavens we behold will vanish away like the cloud that covers them; and the earth we tread will dissolve like a morning dream; but thou art, from everlasting to everlasting, God over all, unchangeably the same, and thy years shall not fail.

Infinitely great and glorious as thou art, we are thy offspring and thy care. Thy hands have made us and fashioned us. Thou hast watched over us with more than parental tenderness. Thou hast held our soul in life, and not suffered our feet to be moved. Thy divine power has given us all things, not only necessary for life, but godliness. Bless the Lord, O our souls, and forget not all his benefits;

who forgiveth all our iniquities; who healeth all our diseases; who redeemeth our lives from destruction; who crowneth us with loving-kindness and tender mercies; who satisfieth our mouth with good things, so that our youth is renewed like the eagle's.

We raise this evening a fresh memorial, and inscribe it to the God of our salvation. We have passed, not only through another day, but through another week. The sun has not smitten us by day, nor the moon by night. We have been preserved in our going out, and coming in. Thine have been the supplies that have nourished us. Thine the comforts that have indulged us. Thine the relations and friends that have delighted us. Thine have been the means of grace which have edified us; and thine the book, which, amidst all our enjoyments, has told us, that this is not our rest; and in all our successes, that one thing is yet needful.

Nothing can equal the number of thy mercies, but our imperfections and sins. These, O God, we would not conceal, or palliate; but confess them, with a broken heart and contrite spirit.

In what a condition would we be this evening, were it not for the assurance that there is forgiveness with thee, that thou mayest be feared, and that with thee there is plenteous redemption! Yet, while we hope for pardon through the blood of the cross, we pray to be clothed with humility; to be quickened in thy way; and to be more devoted to the things that belong to our everlasting peace.

How soon has the week rolled away! So will all our days flee; so will they all appear when the end arrives. Oh, help us to keep that end in remembrance; and endeavor to view things now, as they will appear from the borders of the grave. May we know how frail we are, that we may be cured of the folly of delay and indecision; and so number our days, that we may apply our hearts unto wisdom.

(Occasional Prayers.)

May we call the approaching Lords Day a delight, the holy of the Lord, honorable; and may we honor thee, in not doing our own ways, nor finding our own pleasures, nor speaking our own words. May the private moments of the day be sacred; and the social—innocent and edifying. And may we keep our foot, when we go to the house of God, and offer not the sacrifice of fools.

Preserve us from trifling with the things of the soul and eternity, or trusting in those privileges which, unimproved, will only augment our guilt and our misery.

Oh, let us not perish under means designed to save us. Oh, let not the savor of life unto life prove to us only the savor of death unto death.

Make the place of thy feet glorious. Bring us to thy holy mountain, and if we are not made joyful in thy house of prayer, convince us, alarm us, humble us, banish the spirit of the world from our hearts, and fill us with all the fullness of God.

So we thy people, and the sheep of thy pasture, will give thee thanks for ever, we will show forth thy praise throughout all generations. *Amen.*

SECOND WEEK

LORDSDAY MORNING

Scripture Lesson
(OR PSALM 122)

Psalm 25:10: All the paths of the Lord are mercy and truth unto such as keep his covenant and his testimonies. The secret of the Lord is with them that fear him, and he will show them his covenant.

Eph. 1:3: Blessed be the God and Father of our Lord Jesus Christ, who hath blessed us with all spiritual blessings in heavenly places in Christ. According as he hath chosen us in him before the foundation of the world, that we should be holy, and without blame before him in love.

Ps. 84:4: Blessed are they that dwell in thy house; they will still be praising thee. For a day in thy courts is better than a thousand. I had rather be a door-keeper in the house of my God, than to dwell in the tents of wickedness. For the Lord is a sun and a shield: he will give grace and glory; and no good thing will he withhold from them that walk uprightly.

Is. 56:7: Them will I bring to my holy mountain, and make them joyful in my house of prayer: their burnt-offerings and their sacrifices shall be accepted upon mine altar; for my house shall be called an house of prayer for all people.

Is. 52:7: How beautiful upon the mountains are the feet of him that bringeth good tidings, that publisheth peace, that bringeth good tidings of good, that publisheth salvation, that saith unto Zion, thy God reigneth. Thy watchmen shall lift up the voice, with the voice together shall they sing; for they shall see eye to eye, when the Lord shall bring again Zion.

Ps. 92:13: Those that be planted in the house of the Lord, shall flourish in the courts of our God.

Prayer

O ALMIGHTY God, Creator, Governor, and Upholder of all things, who, after making the heaven and the earth, didst rest the seventh day, and bless and sanctify it, teach us now, resting from our worldly labors, to devote the day to thy service. O thou, whose Son did, on this day, rise again from the dead, grant us grace to rise from the death of sin, to the life of righteousness. Help us now, in his name, to seek thy blessing on those holy duties to which the Lordsday is set apart.

We thank thee for the knowledge of Jesus Christ; for free justification and salvation through his life, death, and resurrection. We praise thee for the gift of thy Holy Spirit. Blessed, forever blessed, be thou, the God and Father of our Lord Jesus Christ, for these thy benefits.

With shame we confess that we have slighted thy goodness, and carelessly regarded thy great salvation. How many Lordsdays have we misapplied! how many invitations of mercy have we neglected! with how many warnings and threatenings have we trifled! how cold have been our prayers! how inexcusable our unbelief!

Forgive us, Oh forgive us all our sins. To the Lord our God belong mercies and forgiveness, though we have rebelled against him. Return again and bless us. Graciously be present with us through all the solemn services of this day. Enable us to go to thy house in the spirit of prayer. Pour out upon us, and all that shall meet in thy name, the spirit of grace and supplication. Let none of us draw near to thee with our lips only, while our hearts are far from thee; but enable us to worship thee in spirit and in truth. Cause thy face to shine upon us. Prepare our hearts to receive thy holy word, that it may be sown in good ground, and bring much fruit to perfection.

Help all of us, not only to abstain from engaging in our usual business and occupation, but also keep us from worldly conversation, and from vain thoughts. Raise our affections to things above, and let our conversation be in heaven. Enable us to give this day to reading and hearing thy word, to meditation, self-examination, and prayer; and be thou with us, to bless us in our retired devotions.

And, Father of mercies, we beseech thee to bless all who minister in holy things. Multiply unto them thy grace, that they may be faithful, diligent, and laborious. Grant them humility, disinterestedness, watchfulness, and zeal; may all have grace to take heed to themselves, and to the flock over which the Holy Ghost has made them overseers, feeding the church of God which he has purchased with his own blood. Stand by and strengthen them this day. Open thou their mouths, and enable them to testify boldly the gospel of the grace of God. We especially pray for him who ministers among us. May he this day be enabled to speak a word in season to us, and to all that hear him.

And, we beseech thee, grant that this thy Lords-day may be distinguished by great and singular mercies to thy church. Be thou with all Christian congregations meeting to worship thee. By the ministry of thy word this day, convert many sinners; heal those that have backslidden, strengthen those that are weak, and confirm those that are strong. Give thy holy word free course, and let it be glorified in every land, and among every people.

(Occasional Prayers.)

Hear us, and answer us, for our Lord Jesus Christ's sake. *Amen.*

LORDSDAY EVENING

Scripture Lesson
(OR MATTHEW 13:1–23)

John 5:39: Search the Scriptures; for in them ye think ye have eternal life; and they are they which testify of me.

Rom. 9:5: Christ who is over all, God blessed forever. Amen.

Rev. 1:8: I am the Alpha and Omega, the beginning and the ending, saith the Lord, which is, and which was, and which is to come, the Almighty.

Rev. 21:6: I will give unto him that is athirst of the fountain of the water of life freely. He that overcometh shall inherit all things; and I will be his God, and he shall be my son.

1 *Tim.* 3:16: And without controversy, great is the mystery of godliness. God was manifest in the flesh, justified in the Spirit, seen of angels, preached unto the Gentiles, believed on in the world, received up into glory.

Isa. 9:6: Unto us a child is born, unto us a son is given: and the government shall be upon his shoulders: and his name shall be called Wonderful, Counsellor, the Mighty God, the Everlasting Father, the Prince of Peace.

Matt. 1:23: And they shall call his name Emmanuel, which being interpreted is, God with us.

Tit. 1:3: According to the commandment of God our Savior. (*Acts* 20:23.) Feed the church of God, which he hath purchased with his own blood.

Col. 1:16: By him (Christ) were all things created, that are in heaven, and that are in earth, visible and invisible, whether they be thrones, or dominions, or principalities, or powers; all things were created by him, and for him.

Heb. 3:4: For every house is builded by some man; but he that built all things is God. *John* 1:1: The Word was God. *Col.* 2:9: For in him dwelleth all the fullness of the Godhead bodily. *Heb.* 13:8: Jesus Christ the same yesterday, to-day, and forever.

Prayer

O LORD, God of our salvation, we present our supplications before thee; knowing that thy arm is not shortened that it cannot save, nor thy ear heavy that it cannot hear. Let our prayers enter into thy presence, and incline thine ear unto our calling. Let not our iniquities separate between us and thee our God. Cast us not away from thy presence, and take not thy Holy Spirit from us.

We acknowledge, merciful Father, the imperfection of our best services, during the day which is now closing. The wanderings of our thoughts, the coldness of our devotions, our carelessness, and hardness, are all known to thee. Pardon, O Lord, all our infirmities, and quicken us to greater diligence and fidelity in the performance of our duty to thee, to our neighbor, and to ourselves. Enable us to devote ourselves, with all our powers, to thee and thy service. May we keep in lively remembrance the truths which have been delivered to us this day; that the words which we have heard with our outward ears, may be ingrafted inwardly in our hearts, and bring forth in us the fruit of good living. Give us thy Holy Spirit, to enlighten our understanding, and purify our hearts; that all our wishes and desires may centre in what thou hast commanded. Make us instrumental, according to our opportunity, in promoting the salvation of all men, and especially of those who are the most closely united to us in the bonds of friendship and society. Be thou ever with us in the performance of our several duties; in prayer, to quicken our devotion; in praises, to heighten our love and gratitude; and in all our works, to set a bright example to those around us.

We intercede with thee, heavenly Father, for thy church militant on earth; for her ministers and people; and for all who call themselves Christians. Guard thy flock, O thou gracious Bishop and Shepherd of our souls, and lead them into green pastures, and beside the still waters of salvation.

(Occasional Prayers.)

Almighty God, we commit ourselves to thy care and keeping this night. We are weak, exposed to dangers on every side, and unable to help ourselves. Keep us outwardly in our bodies, during the unguarded hours of repose; that no evil may befall us, nor any alarm or terror disturb us. Keep us also inwardly in our souls; that no wicked or hurtful thoughts, no corrupt imaginations, no wiles of the adversary, may assail us. Defend us from all adversities; and bring us in peace and safety to the beginning of another day; that being refreshed in body, and strengthened by thy Spirit in the inner man, we may enter upon our respective duties with increasing trust and confidence in thy mercy, and with renewed purpose of serving thee faithfully and truly to the end of our days. We ask these blessings for ourselves, and for all our friends, relatives, and brethren, for the sake of Jesus Christ our Lord, in whose name and words we conclude our petitions:—

Our Father, who, &c. *Amen.*

MONDAY MORNING

Scripture Lesson
(OR JOHN 3:1–21)

Psalm 91:1: He that dwelleth in the secret place of the Most High, shall abide under the shadow of the Almighty. I will say of the Lord he is my refuge and my fortress; my God, in him will I trust. He shall cover thee with his feathers, and under his wings shalt thou trust: His truth shall be thy shield and buckler. There shall no evil befall thee, neither shall any plague come nigh thy dwelling.

Ps. 121:1: I will lift up mine eyes unto the hills, from whence cometh my help. My help cometh from the Lord, which made heaven and earth. Behold, he that keepeth Israel shall neither slumber nor sleep. The Lord is thy keeper: the Lord is thy defense upon thy right hand. The sun shall not smite thee by day, nor the moon by night. The Lord shall preserve thee from all evil; he shall preserve thy soul. The Lord shall preserve thy going out, and thy coming in, from this time forth, and even for evermore.

Ps. 37:3: Trust in the Lord and do good, so shalt thou dwell in the land, and verily thou shalt be fed.

Matt. 6:26: Behold the fowls of the air, for they sow not, neither do they reap, nor gather into barns; yet your heavenly Father feedeth them; are ye not much better than they?

Matt. 6:25: I say unto you, take no thought for your life what ye shall eat, or what ye shall drink; nor yet for the body, what ye shall put on: is not the life more than meat, and the body than raiment? Wherefore if God so clothe the grass of the field, which to-day is and to-morrow is cast into the oven, shall he not much more clothe you, O ye of little faith? Therefore take no thought, saying, What shall we eat? or what shall we drink? or wherewithal shall we be clothed? For your heavenly Father knoweth that ye have need of all these things.

Prayer

ALMIGHTY and most merciful Father! thou art a God that hearest prayer; and we are encouraged to draw nigh unto thy throne of grace, most humbly beseeching thee to look upon us, according to thy tender mercy in Jesus Christ. We confess our daily offenses against thee in thought, word, and deed. If thou shouldst be extreme to mark what is done amiss, O Lord, who might abide it? Deal not with us after our sins, neither reward us after our iniquities. We bless thee for that all-prevailing Advocate, Jesus Christ, the righteous: by his cross and intercession, Lord, deliver us.

We are now about to enter upon the worldly employments of another week; strengthen us with thy grace, that these may not withdraw our hearts from thee, nor make us negligent of our souls, and our salvation. May the influences of the Lords Day rest upon us through the week, and may the solemn and blessed truths which we heard yesterday, in the house of prayer, abide in our memories, and direct our conduct!

With many thanks for thy mercies during the past night, we now cast ourselves upon thy protection, not knowing what this day may bring forth, but trusting in that wisdom which cannot err, and in that love which cannot fail. Father, not our will, but thine be done! Preserve us from temptation; preserve us from sin; preserve us from our own evil hearts; and if we are permitted to see the close of this day, may it be our happiness to look back upon it as one in which we have walked with God.

Send thy good Spirit to direct us in the ways and works of godliness; purify our affections; enliven our devotion; teach us how to pray, and how to hear, and read, and profit by thy holy word. Make us Christians, not only in name, but also in heart and in hope. Teach us the value of our souls, and of the salvation which has been wrought for them by Christ Jesus. May we never be ashamed to confess him before men, but, amidst all discouragement and difficulties, give us boldness to show ourselves his true disciples.

Let our conversation be such as becometh his gospel; and whatsoever we do in word or in deed, let us do all in his name, giving thanks to God and the Father through him. Let the words of our mouths, and the meditations of our hearts, be acceptable in thy sight, O Lord, our strength, and our Redeemer. *Amen.*

(Occasional Prayers.)

MONDAY EVENING

Scripture Lesson
(OR PSALM 91)

Gal. 3:20: I am crucified with Christ, nevertheless I live, yet not I, but Christ liveth in me: and the life which I now live in the flesh, I live by the faith of the Son of God, who loved me, and gave himself for me.

Deut. 33:27: The eternal God is thy refuge, and underneath are the everlasting arms, and he shall thrust out the enemy from before thee, and shall say, Destroy them. Happy art thou, O Israel! Who is like unto thee, O people, saved by the Lord, the shield of thy help, and who is the sword of thy excellency?

1 John 5:18: We know that whosoever is born of God, sinneth not; but he that is begotten of God keepeth himself, and the wicked one toucheth him not.

1 Cor. 10:12: Wherefore let him that thinketh he standeth, take heed lest he fall.

1 Cor. 10:13: There hath no temptation taken you but such as is common to man: but God is faithful, who will not suffer you to be tempted above that ye are able; but will with the temptation also make a way to escape, that ye may be able to bear it.

Phil. 1:6: Being confident of this very thing, that he which hath begun a good work in you, will perform it until the day of Jesus Christ.

2 Pet. 1:10: Wherefore, the rather, brethren, give diligence to make your calling and election sure; for if ye do these things, ye shall never fall.

Prayer

O LORD our God! thou art infinitely great, and infinitely good. Thy glory is above all our thoughts, and thy mercies are over all thy works. And above all thy mercies, have we cause to praise thee for those mercies which, in so large a measure, and especial manner, thou hast been pleased still to vouchsafe unto us, who are daily objects of thy bounty, and who continue still the living monuments of thy goodness.

Thou didst create us, O Lord, after thine own blessed linage, in a holy and happy estate; but we have made ourselves vile and miserable, averse to good and prone to evil. But thou hast so far declared thy willingness to be reconciled even to thy enemies, that thou hast sent thy only Son into the world, that whosoever believes in him, should not perish in their sins, but have everlasting life, for his sake. O Lord, we believe, help our unbelief; and give us true repentance toward God, and faith in our Lord Jesus Christ; that we may be of the number of those who do indeed repent and believe, to the saving of the soul.

And save us, O good Lord, from our sinful selves, and from the love and course of this present evil world, and from every self-destroying way which we are tempted to follow. Make us a way to escape out of all the snares of temptation, wherewith we have been entangled and held, and hindered in running the race set before us.

Make thy ways plain before us. Strengthen and establish us, O Lord, that going forth in thy strength, we may do thy will to all well-pleasing; and continue in thy fear and love to our life's end.

These things we beg, not for ourselves alone, but also in behalf of all for whom we ought to entreat thy mercy in our prayers. Oh bring nigh unto thee all those that are afar off; and make manifest the savor of thy knowledge in every place; that such as yet sit in darkness and in the shadow of death, may come to see the light of thy truth, and the joy of thy salvation. Oh that all who name the name of Christ may depart from iniquity, and so live up to their high and holy profession, that they may give no just occasion to the enemies of the Lord to blaspheme; but adorn the doctrine of God, our Savior, in all things, and so put to silence the ignorance of foolish men by well-doing.

Be gracious, O Lord, in an especial manner, to thy church. Arise, O God, and plead thy own cause, and maintain thy true and holy religion, which thou hast so long and so wonderfully owned and asserted. May all that espouse thy cause, and stand up for the honor and defense of thy truth, be prosperous in all their pious designs; and still have cause to say, the Lord be magnified, who has pleasure in the prosperity of his servants.

Comfort all that want the comforts which we enjoy. Remember with the favor which thou bearest to thy people, our friends, our kindred after the flesh, and all whosoever are dear to us on any other account. Forgive our enemies, and turn their hearts; and turn ours to forgive them. And direct all our ways to please thee, that thou mayest make even our enemies to be at peace with us.

Hear us, O God of the spirits of all flesh; hear us for ourselves and others; others for themselves and us: and hear the Son of thy love, the lover of our souls, for us and all the members of thy church militant here on earth, whereof Christ Jesus in heaven is the glorious head. For him and to him with thine eternal self, most holy Father, and the blessed Spirit of grace, our Guide and Comforter, be all thanks and praise, and honor, and glory, humbly and heartily rendered and ascribed of us, and all thy people, now and for evermore.

(Occasional Prayers.)

And on this day, set apart by many of thy people as a season of prayer for thy mercy on Sunday-schools, we humbly implore thy blessing on all who are engaged in those schools as teachers, or learners. Enlighten by the Holy Spirit all teachers, that they may truly understand thy word. Make them the true friends of Jesus Christ. May they be endowed with his spirit of self-denial, patience, humility, and prayer. May they evermore copy the example of Him who, when on earth, said, Suffer little children, and forbid them not to come unto me. While engaged in instructing the rising generation, in leading others to the cross of Christ, may they themselves be interested in thy promises, and sanctified in all their efforts to promote thy glory. And grant, O gracious God, that their labors may be attended with thy blessing. Do thou send down thy Spirit on all Sunday-schools, that the rising generation may grow up in the knowledge of Jesus Christ, and in preparation for great usefulness in the church, and in the state. May schools be established in all the destitute places of our land; and all the means used to enlarge and perpetuate these blessings be crowned with success. Never suffer the zeal of thy people to languish in this cause, or thy ministers to forget their obligations to use every influence in their power to promote the religious training of the rising generation. Hear and answer the prayers which this day may have been offered in behalf of Sunday schools; excite in all thy people a spirit of benevolence; and fill the earth with thy glory. *Amen.*

TUESDAY MORNING

Scripture Lesson
(OR PSALM 1)

Isaiah 28:16: Behold, I lay in Sion, for a foundation, a stone, a tried stone, a precious corner-stone, a sure foundation.

1 *Pet.* 2:6: He that believeth on him shall not be confounded.

Isa. 14:22: Look unto me and be ye saved, all the ends of the earth.

Mark 4:23: If thou canst believe, all things are possible to him that believeth.

John 1:12: As many as received him, to them gave he power to become the sons of God, even to them that believe on his name.

John 3:16: God so loved the world, that he gave his only begotten Son, that whosoever believeth on him should not perish, but have everlasting life.

Jer. 31:33: This shall be the covenant that I will make with the house of Israel, after those days, saith the Lord, I will put my law in their inward parts, and Write it in their hearts: and I will be their God, and they shall be my people.

Eph. 2:10: We are his workmanship, created in Christ Jesus unto good works, which God hath before ordained, that we should walk in them.

2 *Cor.* 3:5: Not that we are sufficient of ourselves to think anything as of ourselves; but our sufficiency is of God.

Prayer

OUR voice shalt thou hear in the morning, O Lord: in the morning will we direct our prayer unto thee, O thou Most High! Many, during the past night, have had no place where to lay their head. Many, the victims of disease, have been full of tossing to and fro, until the dawning of the day; so that their bed has not comforted them, nor their couch relieved their complaint. Many have been deprived of rest while watching over their connections in pain and sorrow. Many have slept the sleep of death. Others, whose lives are prolonged, have risen to be surrounded with want and woe: and thousands who have all things richly to enjoy, have risen to live another day without God in the world.

Thou, O God, hast remembered, and distinguished, and indulged us. Bless the Lord, O our souls, and all that is within us bless his holy name! Oh magnify the Lord, and let us exalt his name *together*.

Thy mercies have been new every morning, yea, every moment. All our desires have not been gratified; but it was love that denied us, when the accomplishment of our wishes would have proved our ruin or our injury. We have had our trials, but they have been few compared with our sins; they have been attended with numberless alleviations.

Thou hast often wiped away our tears, and restored peace to thy mourners. Thou hast never chastened us but for our profit. We believe that thou hast done all things well, and that thy work is perfect.

But, oh, what do we owe thee for the word of thy truth—the throne of thy grace—the Son of thy love—thy unspeakable gift! what do we owe thee, that we have any reason to hope that we are in Christ, and free from all condemnation; and that when he, who is our life, shall appear, we shall also appear with him in glory, and be forever with the Lord?

Surely, gratitude becomes us that will not end in a morning acknowledgment with the lip, but such as will keep us in the fear of the Lord all the daylong. We, therefore, by the mercies of God, present our bodies a living sacrifice, holy and acceptable unto thee, which is our reasonable service.

(Occasional Prayers.)

And now, O thou Author of all good, we come to thee for the grace another day will require. We know that we are stepping into a wicked world, and that we carry about us an evil heart. We, therefore, desire to commit ourselves into thy holy keeping. Hold *thou* us up, and we shall be safe. Preserve our understandings from error; our affections from idols; our senses from the ungovernable impressions of outward objects; our character from every stain of vice, and our profession from every appearance of evil. May the God of peace sanctify us wholly; and may our whole spirit, soul, and body, be preserved blameless unto the coming of our Lord Jesus Christ.

May we engage in nothing on which we cannot implore thy blessing, and to which we cannot welcome thy inspection. Prosper us in our lawful undertakings, or prepare us for disappointment. Give us neither poverty nor riches. Feed us with food convenient for us, lest we be full and deny thee, and say, who is the Lord? or lest we be poor, and steal, and take the name of our God in vain.

Enable us to improve our talents, and to redeem our time. May we walk in wisdom toward them that are without, and in kindness toward them that are within; and do good as we have opportunity unto all men, especially unto them that are of the household of faith.

And unto Him that is able to keep us from falling, and to present us faultless before the presence of his glory with exceeding joy: to the only wise God, our Savior, be glory, and majesty, dominion, and power, both now and ever. *Amen.*

TUESDAY EVENING

Scripture Lesson
(OR 1 CORINTHIANS 2)

Rom. 8:11: If the Spirit of him that raised up Jesus from the dead dwell in you, he that raised up Christ from the dead shall also quicken your mortal bodies by his Spirit that dwelleth in you.

John 6:63: It is the Spirit that quickeneth; the flesh profiteth nothing: the words that I speak unto you, they are spirit, and they are life.

Rom. 8:26: Likewise the Spirit also helpeth our infirmities: for we know not what we should pray for as we ought: but the Spirit itself maketh intercession for us with groanings which cannot be uttered.

Gal. 5:22: But the fruit of the Spirit is love, joy, peace, long-suffering, gentleness, goodness, faith, meekness, temperance: against such there is no law. And they that are Christ's have crucified the flesh, with the affections and lusts. If we live in the Spirit, let us also walk in the Spirit.

Heb. 6:4: For it is impossible for those who were once enlightened, and have tasted of the heavenly gift, and were made partakers of the Holy Ghost, and have tasted the good word of God, and the powers of the world to come, if they shall fall away, to renew them again unto repentance, seeing they crucify to themselves the Son of God afresh, and put him to an open shame.

1 *Cor.* 6:9–11: Know ye not that the unrighteous shall not inherit the kingdom of God? Be not deceived; neither fornicators, nor idolaters, nor adulterers, nor thieves, nor covetous, nor drunkards, nor revilers, nor extortioners, shall inherit the kingdom of God. And such were some of you: but ye are washed, but ye are sanctified, but ye are justified in the name of the Lord Jesus, and by the Spirit of our God.

Prayer

ALMIGHTY and most merciful Father, who, for our many sins committed against thee, mightest most justly have cut us off in the midst of our days, we humbly thank thee, that in the multitude of thy mercies thou hast hitherto spared us.

Accept, we beseech thee, our unfeigned sorrow for our past transgressions; and grant that we may never so presume upon thy mercy, as to despise the riches of thy goodness: but let a sense of thy forbearance and long-suffering work in us repentance and amendment of life, to thy honor and glory, and to our final acceptance in the last day, through the merits of our Savior Jesus Christ.

Keep alive in us, O Lord, a true spirit of devotion; and preserve us from the great sin of praying to thee with our lips only, and not with our heart and mind.

Convince us of our entire dependence upon thee; quicken us in the pursuit of things eternal; that we may continually press forward to obtain the prize of our high calling in Christ Jesus.

Dispose us, we beseech thee, rightly to discharge all our duties. Watch over our path; compass us about with thy favor; preserve us in our going out and coming in; and direct all our steps in the way of thy commandments.

Make us truly honest and conscientious in all our dealings; diligent in the performance of our duty; innocent in our conversation; meek, charitable, and forgiving toward others; watchful over ourselves, and ever mindful of thy presence.

Sanctify unto us our trials and crosses, if it be thy good pleasure to afflict us; and give us such a measure of patience and godly resolution, that we may be willing to take up our cross daily, and to follow the Lamb, whithersoever he goeth.

(Occasional Prayers.)

O Lord, if we have now asked anything amiss, we pray thee pardon our ignorance and infirmity; and whatsoever is good for us, even if we ask it not, be pleased to grant to us, in the name and for the sake of thy dear Son Jesus Christ, our only Mediator and Advocate. *Amen.*

WEDNESDAY MORNING

Scripture Lesson
(OR 1 CORINTHINS 13)

Romans 3:10: It is written, There is none righteous, no, not one: there is none that understandeth, there is none that seeketh after God. They are all gone out of the way, they are together become unprofitable; there is none that doeth good, no, not one.

Ezek. 11:19: But I will give them one heart, and I will put a new spirit within them; and I will take the stony heart out of their flesh, and will give them a heart of flesh.

Matt. 18:3: Jesus said, Verily, I say unto you, except ye be converted, and become as little children, ye shall not enter into the kingdom of heaven.

Luke 13:3: Except ye repent, ye shall all likewise perish.

Rom. 8:6: For to be carnally minded is death; but to be spiritually minded is life and peace: because the carnal mind is enmity against God: for it is not subject to the law of God, neither indeed can be.

Acts 3:19: Repent ye, therefore, and be converted, that your sins may be blotted out, when the times of refreshing shall come from the presence of the Lord.

Ps. 51:1: Have mercy upon me, O God, according to thy loving kindness: according to the multitude of thy tender mercies blot out my transgressions. Wash me thoroughly from mine iniquity and cleanse me from my sin. For I acknowledge my transgressions, and my sin is ever before me. Hide thy face from my sins, and blot out all mine iniquities. For thou desirest no sacrifice, else would I give it: thou delightest not in burnt-offering. The sacrifices of God are a broken spirit: a broken and a contrite heart, O God, thou wilt not despise.

Prayer

O THOU, whose name is Jehovah, the Most High over all the earth, we desire to adore the perfections of thy nature, and to admire the works of thy hands. Heaven is thy throne, and the earth is thy footstool. The universe, with all its creatures, was made by thy word, and is upheld by thy power; and thou doest according to thine own will in the army of heaven, and among the inhabitantsts of the earth; none can stay thy hand, or say unto thee, What doest thou?

But thou art the Father of mercies, the God of all grace, and the God of all comfort. Even we, poor, mean, dying creatures, are not beneath thy care. Thou hast been mindful of us; thou hast visited us;

and thy visitation hath preserved our spirits. The lines are fallen to us in pleasant places; yea, we have a goodly heritage; we live in a land of light; we have the Scriptures in our hands, and our ears hear the joyful sound of the gospel. We know that thou hast not spared thine own Son, but delivered him up for us all. We know that he has borne our griefs, and carried our sorrows: that his blood cleanseth from all sin, and that whosoever believeth on him shall not perish, but have everlasting life.

We come in *his* name, and make mention of his righteousness only. May we be justified by his blood; and may we be saved by his life. May we be joined to the Lord, and be of one spirit with him. May we deny ourselves, and take up our cross, and follow him. May the agency of thy Holy Spirit prepare us for all the dispensations of thy providence. May we be willing that the Lord should choose our inheritance for us, and determine what we shall retain or lose; what we shall suffer or enjoy.

If indulged with prosperity, may we be secured from its snares, and use its advantages as not abusing them. And may we patiently and cheerfully submit to those afflictions which are necessary to hedge up our way when we are tempted to wander, to excite an abhorrence of sin, to wean us from the present evil world, and to make us partakers of thy holiness. In whatsoever state we are, may we be therewith content.

May our friends and relations be fellow-heirs with us of the grace of life. Let our house be the tabernacle of the righteous: let our children and servants be a seed to serve thee: and among none of those who surround this family altar, may there be weeping and wailing, and gnashing of teeth, when they shall see Abraham, and Isaac, and Jacob, in the kingdom of God, and they themselves shut out.

(Occasional Prayers.)

In the duties of this day, be graciously pleased to be with us. Preserve us from temptations, and the allurements of the world. Defend us from danger, and prepare us for whatever may be thy will in regard to us. In all circumstances may we evince the Christian spirit; be kept from anger, and pride, and ambition; from envy, hatred, and malice, and all uncharitableness. May we be diligent in business; fervent in spirit; serving the Lord; rejoicing in hope; patient in tribulation; continuing instant in prayer; distributing to the necessity of saints; given to hospitality. May we rejoice with them who do rejoice, and weep with them who weep. Help us to provide things honest in the sight of all men; and to live peaceably with all. To the end of our lives may we be the humble and consistent followers of

Jesus Christ, so that at last, through his merits, we may, with all thy people, be admitted to the joys of thy kingdom above.

And to the only wise God, our Savior, be praise and glory everlasting. *Amen.*

WEDNESDAY EVENING

Scripture Lesson
(OR 2 CORINTHIANS 5)

Jer. 31:33: This shall be the covenant that I will make with the house of Israel, after those days, saith the Lord, I will put my law into their inward parts, and write it in their hearts: and I will be their God, and they shall be my people.

Eph. 2:10: We are his workmanship, created in Christ Jesus unto good works, which God hath before ordained, that we should walk in them.

2 *Cor.* 3:5: Not that we are sufficient of ourselves, to think anything as of ourselves; but our sufficiency is of God.

2 *Thess.* 2:13: We are bound to give thanks always to God for you, brethren, beloved of the Lord, because God hath from the beginning chosen you to salvation, through sanctification of the Spirit, and belief of the truth.

John 17:11: Holy Father, keep through thine own name those whom thou hast given me, that they may be one, as we are.

Rom. 8:38: I am persuaded, that neither death, nor life, nor angels, nor principalities, nor powers, nor things present, nor things to come, nor height, nor depth, nor any other creature, shall be able to separate us from the love of God, which is in Christ Jesus our Lord.

Phil. 1:6: Being confident of this very thing, that he which hath begun a good work in you, will perform it until the day of Jesus Christ.

Rom. 8:1: There is, therefore, now no condemnation to them which are in Jesus Christ, who walk not after the flesh, but after the spirit. Who shall lay anything to the charge of God's elect? It is God that justifieth. Who is he that condemneth? It is Christ that died; yea rather is risen again, who is even at the right hand of God, who also maketh intercession for us.

Phil. 2:12: Work out your own salvation with fear and trembling. For it is God which worketh in you both to will and to do his good pleasure.

Prayer

O MERCIFUL God and heavenly Father, Maker of all things, and Judge of all men, we, the helpless creatures of thy bounty, and the humble dependents on thy will, desire now to offer up our acknowledgments to thee, for all thy goodness, and especially for thy over ruling care and protection during the past day. We approach thy throne as unworthy sinners, and implore thy forgiving mercy. We lament the trespasses which we daily commit against thee. Thou knowest all our infirmities, and seest all our hearts, and searchest out all our ways. Pity, we beseech thee, our blindness and ignorance, and our proneness to err from the paths of uprightness. Our hearts are deceitful above all things, and desperately wicked; and we know not in how many things we constantly offend. But we beseech thee, for Jesus Christ's sake, to pardon whatever evil we have thought, or said, or done this day. Turn away thy face from the multitude of our iniquities, and enable us to examine our hearts and lives by the light of thine unerring word, that we may repent and turn from our transgressions, that iniquity may not be our ruin.

We pray thee to pour down upon us the gift of thy Holy Spirit, that we may amend our ways, and purify our hearts, and walk before thee in newness of life. Teach us to improve the means of grace and knowledge with which we are favored: remembering always, that unto whom much is given, of them will much be required. May we cultivate those tempers, and abound in those works, which the gospel requires. May the graces of meekness and patience, of kindness and forbearance, of benevolence and charity, be the ornaments of our lives. Being established in the love of God, may we also love our fellow-men with pureness and singleness of heart. And let us abound in all the fruits of righteousness, which are by Jesus Christ, to the praise and glory of God.

(Occasional Prayers.)

We beseech thee, heavenly Father, to bless unto us the events of thy holy providence; and so to order all things, during the remainder of our days, that they may issue in our eternal good. Make us duly sensible, at all times, of the shortness and uncertainty of human life. Teach us to realize the solemn truth, that we know not what a day may bring forth. Sanctify to us all the changes through which we are called to pass, whether prosperity or adversity, health or sickness, joy or sorrow. May we consider all things as coming from thy Fatherly hand; that we may neither repine under thy chastisements, nor prove forgetful of thy mercies. In cheerfulness and contentment, and in reconciliation with thee, our God, may we enjoy peace within ourselves and live in perfect charity with all mankind.

We ask for all, for ourselves, and in behalf of those who are near and dear to us, in the name of Jesus Christ, our blessed Lord and Savior. *Amen.*

THURSDAY MORNING

Scripture Lesson
(OR MATTHEW 17:1–13)

1 *John* 3:2–3: Beloved, now are we the sons of God, and it doth not yet appear what we shall be; but we know that, when he shall appear, we shall be like him: for we shall see him as he is. And every man that hath this hope in him purifieth himself even as he is pure.

2 *Pet.* 3:13: We, according to his promise, look for new heavens and a new earth, wherein dwelleth righteousness.

John 17:24: Father, I will that they also whom thou hast given me, be with me where I am, that they may behold my glory, which thou hast given me.

Rev. 7:15: They are before the throne of God, and serve him day and night in his temple: and he that sitteth on the throne shall dwell among them. They shall hunger no more, neither thirst any more, neither shall the sun light on them, nor any heat; for the Lamb which is in the midst of the throne shall feed them, and shall lead them unto living fountains of water: and God shall wipe away all tears from their eyes.

2 *Tim.* 4:8: There is laid up for me a crown of righteousness, which the Lord the righteous judge shall give me at that day; and not to me only, but unto all them also that love his appearing.

1 *Pet.* 1:3–5: Blessed be the God and Father of our Lord Jesus Christ, which, according to his abundant mercy, hath begotten us again unto a lively hope by the resurrection of Jesus Christ from the dead. To an inheritance incorruptible, and undefiled, and that fadeth not away, reserved in heaven for you. Who are kept by the power of God through faith unto salvation.

Heb. 4:9: There remaineth therefore a rest for the people of God.

Prayer

O MOST merciful God, behold with compassion thy weak and sinful creatures, waiting for thy blessing at the throne of grace. Grant us a spirit of prayer and supplication, that we may approach thee in a time acceptable, and offer unto thee the sincere devotions of humble and contrite hearts. Hear us, we beseech thee, and in the multitude of thy tender mercies, draw nigh unto thy servants, whom thou hast redeemed with the precious blood of thy dear Son.

We bow the knee before thee in the name of him, whom thou thyself hast made the Lord our righteousness. And through him we pray thee to show us thy mercy, and to grant us thy salvation.

May we now go forth to the discharge of our several duties, in thy fear, and in humble dependence on thy protection. Grant us thy Holy Spirit, to guide and direct us in all the relations of life, and to restrain us from every vain and sinful indulgence. Enable us to abstain from those luxuries and pleasures which turn away the heart from serving thee, and endanger the peace and welfare of the soul. Preserve us from the snares and enticements of the wicked. Keep our feet from falling, and our souls from death, that we may walk before thee in the light of the living. Dispose us, day by day, to give all diligence, to add to our faith virtue, and to virtue knowledge, and to knowledge temperance, and to temperance brotherly kindness, and to brotherly kindness charity. Grant that these, and all other heavenly dispositions, may be in us and abound, that we may not be idle or unfruitful in the knowledge of our Lord and Savior Jesus Christ.

(Occasional Prayers.)

Prepare us, O God, for the various changes of this mortal life. In every visitation, may we see thy over-ruling hand; that we may humble ourselves in adversity, and receive thy bounties with devout and thankful hearts. Regard with compassion all sorts and conditions of men. Preserve the rich from temptation; and teach them to trust not in uncertain riches, but in thee the living God. To the poor, give contentment and submission; that they may be rich in faith, and heirs of the kingdom which thou hast promised to them that love thee. Save and defend all the faithful in Christ Jesus. Holy Father, keep through thine own name those whom thou hast given him; that they all may be one, as thou; Father, art in him, and he in thee; that they also may be one, even as ye are one.

Comfort the afflicted; succor the tempted; strengthen the weak; instruct the ignorant; and reclaim the wandering: and grant unto all men, that godliness which is profitable unto all things; having the promise of the life that now is, and of that which is to come.

We ask for all, in the name and for the sake of Jesus Christ our Lord, to whom, with thee, O Father, and the Holy Ghost, be all honor and glory, world without end. *Amen.*

THURSDAY EVENING

Scripture Lesson
(OR MATTHEW 19:16–29)

Psalm 34:7: The angel of the Lord encampeth round about them that fear him, and delivereth them.

Ps. 91:11: He shall give his angels charge over thee, to keep thee in all thy ways. They shall bear thee up in their hands, lest thou dash thy feet against a stone.

Matt. 18:10: Take heed that ye despise not one of these little ones, for I say unto you, that in heaven their angels do always behold the face of my Father, which is in heaven.

Heb. 1:14: Are they not all ministering spirits, sent forth to minister for them who shall be heirs of salvation.

Deut. 33:12: The beloved of the Lord shall dwell in safety by him; and the Lord shall cover him all the day long.

Prov. 18:10: The name of the Lord is a strong tower; the righteous runneth unto it, and is safe.

Ps. 16:8: I have set the Lord always before me; because he is at my right hand, I shall not be moved.

Ps. 27:1: The Lord is my light, and my salvation, whom shall I fear? The Lord is the strength of my life, of whom shall I be afraid?

Matt. 6:33: Seek ye first the kingdom of God, and his righteousness, and all these things shall be added unto you.

Isa. 43:2: When thou passest through the waters, I will be with thee; and through the rivers, they shall not overflow thee: when thou walkest through the fire, thou shalt not be burnt; neither shall the flame kindle upon thee. For I am the Lord thy God, the Holy One of Israel, thy Savior.

Isa. 1:18: Though your sins be as scarlet, they shall be as white as snow; though they be red like crimson, they shall be as wool.

1 *John* 1:7: The blood of Jesus Christ cleanseth us from all sin. If we confess our sins, he is faithful and just to forgive us our sins, and to cleanse us from all unrighteousness.

Prayer

O FATHER of mercies, and God of all comfort, who art our constant protector, and the giver of every blessing; we humbly and heartily thank thee for thy mercies during the past day; and we pray thee to preserve us through the night, and to cause thy peace at this time to rest upon us. We ask the forgiveness of all our sins. Remember not against us the transgressions of this day, or of our past lives: but grant unto us true repentance, and a saving faith in our Lord Jesus Christ. Give us a due sense of our great unworthiness, and of the manifold transgressions which we have committed against thee. Help us to exercise that godly sorrow which worketh repentance unto salvation. And when we appear before thee, weary and heavy-laden with the burden of our sins, we beseech thee to show unto us the light of thy reconciled countenance, and grant us the comforts of thy Holy Spirit; that we may go to our rest in peace, and in the hope of pardon of all our sins, through the all-prevailing merits of our dear Redeemer.

Teach us, O Lord, so to number our days, that we may apply our hearts unto wisdom. Let us remember, that we are daily and hourly drawing nearer to the grave. May we learn, by every instance of mortality, that our hold on life is feeble and uncertain, and that we know not how soon it may please thee to bring it to an end. O blessed Lord, by whose mercy we have been spared another day, give us grace to redeem the time that yet remains, and to use all diligence to fill up the measure of our duties, and to finish the work which thou hast given us to do, before we be called hence to give up our account to thee.

(Occasional Prayers.)

Bless, we pray thee, all our relatives, friends, and brethren. Make them thy children by adoption and grace, and extend to them all the benefits of thy gospel. Have mercy on our native land; and continue to us, if it please thee, the blessings which we have so long and so unthankfully enjoyed. Save us from national judgments; and punish us not according to our deserts. But spare us, good Lord; spare us, for the sake of thy dear Son. Give wisdom and integrity, we beseech thee, to our civil rulers and magistrates. May they rule in thy fear, and seek thy glory. Endue them, and the people under them, with that righteousness which exalteth a nation; and save them from those sins which are a reproach to any people.

These and all other things needful for our bodies and our souls, for our temporal and eternal interests, we humbly ask, in the name of our only mediator and intercessor, Jesus Christ. *Amen.*

FRIDAY MORNING

Scripture Lesson
(OR EPHESIANS 4:1–16)

As I live, saith the Lord God, I have no pleasure in the death of the wicked; but that the wicked turn from his way and live: turn ye, turn ye, from your evil ways; for why will ye die, O house of Israel? Ezek. 33:11. But if the wicked will turn from all his sins that he hath committed, and keep all my statutes, and do that which is lawful and right, he shall surely live, he shall not die. All his transgressions that he hath committed, they shall not be mentioned unto him: in his righteousness that he hath done he shall live. Ezek. 18:21. The manifestation of the Spirit is given to EVERY MAN to profit withal. 1 Cor. 12:7. He said unto me, my grace is sufficient for thee; for my strength is made perfect in weakness. 2 Cor. 12:9. Have we not all one father? Hath not one God created us? Mal. 2:10. God is no respecter of persons: Acts 10:34; but is long-suffering toward us, not willing that any should perish, but that ALL should come to repentance. 2 Pet. 3:9. For there is one God, and one mediator between God and men, the man Christ Jesus; who gave himself a ransom for ALL. 1 Tim. 2:5. He is the propitiation for our sins; and not for ours only, but also for the sins of THE WHOLE WORLD. 1 John 2:2. As by the offense of one, judgment came upon all men to condemnation; even so by the righteousness of one the free gift came upon ALL MEN unto justification of life: Rom. 5:18: for God hath concluded them all in unbelief, that he might have mercy upon all. Oh the depth of the riches both of the wisdom and knowledge of God! how unsearchable are his judgments, and his ways past finding out—Rom. 11:32—that he, by the grace of God, should taste death FOR EVERY MAN! Heb. 2:9.

Prayer

O LORD GOD, our heavenly Father, grant us grace, at this time, to present our bodies a living sacrifice, holy, acceptable unto thee, which is our reasonable service. Let us come before thee, under a grateful sense of all thy goodness. We will exalt thee: we will praise thy name; for thou hast done wonderful things in thy righteousness.

We commend ourselves, O God, to thy care and protection this day. Defend us with thy mighty power. Stretch forth thine hand to deliver us from every danger. Guide us by thy good Spirit; that we may shun every evil way, and walk securely in thy commandments. Grant us grace, that we fall not under the power of temptation, nor indulge in any secret or open sin. Purify our hearts, and regulate our desires, and restrain our passions, that all our doings, being ordered by thy holy precepts, may be righteous in thy sight, through Jesus Christ our Lord.

(Occasional Prayers.)

We bless thee, O God, that thou hast caused thy holy scriptures to be written for our learning: and we beseech thee to grant that they may prove profitable to us, for doctrine, for reproof, for correction, for instruction in righteousness; that we may be perfected in obedience, and thoroughly furnished unto all good works. May we all be so taught of thee, that thy law being written in our hearts, we may call upon thee as our God, and be acknowledged as thy people.

Grant, O Lord, that the ministers of thy word may go forth into all the world, preaching the unsearchable riches of Christ. Grant that the dark regions of the earth may hear the voice of redeeming love. Hasten the day, when the mountain of the Lord's house shall be established in the top of the mountains, and shall be exalted above the hills, and all nations shall flow unto it. May many people go and say, Come ye, and let us go up to the mountain of the Lord, to the house of the God of Jacob; and he will teach us of his ways, and we will walk in his paths. May the day soon arrive, when the nations of the earth shall beat their swords into plowshares, and their spears into pruning-hooks; when nation shall not lift up sword against nation, neither learn war anymore; when all may walk in the light of the Lord, and great shall be the peace of thy children.

Prepare us, O God, for the hour of death, and for the day of judgment; that when thy blessed Son, who has ascended into heaven, and sitteth on thy right hand, shall come again, with glory, to judge both the quick and dead, we may be ready to say, Lo, this is our God; we have waited for him, and he will save us. Grant this, for Jesus Christ's sake, to whom, with thee, O Father, and the Holy Ghost, be all honor and glory, now and forever. *Amen.*

FRIDAY EVENING

Scripture Lesson
(OR 1 JOHN 3)

James 1:12: Blessed is the man that endureth temptation: for when he is tried, he shall receive the crown of life, which the Lord hath promised to them that love him.

Heb. 12:5: My son, despise not thou the chastening of the Lord, nor faint when thou art rebuked of him: for whom the Lord loveth he chasteneth, and scourgeth every son whom he receiveth. If ye endure chastening, God dealeth with you as with sons: for what son is he whom the father chasteneth not? Furthermore, we have had fathers of our flesh which corrected us, and we gave them reverence: shall we not much rather be in subjection to the Father of spirits, and live? For they verily for a few days chastened us after their own pleasure; but he for our profit, that we might be partakers of his holiness. Now no chastening for the present seemeth to be joyous, but grievous: nevertheless, afterward it yieldeth the peaceable fruit of righteousness unto them which are exercised thereby. Wherefore, lift up the hands which hang down, and the feeble knees.

James 5:7: Be patient, brethren, unto the coming of the Lord. Behold, the husbandman waiteth for the precious fruit of the earth, and hath long patience for it, until he receive the early and latter rain. Be ye also patient; establish your hearts: for the coming of the Lord draweth nigh.

1 *Pet.* 4:12: Beloved, think it not strange, concerning the fiery trial which is to try you, as though some strange thing happened unto you: but rejoice, inasmuch as ye are partakers of Christ's sufferings; that, when his glory shall be revealed, ye may be glad also with exceeding joy.

2 *Cor.* 4:16: For which cause we faint not; but though our outward man perish, yet the inward man is renewed day by day. 17.—For our light affliction, which is but for a moment, worketh for us a far more exceeding and eternal weight of glory.

1 *Pet.* 5:6: Humble yourselves, therefore, under the mighty hand of God, that he may exalt you in due time: casting all your care upon him: for he careth for you. And the God of all grace, who hath called us unto his eternal glory by Christ Jesus, after that ye have suffered awhile, make you perfect, stablish, strengthen, settle you.

Prayer

ALMIGHTY God, the Giver of every good and perfect gift, we bless thee for another opportunity of coming into thy presence; and we beseech thee, of thy great goodness, to accept our thanksgivings and receive our prayers. May we approach thy throne with due reverence and godly fear; knowing that thou art everywhere present, and searchest out all our ways; that there is not a word in our tongue, nor a thought of our heart, but thou, O Lord, knowest it altogether.

We acknowledge our sinfulness. We have gone astray like lost and wandering sheep. But, O thou Shepherd of Israel, who didst come to seek and to save that which was lost, may we hear thy voice, and return unto thee. We beseech thee to have compassion upon us; bind up the broken; reclaim the wandering, and restore us to the paths of righteousness and peace.

When compassed about with infirmities, and sorrows, and sufferings, may we repose in perfect confidence on thy promise, that thou wilt swallow up death in victory, and wipe away tears from off all faces. May we look upon our blessed Savior as he is revealed to us, a King reigning in righteousness. May he be unto us as a hiding-place from the wind, and a covert from the tempest; as rivers of water in a dry place; as the shadow of a great rock in a weary land.

(Occasional Prayers.)

Have mercy, O God, upon the poor, the desolate, and the oppressed. Be thou the widow's God, and a father to the fatherless; and raise up, we beseech thee, friends and benefactors for the needy and the destitute; that they may be defended in all adversities, and provided for in all their necessities.

We pray for our enemies, persecutors, and slanderers. Have pity and compassion upon them; and grant them grace to see their wickedness, and turn from their sins. Forgive them, O Lord, in thy mercy; and grant us a spirit of forgiveness, that we may be ready to do unto others, as we would that they should do unto us.

Extend thy compassion, heavenly Father, to those who are spiritually blind and ignorant. Cause the wicked to forsake his way, and the unrighteous man his thoughts, that he may turn unto thee, and be abundantly pardoned.

Send out the light of thy everlasting gospel to the benighted heathen, and to all who are dwelling in darkness and the shadow of death. May the glad tidings of salvation be heard among them, as the voice of one crying in the wilderness, Prepare ye the way of the Lord, and make his paths straight.

We ask for all, in the name and for the sake of Jesus Christ our Lord, to whom, with thee, O Father, and the Holy Ghost, be all honor and glory, world without end. *Amen.*

SATURDAY MORNING

Scripture Lesson
(OR EPHESIANS 2)

Col. 3:1: If ye then be risen with Christ, seek those things which are above, where Christ sitteth on the right hand of God. Set your affections on things above, not on things on the earth. For ye are dead, and your life is hid with Christ in God. When Christ, who is our life, shall appear, then shall ye also appear with him in glory. Mortify therefore your members which are upon the earth; fornication, uncleanness, inordinate affection, evil concupiscence, and covetousness, which is idolatry. For which things' sake the wrath of God cometh on the children of disobedience: but now ye also put off all these; anger, wrath, malice, blasphemy, filthy communication out of your mouth. And have put on the new man, which is renewed in knowledge after the image of him that created him.

Rom. 6:21–23: What fruit had ye then in those things whereof ye are now ashamed? for the end of those things is death. But now being made free from sin, and become servants to God, ye have your fruit unto holiness, and the end everlasting life. For the wages of sin is death; but the gift of God is eternal life through Jesus Christ our Lord.

Prayer

ALMIGHTY and everlasting God, who has taught us, in thy holy word, to make prayers, and supplications, and intercessions, and to give thanks for all men; we humbly beseech thee favorably to receive these our prayers, which we offer unto thy divine majesty. We bless thee for thy great mercy, in opening a door of access to thy throne, through the intercession of thy dear Son, who is revealed to us as the way, the truth, and the life. We bless thee for thy gracious promise, that whatsoever we shall faithfully ask of thee in his name, shall be given unto us. We come before thee, pleading this thy unfailing assurance; and we beseech thee to look down upon us in mercy, and grant our petitions for Jesus Christ's sake.

We pray for thy holy church throughout the world. Inspire its ministers and members with the spirit of truth, unity, and concord; that it may be delivered from all false doctrine, from hardness of heart, and contempt of thy word and commandment; and grant that all those who confess thy holy name may agree in the truth of thy holy word, and live in peace, and harmony, and godly love.

We pray for all Christian rulers and magistrates; beseeching thee so to direct and dispose their hearts, that they may truly and impartially administer justice, to the punishment of wickedness and vice, and to the maintenance of thy true religion and virtue.

We pray for our common country; that its civil, religious and benevolent institutions may enjoy thy blessing; that its schools and seminaries of learning may flourish and prosper; that health, and peace, and plenteousness may abound; that righteousness, which alone exalteth a nation, may prevail; and that sin, which is a reproach to any people, may not be our ruin.

We pray for all sorts and conditions of men; that thou wouldst give them thy heavenly grace, and especially to this family here assembled in thy name and presence; that with meekness of heart and due reverence, they may hear and obey thy commandments, truly serving thee in holiness and righteousness all the days of their life.

We pray for all those, who, in this transitory life, are in sorrow, sickness, or any other adversity. Of thy great goodness, O Lord, comfort and succor them. Show them the light of thy countenance; sustain them in all their trials, and make all things to work together for their present and eternal welfare.

(Occasional Prayers.)

We ask for all, in the name and for the sake of Jesus Christ our Lord, to whom, with thee, O Farther, and the Holy Ghost, be all honor and glory, world without end. *Amen.*

SATURDAY EVENING

Scripture Lesson
(OR PSALM 119:1–16)

Acts 24:16: Herein do I exercise myself, to have always a conscience void of offense toward God, and toward men.

2 *Cor.* 1:12: For our rejoicing is this, the testimony of our conscience, that in simplicity and godly sincerity, not with fleshly wisdom, but by the grace of God, we have had our conversation in the world.

Isa. 57:15: Thus saith the high and lofty One that inhabiteth eternity, whose name is Holy: I dwell in the high and holy place, with him also that is of a contrite and humble spirit, to revive the spirit of the humble, and to revive the heart of the contrite ones. But the wicked are like the troubled sea, when it cannot rest, whose waters cast up mire and dirt. There is no peace, saith my God, to the wicked.

Heb. 10:22: Let us draw near with a true heart, in full assurance of faith, having our hearts sprinkled from an evil conscience, and our bodies washed with pure water.

Tit. 1:15: Unto the pure all things are pure; but unto them that are defiled and unbelieving is nothing pure; but even their mind and conscience is defiled. They profess that they know God; but in works they deny him, being abominable and disobedient, and unto every good work reprobate.

Luke 13:24: Strive to enter in at the straight gate; for many, I say unto you, will seek to enter in, and shall not be able.

1 *Tim.* 4:2: Having their conscience seared with a hot iron.

Jer. 17:9: The heart is deceitful above all things, and desperately wicked: who can know it?

Prayer

IN an humble acknowledgment of our manifold sins and iniquities, which we from time to time, and also this day, have committed against thee, in thought, word, and deed, we now prostrate ourselves before thee, O Lord of heaven and earth. We beseech thee, for the sake of Jesus Christ, our only Savior, to be merciful unto us. Forgive us that we have not rendered unto thee according to thy mercy and loving-kindness; that we have been forgetful and disobedient, and have sinned against heaven, and in thy sight. Let thy Holy Spirit sanctify us throughout, and give us more and more grace and strength, whereby we may be enabled to subdue all our sinful affections; grant that we may improve the remainder of our days with all possible care, and give all diligence to make our calling and election sure, that we may so persevere therein unto death, that at last we may attain everlasting life.

Accept our thanksgivings for all thy mercies vouchsafed to us in this life, and for the hopes of a better. And now that we are going to take our rest and sleep, may we consider that thou, Lord, only makest us to dwell in safety; whether we sleep or wake, live or die, may we be found thine own, to thy eternal glory, and our everlasting salvation, through Jesus Christ.

O our God, another week has just passed away, and we are still in the land of the living, while so many of our fellow-creatures have passed from time into eternity. Blessed be God for the continuance of life and health, and for prolonged opportunities of preparing for death and judgment.

O gracious God, let not this continuance of mercy increase our condemnation, by encouraging us to commit sin, because hitherto thine anger has been withheld from falling upon us. Let us not treasure up wrath unto ourselves against the day of wrath; but teach us to number our days, that we may apply our hearts unto wisdom.

(Occasional Prayers.)

Prepare us, most blessed God, by sleep and rest, to take our part in the duties of the Sabbath to-morrow. Give us that sense of sin which leads to a full confession of its guilt, and to faith in the atonement of Christ for its pardon. Give us that adoring gratitude for all thy mercies, more especially for the great mercy of a Savior, which may incline us to praise thee with joyful lips. Give us that sense of the value of our souls, and of the greatness of thy salvation, which may lead us to seek life and mercy with all our hearts. O may the coming Sabbath be so improved, by the means of grace, as to advance our meetness for the service of that eternal Sabbath that remaineth for the people of God; through the merit and mediation of Jesus Christ. *Amen.*

THIRD WEEK

LORDSDAY MORNING

Scripture Lesson
(PSALM 19)

Prayer

O THOU Lord of the Sabbath! enable us, on this morning of thy holy day, to worship thee in spirit and truth. May we find it good to draw near to thee in prayer. We thank thee for the consecration of one day in seven to thy immediate service. This is the day the Lord hath made; we will rejoice and be glad in it. Grant us thy gracious presence and blessing. Take off our thoughts from the vanities of time and sense, and place them upon divine and heavenly things. We would cease from our own works, as God on the seventh day did from his, and call the Lords Day a delight, the holy of the Lord, honorable; and honor him, not doing our own ways, nor finding our own pleasure, nor speaking our own words; but delighting in the Lord. We confess before thee our manifold transgressions. With the leper under the law, we cry, unclean, unclean; and with the humble publican, God! be merciful to us, sinners. Like penitent Job, we would abhor ourselves, and repent in dust and ashes. O thou God of salvation! have mercy on us. Make bare thine almighty arm for our deliverance: save us, or we perish. Make us the trophies of thy victorious grace. Wilt thou, who didst at first command light to shine out of darkness, shine in our hearts, to give the light of the knowledge of the glory of God in the face of Jesus Christ. We bless thee, O God! for our creation and preservation; for the kind care thou hast taken of us from the commencement of our existence to the present moment. We thank thee especially for the gift of thy Son, and for the method of salvation by him. What shall we render unto the Lord for all his benefits toward us? We will offer to thee the sacrifice of thanksgiving, and call upon the name of the Lord. We would present our bodies a living sacrifice, holy and acceptable unto God, which is our reasonable service. If permitted to wait upon thee in thine earthly courts, grant us thy blessing. If thy presence go not with us, wherefore should we go up to thy house? Help us to keep our feet, when we go to the house of God, and to be more ready to hear, than to offer the sacrifice of fools. Be with all thy worshiping assemblies everywhere this day. Give them fellowship with thee in thine ordinances, and, while in thy banqueting-house, may thy banner over them be love. Let none be disposed unnecessarily to forsake the assembling of themselves together as the manner of some is. Impart unto the ministers of the gospel, a double portion of thy Holy Spirit. May they show themselves approved unto God, workmen that need not be ashamed, rightly dividing the word of truth. Bless the minister whom thou hast placed over us. Make him wise to win souls unto Christ. May this Lords Day be a spiritual birth-day to thousands. Open thou blind eyes, unstop deaf ears, and break hard hearts. Instruct the ignorant, reclaim the wandering, and edify thy people.

(Occasional Prayers.)

We thank thee, gracious Father! for the mercies of the past night, and for the light and blessings of this holy morning. Let thy good providence preserve and defend us this day, and thy Holy Spirit guide and comfort us. Prepare us for all the duties and events of subsequent life, and especially for death, judgment and a happy eternity. And now, O thou prayer-hearing and prayer-answering God! hear our supplications, and grant us an answer in peace through Jesus Christ; to whom, as the Lamb that was slain to redeem us to God by his blood, be blessing, and honor, and glory, and power forever and ever. *Amen.*

LORDSDAY EVENING

Scripture Lesson
(JOHN 1:1–18)

Prayer

HOLY, holy, holy Lord God Almighty, which art, and wast, and art to come! thy name endureth forever, and thy memorial unto all generations. Help us, at the close of this thy holy day, to bow before thee with profound veneration. We thank thee for the Lords Day and its sacred privileges; that we have been permitted to worship thee in the family, and in the house of our holy solemnities. Accept, through the mediation of the heavenly Advocate, our thanksgivings; hear our supplications; and sanctify to us the instructions of thy word. May what we have this day heard, read and meditated upon, of a religious nature, deeply impress our minds and do us good, as thy word doth the upright in heart. If we have misspent or profaned any portion of thy holy day, pardon us, we beseech thee. May the services of thy people, in all parts of Christendom, come up in acceptable remembrance before thee. Wherein their worship has been defective or defiled, forgive. Let what they have this day learned of God and his law, of their depravity and ruin, of Christ and his gospel, powerfully impress their hearts, and influence their practice. May thy word, this day dispensed, be quick and powerful, and sharper than a two-edged sword, piercing even to the dividing asunder of soul and spirit, and of the joints and marrow. Cause a heavenly wind to blow, that dry bones may be enlivened, and the dead in trespasses and sins be quickened. Bless all thy churches. Build them up in the faith, order, and purity of the gospel. May all, who minister at thy holy altar, be richly furnished for the services of the sanctuary, and be inspired with an ardent love for the souls of men. Bless thy servant, who ministers in spiritual things unto us. May he be instant in season and out of season, laboring abundantly in word and doctrine, not teaching for doctrines the commandments of men, but the pure word of God.

(Occasional Prayers.)

Bless all attempts to spread the gospel to the ends of the earth, and to save a perishing world. O Lord! graciously regard us, who are now worshiping before thee. Behold! we are vile, what shall we answer thee? With the disciple of Christ we pray, Lord! save or we perish. O thou who art exalted to give repentance to Israel and remission of sins! give us that godly sorrow which worketh repentance to salvation not to be repented of. Pardon us, we beseech thee, and accept us in thy beloved. We thank thee, heavenly Father! that thou hast so tenderly loved us, as to give thine only begotten Son to die for us. Praised be thy name, that eternal redemption may be obtained through the blood of sprinkling. We give thee thanks for the blessings of life, and of the past day in particular. We commit ourselves into thy hands for keeping this night. May we lie down to rest in safety, and in peace with God and man. Bring us to behold the morning, rejoicing in its light and in thy loving-kindness. Ever may we act in thy fear, and live to thy glory. When the evening of life shall arrive, and we are called to close the day of toil and trouble, may we fall asleep in Jesus, and, in the morning of the resurrection, awake to a glorious and blissful immortality. Hear our prayer, O Lord! and give ear to our supplications. Now unto the King eternal, immortal, invisible, the only wise God, be honor and glory forever. *Amen.*

MONDAY MORNING

Scripture Lesson
(JOHN 4:1–26)

Prayer

THE heavens declare thy glory, O God, and the firmament showeth thy handiwork. Day unto day uttereth speech, and night unto night showeth knowledge, and there is no speech nor language where their voice is not heard. We behold displays of thy wisdom, power and goodness, in all thy works, from the largest to the least.

But thou hast magnified thy word above all thy name; and we can never be sufficiently thankful for the revelation of thy will in the Scriptures of truth. We bless thee that these sacred Scriptures have been preserved, and translated, and published, and multiplied, so that we all have it in our possession, and can read, in our own tongue, the wonderful works of God. Here we see mercy and truth meeting together, righteousness and peace kissing each other. Here thou hast shined in our hearts, to give us the light of the knowledge of thy glory in the face of Jesus Christ.

For in Him thou hast reconciled the world unto thyself, not imputing their trespasses unto them. Thou hast made him to be sin for us, who knew no sin, that we might be made the righteousness of God in him. And thou hast raised Him up from the dead, and given him glory, that our faith and hope may be in God. At the view of this infinite kindness, may we resign all our unworthy and suspicious thoughts; and, placing our confidence in thee, return and say—Lord, I am thine, save me. Look thou upon me and be merciful unto me, as thou art unto those that love thy name.

(Occasional Prayers.)

May our heart be right with God, and our life such as becometh the gospel. May we maintain a supreme regard to another and a better world, and feel and confess ourselves to be only strangers and pilgrims in this. How often, by bodily infirmities and pains, have we been told that this is not our rest! O God, not only command, but enable us, to arise and depart hence. Afford us all the direction, all the defense, all the support, all the consolation our journey will require. Give us, in large abundance, the supply of the spirit of Jesus Christ, that we may be prepared for every duty; that we may love thee in all our mercies; that we may submit to thee in every trial. May we trust thee when we walk in darkness, and have no light; and amidst all the changes of the present, and the uncertainties of the future, may our minds be kept in perfect peace, being stayed upon God.

Hast thou not made with us an everlasting covenant, ordered in all things and sure? The very hairs of our head—are they not all numbered? Are not all thy ways mercy and truth? Lord, we believe, help thou our unbelief. And now unto him that is able to keep us from falling, and to present us faultless before the presence of his glory, with exceeding joy,—to the only wise God our Savior, be glory and majesty, dominion and power, both now and forever. *Amen.*

MONDAY EVENING

Scripture Lesson
(ISAIAH 35)

Prayer

O THOU exalted God and Father! we come, loaded with thy mercies, to present to thee our evening sacrifice of prayer and thanksgiving. With more than parental solicitude thou hast watched over us this day, and brought us to see its close in peace and safety. How unworthy are we of all thy favors! We feel and acknowledge that this very day we have been guilty of many sins and short-comings. Our hearts are ever prone to forget thee; and though the spirit is willing, the flesh is weak. Have mercy upon us, O God, according to thy loving-kindness; according to the multitude of thy tender mercies, blot out our transgressions. Sprinkle our souls afresh with the atoning blood of Christ. Cleanse thou us from secret faults. We know that our sins are great, but thy mercy is greater, and hence we trust in our Lord and Savior, Jesus Christ. May we be enabled hereafter carefully to avoid whatever was wrong or sinful in us to-day. May we be more watchful against temptation, more zealous in thy service, more devout in prayer, more spiritual in our conversation, and more holy in our walk.

Hitherto thou hast helped us, provided for our necessities, and crowned our lives with loving-kindness. Truly our hope is in thee, and under the shadow of thy wings will we put our trust. Let thy goodness continue to follow us; and enable us to express our thankfulness by a more holy walk and sincere obedience to thy laws.

(Occasional Prayers.)

We now retire to rest. Give thy holy angels charge concerning us, that no evil, seen or unseen, may befall us. Help us to remember that as we now lay our bodies upon our bed of sleep, so we will soon have to be laid in our grave to awake no more until the morning of the resurrection. Let every future day and night of our lives be spent in such a manner, that whenever thou shalt call us hence, we may depart as peacefully as we now retire to rest. If this should be the night of our death, may we sleep in Jesus. Our God is ours, and we are his: what enemy have we to fear?

We would supplicate the same blessings for all that are near and dear to us. Have mercy upon our enemies, and bless their souls. May they not be thine enemies. May we be enabled to act in such a manner towards them, that they may take knowledge of us, that we have been with Jesus, and have learned of him. Remember graciously all the sick and afflicted, and administer to their wants. Pity a world that lieth in sin, and send abroad thy light and truth into all the earth. May we be invigorated and refreshed by sleep, so that, if it be thy will, we may behold the coming morning in health and peace, and be well prepared for the duties and labors of the new day. And now unto God the Father, Son and Holy Spirit, be present and eternal praises given. *Amen.*

TUESDAY MORNING

Scripture Lesson
(MARK 2:1–17)

Prayer

BLESSED be God, the Creator of heaven and earth! Blessed be the Lord God, the God of Israel, who only doeth wondrous things! And blessed be his glorious name forever! who hath created the day and the night, and divided the light and the darkness, and who hath ordained that as long as time shall be, they shall not cease; in order that mankind may rest in the hours of silent darkness and return by morning light to their daily avocations. Lord, how manifold are thy works! in wisdom hast thou made them all; the earth is full of thy goodness. For these thy mercies we desire to praise thee, and draw nigh unto thee with the dawn of the morning. Therefore do we now again appear in thy presence, to praise thee for the quiet repose and refreshing sleep which in the past night we have enjoyed, and that we are this morning again permitted to rise in health and gladness. We beseech thee, preserve our souls this day as it were in the hollow of thy hand, and keep our bodies in health and safety, secure from the multiplied calamities which surround us. Be thou unto us a mighty protection and a strong stay, a preservation from stumbling and a help from falling, [Sir. 34:16,] that no calamity overtake us.

(Occasional Prayers.)

O merciful God, grant that, as knowing the time, that now it is high time to arise out of the sleep of sin and unrighteousness, for now our salvation is nearer than when we believed, and since the night is far spent and the day is at hand, O grant that we may therefore cast off the works of darkness, and put on the armor of light, that we may walk honestly as in the day: not in rioting and drunkenness, not in chambering and wantonness, not in strife and envying, but that we may put on the Lord Jesus Christ in true faith and goodness. Waken us, O Lord, in the morning, and incline our ears to hear thy word, that we may receive the same in faith and treasure it up in our hearts— and, complying with its directions, listen to the cries and supply the wants of the poor and distressed; and when again in days of distress we call upon thee, O lend a listening ear to the voice of our supplications, and despise not the prayer of our souls when death draws nigh. Early shall our prayers come before thee; incline thine ear to our cries, and in the morning fill us with thy grace; then shall we delight and rejoice in thee all our days. *Amen.*

TUESDAY EVENING

Scripture Lesson
(MATTHEW 11)

Prayer

O THOU powerful and everlasting God, Father of our Lord Jesus Christ, we would tender unto thee our heartfelt and grateful acknowledgments, that, through thy divine protection, this day has been spent free from all danger and harm. That we have not come into dangers, threatening both body and soul, we have to attribute to thy mercy, for thou hast preserved us in all our ways. We beseech thee now furthermore, pardon all the sins we have committed against thee in former times, and take us and all those who are near and dear unto us into thy keeping, this night and through the remainder of our pilgrimage here below; guide them and us by thy unerring Spirit. In mercy preserve us from all fear and distress, from the delusions and craftiness of the devil, wherewith he endeavors to subdue us both by day and by night; preserve us from the pestilence that walketh in darkness, and from the snares of the enemy: deliver us from the net and the snares laid to entrap our souls. Leave us not, neither forsake us, O thou God of our salvation. Let not the temptations of the evil one be greater than our strength, but rescue us, O Lord, from every danger which may threaten either body or soul; for thou, Lord, art our rock and our fortress and our deliverer: our God, our strength, in thee will we trust, our buckler and the horn of our salvation and our high tower. [Ps. 18:3.] Therefore, thou ever-faithful God, let thy waking eyes be upon us, and prove thou our defense from the power and attacks of the great enemy; be our watch and guard, surround us with thy protection as with a wall, that nothing can harm us, for in thee alone is our salvation—to thee do we raise our eyes, from thee alone cometh our help. Our help cometh from the Lord who hath created heaven and earth. Behold, as the eyes of servants look unto the hand of their masters, and as the eyes of a maiden unto the hand of her mistress, so our eyes wait upon the Lord our God, until that he have mercy upon us. Have mercy upon us, O Lord, have mercy upon us. Lift upon us the light of thy countenance, that we may not sleep the sleep of death, O thou that livest and reignest throughout eternity. *Amen.*

(Occasional Prayers.)

WEDNESDAY MORNING

Scripture Lesson
(PSALM 23)

Prayer

ALMIGHTY and heavenly Father, who art about our path, and beholdest all our ways; we come to thee in the name of thy beloved Son, to supplicate thy mercy as we enter upon the duties of another day.

Thou, O Lord, art a shield for us, our glory, and the lifter up of our heads. We laid us down, and slept; we have awaked, for thou, Lord, hast sustained us. May our souls, and all that is within us, magnify God for all his goodness, and especially for his wonderful mercy in redeeming sinners by Jesus Christ; for the light of that Sun of Righteousness, which arises with healing in his wings on benighted souls; for all the blessings of free salvation through him, all the means of grace, and the hope of future glory.

Sad are the returns which we have made for so many mercies. How ungrateful have we been! We acknowledge and bewail our manifold sins and rebellions. We were born in sin, and we find continually the flesh lusting against the spirit, and the spirit against the flesh, so that we cannot do the things that we would. We are guilty, sinful and weak. Lord, save us, or we perish. We entirely depend on thy mercy, in Christ Jesus, for the gift and continuance of every good, and for deliverance from all those evils which we have justly deserved.

For that mercy we now earnestly look to thee, O Father of mercies. Remember us, O Lord, with the favor that thou bearest unto thy people. May the grace of God which bringeth salvation, teach us, and all men, to deny ungodliness and worldly lusts, and to live soberly, righteously and godly, in this present world.

Give us grace to be continually looking to thee, through this day, for direction, assistance, and strength. Be thou in all our thoughts, and let us acknowledge thee in all our ways. Incline our hearts, we beseech thee, to thy precepts. Endue us with that simplicity and godly sincerity, which are well pleasing unto thee.

Give us the same mind that was in Christ Jesus, that we may be humble, patient, gentle, and full of love, even as he was. Teach us to be poor in spirit, and meek; to mourn for sin, and to hunger and thirst after righteousness. Grant that we may love that Savior whom we have not seen, and believing in him, may we rejoice with joy unspeakable and full of glory.

And here, constrained by thy mercies, we would afresh present our bodies a living sacrifice, holy and acceptable unto thee, which is our reasonable service. We renew in thy presence all our solemn vows, renouncing the world, the flesh and the devil; and steadfastly purposing, by thy help, to keep thy holy will and commandments. We take thee, O God, for our portion, and thy laws as our rule, and thy service as our duty, entreating thee to give us grace that we may be wholly thine.

(Occasional Prayers.)

May all mankind know and serve thee. Grant that the kingdom which is righteousness, and peace, and joy in the Holy Ghost, may be established in every land, in every heart. We beseech thee also to bless our more immediate relations. Look upon them in mercy, and visit them with thy salvation. Hear these humble petitions for the only sake of the Lord Jesus Christ. *Amen.*

WEDNESDAY EVENING

Scripture Lesson
(1 CORINTHIANS 15:1–28)

Prayer

ALMIGHTY God and most merciful Father! we adore thee as a being possessed of all possible perfections, excellence and glory. Who is like unto thee, O Lord? glorious in holiness, fearful in praises, doing wonders! We approach thee through Jesus Christ, who is Mediator between God and man. In the name of our great High-Priest, who is passed into the heavens, we would come boldly unto the throne of grace, that we may obtain mercy and find grace to help in time of need. We thank thee, that thou didst make man with such noble powers of body and mind. But we have to acknowledge that the crown is fallen from our head; woe unto us that we have sinned! Our hearts by nature are deceitful above all things, and desperately wicked; who shall deliver us from the body of this death? Our flesh trembleth for fear of thee, and we are afraid of thy judgment. Praised be thy name, that thou hast not cut us down as cumberers of the ground, but that we have still a place in thy vineyard. Thou art waiting to be gracious, and calling by the voice of providence and thy glorious word, saying: "turn ye, turn ye, for why will ye die?" Oh that we might obey thy calls, and turn and live! Give us repentance towards God, and faith towards our Lord Jesus Christ. May we have the blessedness of that man, whose iniquities are forgiven, and whose sins are covered. Enable us to exercise ourselves so as to have always a conscience void of offense towards God and towards man. O Lord! graciously regard those who are in a state of impenitence. Teach transgressors thy ways, and let sinners be converted unto thee. Quicken those who are dead in trespass and sins. Bless the aged. Support them in the decline of life, and let the evening of their days be tranquil and happy. Command thy blessing upon the middle-aged and the rising generation. May parents instruct their children and their households after them, that they may keep the way of the Lord, to do justice and judgment. Comfort Zion, make her wilderness like Eden, and her desert like the garden of the Lord, that joy and gladness may be found therein, thanksgiving and the voice of melody.

(Occasional Prayers.)

We thank thee for the favors which thou hast been pleased to bestow upon us. We bless thee for the wonders of redeeming love, for the overtures of mercy, and for the means of grace, and for thine inestimable love in sending thine only-begotten Son, to instruct, to guide, to save us from sin and misery, and elevate us to an inheritance which is incorruptible in heaven. We thank thee for the protection and blessings of another day and evening. We commend ourselves, our friends, and all our interests, to thy holy keeping during this night. May the holy angels encamp around our habitation and defend us. Permit us in safety to see another day, prepared for its duties and events. Guide, guard, and bless us in this state of trial, and at death receive us to mansions of glory, through the atonement and intercession of Jesus Christ. Now unto him that is able to keep us from falling, and to present us faultless before the presence of his glory with exceeding joy; to the only wise God our Savior, be glory and majesty, dominion and power, both now and ever. *Amen.*

THURSDAY MORNING

Scripture Lesson
(JOHN 10:1–18)

Prayer

O THOU high and lofty One that inhabitest eternity, whose name is holy! though thou art exalted as God over all, blessed for evermore; yet thou dost condescend to dwell with those who are of a contrite and humble spirit, to revive the spirit of the humble, and the heart of the contrite. O Lord! in thine infinite condescension look down upon us now prostrate before thee. We humbly confess our guilt. We have erred and strayed like lost sheep. When we have known our Master's will, we have not been careful to perform it, and therefore deserve to be beaten with many stripes. O Lord! have mercy upon us miserable sinners. Spare thou us, who confess our faults. Let us know the plague of our hearts, and see what evil dwells within us. Give us the deepest penitence for sin, for a broken heart, O God! thou wilt not despise. May we think on our ways, and turn unto the Lord, from whom we have so ungratefully revolted. Oh for an interest in Christ, whose blood cleanseth from all sin. We would go unto the glorious Savior, who hath said, Come unto me, all ye that labor and are heavy laden, and I will give you rest. Enable us at all times to possess the temper of Christians, that we may manifest ourselves to be the disciples of the meek and lowly Jesus.

(Occasional Prayers.)

O thou compassionate Father in heaven! be pleased to extend thy grace to the whole family of man. Give thy Son the heathen for his inheritance, and the uttermost parts of the earth for his possession. Let the gospel be preached to every creature under heaven, and be effectual to their conversion and salvation. Give to the ministers of the gospel ardent zeal in their divine Master's service, and eminent success in their high calling. We give thee thanks for thy manifold goodness in redemption. We praise thee, O Lord, for the message of eternal life, published in the gospel; that we are come not unto mount Sinai, that burned with fire, and threatens death; but unto mount Zion, which proclaims mercy to every penitent. We bless thee, too, for the bounties of thy daily providence. Surely goodness and mercy have followed us all our days. We render thee thanks for the mercies of the night past. We laid us down and slept; we awaked, because thou, Lord! hast sustained us. Go forth with us, we beseech thee, in the concerns of this day. Prosper us in our lawful undertakings. Guide us by thine unerring wisdom, all the days of our pilgrimage, and enable us at death to depart this life in the triumphs of a Christian hope. And when absent from the body, may we be present with the Lord, and be permitted to celebrate forever the praises of redeeming love. All which we ask in the name and through the mediation of Jesus Christ; to whom, with the Father, and the Holy Spirit, be equal and everlasting honors. *Amen.*

THURSDAY EVENING

Scripture Lesson
(MATTHEW 21:1–16)

Prayer

SUPREMELY great and glorious God! before thee angels, vailing their faces, bow and worship. Permit us, who dwell on thy footstool, unworthy as we are, to approach thy sacred presence, through the atoning blood of Jesus. It is a good thing to give thanks unto the Lord, and to sing praises unto thy name, O Most High! to show forth thy loving-kindness in the morning, and thy faithfulness every night. Blessed be God, who hath preserved us in our going out and coming in, the day past, and who daily loads us with benefits. We have been the recipients of thy divine bounty continually, and we would gratefully acknowledge the hand that has supplied us. Take care of us, O Lord! this night. Hide us under the shadow of thy wings. May we commune with our own hearts upon our beds, and meditate upon thee in the night-watches. Permit us to behold the light of another day, better prepared to serve thee than ever we have been. Be with us in all subsequent life. As thou hast guarded and blessed us in infancy, in youth, and in riper years; so do thou continue to be our guardian and benefactor. While we rejoice that thou hast given us birth and education in a land of gospel light and liberty, may we not abuse our exalted privileges and blessings. O Lord! we confess that we have been disobedient children. We have violated thy precepts, and despised thy mercy. Our trespasses have reached unto the clouds, and cry aloud for vengeance. It is thine amazing, thine infinite forbearance, that keeps us out of hell. Look in mercy upon us, O God of mercy! Turn us, and we shall be turned; draw us with the cords of thy love, and we shall run after thee; mold us into thine image, and we shall be holy. Ever may we act as accountable creatures, and faithfully discharge the duties of our several relations in life. May we

be dead to this world, and alive to God and divine things, and always live prepared for death, judgment and eternity.
(Occasional Prayers.)

Bless the whole Christian church; purge it from corruptions, heal its divisions, and increase its numbers. Pour out thy Holy Spirit and revive pure religion, and undefiled before God and the Father. Let converts to Jesus be multiplied, and let many be added to the church, who shall finally be saved. Bless thy servant, who labors among us in word and doctrine. Make him faithful and successful, as an ambassador of Christ. Have compassion, O Lord! upon the whole family of man. By thy all-conquering grace suppress all vice, error and delusion. Plant Immanuel's standard in every land. Let thy word have free course and be glorified; and let the earth be full of the knowledge of the Lord as the waters cover the sea, and all flesh see thy salvation. Glory be to the Father, and to the Son, and to the Holy Ghost; as it was in the beginning, is now, and ever shall be, world without end. *Amen.*

FRIDAY MORNING

Scripture Lesson
(PHILIPPIANS 2:1–17)

Prayer

O THOU eternal God! with thee is the fountain of life. Thou art the Father of men and angels. Thou dost from thy throne behold all the dwellers upon earth: and there is not a word on our tongue, or a thought in our heart, but lo! O Lord, thou knowest it altogether. And thou art not a God that has pleasure in wickedness, neither can evil dwell with thee.

How then can we presume to enter thy presence, who have rendered ourselves guilty before thee, and have provoked thy righteous displeasure. Oh wretched creatures that we are! We have wearied thy patience, we have abused thy goodness, we have trampled on thy authority, and we have said unto God, depart from us, we desire not the knowledge of thy ways. We lie at thy mercy. If thou pity us not, we are undone. But thou art longsuffering, not willing that any should perish. Hast thou not sworn by thyself, that thou hast no pleasure in the death of him that dieth? Hast thou not delivered up thine own Son for us all? And wilt thou not with him also freely give us all things?

Through him as the way, the truth, and the life, may we return to thee, and find thee waiting to be gracious. Enlighten us in the knowledge of sin and of ourselves. May we feel our unworthiness, misery, and helplessness. May we rejoice in the suitableness, the all-sufficiency, and the perfect willingness of the Savior; and find in him, for ourselves, individually, wisdom, and righteousness, and sanctification, and redemption. As our Prophet, may we receive his instructions. As our High Priest, may we rely on his sacrifice and intercession. As our Prince, may we obey him. As our example, may we follow him: and whatsoever we do, in word or deed, may we do all in the name of the Lord Jesus.

May we maintain integrity and uprightness. May we be Israelites indeed, in whom is no guile; and herein exercise ourselves, to have always a conscience void of offense towards God and towards man. May the same mind govern us and the same spirit actuate us in prosperity and adversity; alone and in public; in thy house and in our own; may we fulfill our course with diligence and perseverance; and at last finish it with joy. When we have passed the wilderness, and our eyes behold the swellings of Jordan, bid our anxious fears subside;

and give us an abundant entrance into the everlasting kingdom of our Lord and Savior.

But, O Lord, we would not reach that felicity alone. May we awaken the attention of others, and induce them to join us in the path of life; ever remembering, that if we convert a sinner from the error of his way, we shall save a soul from death and shall hide a multitude of sins. May we therefore seek every opportunity of usefulness; may we walk in wisdom towards them that are without; holding forth the word of life, and adorning the doctrine of God our Savior in all things. *Amen.*

(Occasional Prayers.)

FRIDAY EVENING

Scripture Lesson
(PHILIPPIANS 3)

Prayer

ALMIGHTY and everlasting God, dispose our hearts, we beseech thee, to close this day with serious reflection and fervent prayer. Receive with favor the supplications of thy servants, and look down upon us in compassion; not in thine anger, lest thou bring us to nothing.

We thank thee for the daily blessings which thou givest us to enjoy. Enable us to see thy hand and to acknowledge thy providence in all our concerns; and, with true devotion of heart, to trace up every stream of earthly comfort to the fountain of eternal love.

We bless thee especially, heavenly Father, for the light of the everlasting gospel, and for the redemption of the world by the death of our Savior Christ, both God and man; who did humble himself, even to the death of the Cross, for us miserable sinners; who lay in darkness and the shadow of death, that he might make us the children of light and exalt us unto everlasting life. May we always remember the exceeding great love of our only Savior, Jesus Christ, thus dying for us, and the innumerable benefits which, by his precious blood-shedding, he hath obtained for us. And may we give unto thee continual thanks; submitting ourselves to thy holy will and pleasure, and studying to serve thee, in true holiness and righteousness, all the days of our lives.

(Occasional Prayers.)

To the care and protection of thy good providence we commend ourselves, and all who are near and dear to us, this night. Be thou our refuge, and fortress, and house of defense, in whom we may trust. May we abide safely under thy almighty shadow. May thy truth and faithfulness be our shield and buckler. May no evil befall us, nor any plague come nigh our dwelling. Be thou our continual ruler and guide; and teach us so to pass through things temporal, that we finally lose not the things eternal.

We humbly beseech thee, O God, for all sorts and conditions of men; that thou wouldst be pleased to make thy ways known unto them, thy saving health unto all nations. We pray especially for thy church universal; that it may be so guided and governed by thy good Spirit, that all who call themselves Christians may be led into the way of truth, and hold the faith in unity of spirit, in the bond of peace, and righteousness of life. Finally, we commend to thy fatherly goodness all those who are in any way afflicted or distressed, in mind, body, or estate; that it may please thee to comfort and relieve them, according to their several necessities; giving them patience under their sufferings, and a happy issue out of all their afflictions. All which we ask for Jesus Christ's sake; in whose all-prevailing words we sum up these our petitions:—

Our Father who, &c. *Amen.*

SATURDAY MORNING

Scripture Lesson
(COLOSSIANS 2)

Prayer

ALMIGHTY and ever blessed God, whose name alone is Jehovah; thou art the Most High over all the earth; unto thee would we look this morning, through Christ the Mediator, as unto the prayer-hearing and prayer-answering God. We thank thee for thy merciful protection during the past night, and for the refreshing sleep which we have enjoyed. We laid ourselves down and slept, and rose again because the Lord hath sustained us. We thank thee for the light of another day, and for the measure of health with which we are permitted to behold it, and for all our mercies and comforts. But above all, we bless thee for the light of the gospel, and for the gift of him who is the light of the world. Grant us, we beseech thee, thy Holy Spirit, to enlighten our minds, and to sanctify our hearts, that we may perceive Christ to be the chief among ten thousand, and the one altogether lovely; that we may receive him by faith, as the Lord our righteousness, and glorify his holy name by a godly walk and conversation.

We confess our manifold sins and transgressions. We have strayed from thy ways, O God, like lost sheep. We have done those things which we ought not to have done, and we have left undone those things which we ought to have done. We have incurred thy displeasure. We deserve thy wrath. But O most gracious Father, have mercy upon us. Grant us true repentance for all our sins. Look thou upon us in the face of thine anointed; forgive us all our trespasses, and enable us by thy grace to adorn the doctrine of God, our Savior, in all things.

(Occasional Prayers.)

Preserve us this day, O Lord, from all evil, and defend us from every danger to which we may be exposed. Give us a due sense of our dependence on thee, and of our indebtedness to thee, for every good gift we enjoy. Enable us this day to resist temptation, and overcome the evil desires of our own hearts. May we, in thy strength, discharge the duties incumbent on us, and do thy holy will in all things. May we, as a family, be devoted to thy service, and as individuals, may we be the objects of thy providential care, and the subjects of thy saving grace.

O heavenly Father, remember in mercy our absent relatives and friends. May they be interested in the covenant of redemption, and be made partakers of everlasting life. May their lives and health be precious in thy sight, and consecrated to thy service.

Bless all for whom we should pray. Have mercy upon all men, and especially the sick and afflicted. Heal and comfort them. Relieve them according to their necessities. Give them patience under their sufferings, humble resignation to thy will, and a happy deliverance from all their pains and sorrows.

Smile graciously upon thy church universal, and give grace to all who minister in holy things, to be faithful in the same. Let thy kingdom soon come. From the rising of the sun even unto the going down of the same, may thy name be magnified. The grace of, &c. *Amen.*

SATURDAY EVENING

Scripture Lesson
(COLOSSIANS 3:1–17)

Prayer

O ALMIGHTY God, who art exalted far above all praises—how great is thy mercy in opening a way for lost sinners to approach thee, and to spread their wants before thy footstool!

Great God, we might justly have been left under thy wrath for our rebellion—having no way to escape, had not thine own arm brought salvation! Thou hast sent thine incarnate Son to seek and to save the guilty, and thou hast revealed thyself in him as a just God, and yet the justifier of the believer in Jesus. O Lord, save us, we beseech thee; we fall as vile sinners at the footstool of thy sovereign mercy, loathing ourselves in our own sight, on account of our iniquities. We renounce all dependence on any merits of our own. We plead thy promises, and offer before thee no other sacrifice or righteousness but the all-sufficient sacrifice and spotless righteousness of thy beloved Son, in whom thou art ever well pleased.

O thou Holy Spirit, whose province it is to convince the world of sin, of righteousness, and of judgment, discover to us the pride of our nature, and the alienation of our hearts from God. Take of the things of Christ, and exhibit them before us in all their fullness and sufficiency. Cause us to renounce our own wisdom and righteousness, and to be willing to receive pardon, and the hope of eternal life, as the gift of free, unmerited mercy, through Jesus Christ our Lord. Create in us clean hearts, and renew right spirits within us. Subdue our corrupt desires, and set our affections on heavenly things.

We have often erred and strayed from thy fold, yet now again we return to thee hungry and thirsty, weak and defenseless, diseased and perishing. Oh may we hear thy voice and follow thee—may we be supported by thy grace and enjoy thy favor.

Another week has passed, and we are rapidly approaching eternity. Help us, O most merciful Father, to fully realize this momentous truth; and when our end arrives, may we be prepared to yield our spirits in the full assurance of a happy eternity.

(Occasional Prayers.)

With humble and heartfelt thanks for the mercies of the day that is past, we implore thy gracious protection during the dark and silent watches of the night. O thou keeper of Israel, who never slumberest nor sleepest, be thou about our path and about our bed. Defend us from all dangers, refresh our wearied bodies with sleep, and if it should please thy almighty providence to raise us up to behold the light of the returning sun, let us arise with thankful hearts, remembering that the day is the Sabbath of the Lord. Oh may our minds be solemnized, and may we rejoice and be glad in the day which the Lord has made. Be with all thy ministering servants on the morrow, and especially with him who ministers unto us. May they go forth in the fullness of the blessing of the gospel of peace, preaching peace through the blood of the cross; and may the word of thy grace be as the rain that watereth the earth, and maketh it to bring forth and bud; may it accomplish thy good pleasure, and prosper in the thing whereto thou shalt send it. All these things we ask for the sake, and through the intercession of our Lord and Savior Jesus Christ, to whom, in the unity of the Father and the Holy Spirit, be ascribed all honor and glory, now and forever. *Amen.*

FOURTH WEEK

LORDSDAY MORNING

Scripture Lesson
(ISAIAH 55)

Prayer

O THOU King eternal, immortal, invisible, dwelling in the light which no man can approach unto, and whom no eye hath seen, or can see. Yet thou hast been pleased to reveal thyself to man; and by means of thy word we behold thee in every character and relation that can suit our necessities or encourage our hope. Thou art exalted above all blessing and praise: our goodness extendeth not to thee—but unless thine be extended to us, we are undone forever.

We bless thee, that thou hast regarded our souls as well as our bodies; and no less provided for our future interests than our present. When there was no eye to pity us, thou didst remember us in our low estate; and when there was no arm to rescue, thou wast pleased to lay help on one that is mighty; and thou hast sent thy own Son into the world, not to condemn the world, but that the world through him might be saved. To him may we turn and find in him the wisdom, righteousness, sanctification, and redemption which, as perishing sinners, we need. May we know that he has borne our griefs and carried our sorrows; and be able to rejoice in him as our sacrifice, our almighty helper, and our lovely example. May we drink into his spirit. May we place our feet in the very prints of his steps; and follow him till we shall be perfectly like him, and see him as he is.

We desire to acknowledge thee in the dispensations of thy providence; and to own thy agency in all the events that befall us, whether pleasing or painful. Thou hast a right to govern us; and thou knowest what will best advance our welfare. May we commit our way unto the Lord, and be able to say at thy footstool, in unfeigned submission, Here I am, let him do what seemeth him good.

(Occasional Prayers.)

We bless thee for the institutions of religion, in the use of which thou hast promised to draw near to those that draw near to thee. Quicken and elevate our souls, that rising above the formality of devotion, we may come even to thy seat, and enjoy a little of the blessedness of those that have entered thy temple above and are singing the song of Moses and the Lamb. We are about to assemble in the house of prayer—pour upon us the spirit of grace and of supplication; and grant that we may hunger and thirst after righteousness. We are going to the house of praise—awaken in us every grateful and cheerful emotion, and may we speak to ourselves in psalms and hymns, and spiritual songs, singing and making melody in our hearts unto the Lord. We are repairing to the house of instruction—enable us to receive the kingdom of God as a little child. Lead us into all truth. And let us be neither barren nor unfruitful in the knowledge of our Lord and Savior Jesus Christ.

For this purpose, let thy presence go with us; and let thy word come to us in power, and in the Holy Ghost, and in much assurance. Bless all the churches of the faithful; and the ministers of the everlasting gospel, of every name, and of every nation. Clothe thy ministering servants with salvation; and let thy saints shout aloud for joy. May our country prosper in all her lawful interests, both domestic and foreign. Bless the chief magistrate of our nation, and all that are in authority: may they rule in thy fear, and be guided by thy counsel; and may the people lead quiet and peaceable lives in all godliness and honesty.

We especially invoke thy blessing, O Lord, to attend this day all the instructions imparted in Sabbath-schools and Bible classes. We pray that thou wilt be graciously pleased to grant the influences of the Holy Spirit, that that instruction may be impressed deeply on the heart and may produce abundant fruit in the life. Give grace, Almighty God, to those who are teachers in those schools; that they may be deeply impressed with their responsibility; that they may be themselves thy children; and that they may engage in their work with an earnest desire to benefit those entrusted to their charge. May their minds be enlightened, that they may understand thy holy word. May they see clearly the great plan of redeeming mercy. May they be enabled to present thy truth simply, clearly, with affection, and with prayer. May the sacred Spirit—the Comforter—be given them, to guide them into all truth. And do thou be pleased to bless all children in those schools. Preside over them and give to them thy Holy Spirit. Grant them tender, teachable minds. May their hearts be given to the Savior in their early years. May they come to him, who, when on earth, said, Suffer little children and forbid them not to come unto me, for of such is the kingdom of heaven. Take, O blessed Savior, those lambs of the flock into thine arms. Defend them from the perils and temptations of life, and conduct thou them to the joys of thine everlasting kingdom. [May our own children be trained up in the knowledge of thy name; and whatever instruction in accordance with thy word may be imparted to them in the family, the Sunday-school, or the sanctuary, we pray that it may be attended with thy blessing, and be the means of fitting them for the duties of this life, and for the joys of thine eternal kingdom.]

These mercies, and all we need, we humbly ask in the name of thy Son, Jesus Christ, our most gracious Lord and Redeemer. *Amen.*

LORDSDAY EVENING

Scripture Lesson
(LUKE 13:1–17)

Prayer

ALMIGHTY and everlasting God, we bless thee for our creation, preservation, and all the blessings of this life; but, above all, for thine unspeakable love in the redemption of the world by our Lord Jesus Christ; for the means of grace which thou hast bestowed upon us, and for the hope of glory which thou hast set before us. Heavenly Father, make us duly sensible of thy unspeakable gift, whereby we obtain the pardon of our sins and all things necessary for our eternal salvation. We adore thee for the coming of thy blessed Son in the flesh to dwell among us; for the perfect example set before us in his holy life; for his painful atonement for the sins of the world; and for his glorious resurrection from the grave, whereby he hath given us assurance that he is able also to raise our bodies from the dust, and to exalt us to his own right hand in the kingdom of heaven.

We pray thee, O Lord, to impress deeply on our minds the great and solemn truths revealed in thy word; that amidst the cares and occupations of the world, we may neither forget our Christian privileges, nor neglect the duties to which we are called. Convince us of the vanity of the world, of the shortness of life, and of the unspeakable importance of preparing for eternity. Save us from the sins of indifference, carelessness, and levity, as well as from bold and presumptuous transgressions. Purify our hearts by thy Holy Spirit, that we may be cleansed from every secret fault and every unholy passion. And pardon, O Lord, the multitude of our past iniquities. Thou hast nourished and brought us up as thy children, and we have rebelled against thee. Thou hast borne with our infirmities, and withheld thy chastening hand when we deserved nothing but punishment. Thou hast laid us under peculiar obligations to love and serve thee, and to praise and magnify thy holy name. But how little have we honored thee! How little have we done to glorify thee! O

Lord, forgive our ingratitude to thee. Enable us to look up to Jesus, the great Mediator of the new covenant, for the remission of our sins, and for all the benefits of his glorious redemption.

(Occasional Prayers.)

We intercede with thee, gracious God, for all our relatives, friends, and brethren; and especially for those who are in sorrow, sickness, or any kind of trouble. Give them the consolations which thou alone canst bestow. Put into their hearts a holy trust in thee, and a sure hope in thy promises. And may those who are compassed with infirmities, and who feel that their outward man is perishing, be strengthened with might by thy Spirit in the inner man; that so their light affliction, which is but for a moment, may work out for them a far more exceeding and eternal weight of glory.

Take us now, O God, under thy gracious care and protection this night. Let thy blessing attend us, and thy good Spirit rest upon us, through Jesus Christ our Lord. *Amen.*

MONDAY MORNING

Scripture Lesson
(LUKE 9:1–27)

Prayer

O THOU God of the morning, as well as of the evening! help us to worship and bow down, to kneel before the Lord our Maker, and to offer unto thee a sacrifice of praise and prayer. We rejoice that thou hast proclaimed thyself the Lord God, merciful and gracious, long-suffering and abundant in goodness and truth, keeping mercy for thousands, forgiving iniquity and transgression and sin, and that will by no means clear the guilty. O Lord! what is man, that thou art mindful of him? and the son of man, that thou visitest him? We confess we are but sinful dust and ashes. If thou shouldst mark iniquities, who shall stand? But there is forgiveness with thee, that thou mayest be feared. Forgive all our sins, and be at peace with us in the blood of Christ. Work in us both to will and to do of thy good pleasure, that we may work out our salvation with fear and trembling. Ever may it be as our meat and drink to do the will of our Father in heaven; and ever may we resemble those blessed spirits above, whose love is most ardent and whose obedience is perfect. In all that we do, may we aim to promote the glory of God, and to diffuse happiness around us. And may our path be as the shining light, which shineth more and more unto the perfect day. O Lord! as thou hast directed us, so we would make intercession for all men. Cause thy churches to revive and shoot forth as the branches of Lebanon, and kings to become nursing fathers, and queens nursing mothers to the whole Israel of God. Roll on the golden age of light and love, when the holy and happy kingdom of Christ shall embrace the great family of man. Bless the ministers of religion. Give them the heart of the pious, the tongue of the learned, and the zeal of the faithful, and let their labors not be in vain in the Lord. O thou sovereign Ruler! we pray thee to bless all nations, especially the land in which we live. Endue the President of the United States with patriotic principles. Ever may he know what the American Israel ought to do, and have a prevailing desire to promote the highest prosperity of this great nation. Incline all our officers to peace, and our executors of law to righteousness. May our judges honor justice in our courts of judgment.

(Occasional Prayers.)

Accept, O Lord, our acknowledgments for all favors bestowed upon us. We thank thee for the capacities, intellectual and moral, with which thou hast endued us. We rejoice in the overtures of mercy in the gospel, and in the weighty motives to persuade men to embrace the Savior, and live. We bless thee for the guardian care thou didst exercise over us the last night. O thou Shepherd of Israel! praised be thy name, that we were preserved while others slept the sleep of death, that no distressing accident befell us, and that thou hast opened upon us the eyelids of the morning in circumstances so favorable. We commit ourselves into thy hands for keeping this day, as unto a faithful Creator. To thee belong the issues of life and death. Give us grace to do all the work of the day in its day. May we persevere in well doing unto the end of life, and receive a crown of glory that fadeth not away. All which we ask in the name of our ascended and glorified Mediator. Now unto the Three that bear record in heaven, the Father, the Word, and the Holy Ghost, be glory forever. *Amen.*

MONDAY EVENING

Scripture Lesson
(LUKE 12:1–21)

Prayer

O THOU infinitely glorious and merciful Lord God, thou art worthy to receive glory, honor, and power from all thy creatures, for thou hast created all things, and for thy pleasure they are and were created. We would close this day with the solemn acts of self-abasement and humiliation of soul which our great sinfulness requires.

O Lord, when we examine into our own hearts and lives, how ill do we appear to requite thy love! Alas! we are sinners both by nature and by practice. We have erred, and strayed from thy ways like lost sheep, and have preferred the vanities and follies of this world, to thy favor. Yea, even since the blessings of salvation, through our crucified Redeemer, have been set before us, how often have we made light of them, and given way to an evil heart of unbelief!—how often have we abused the mercy which we still implore, and forsaken the fountain of living waters, in order to seek happiness from the broken cisterns of earthly enjoyments and possessions!

Surely it is of thy mercies that we are not consumed. Thou art still the same yesterday, to-day, and forever. Thou hast set no bounds to thy mercy, but dost magnify the freeness and fullness of thy grace, by never rejecting the contrite sighs, or denying the humble requests of those who call upon thee through the merits of thy dear Son. O Lord, for his sake, we again implore thy pardoning grace. Thou knowest our iniquities; remember them not against us, but according to thy mercy in Christ Jesus, remember thou us, O Lord. Wash away our guilt in the fountain that is opened in his precious blood. Cover us with the robe of his justifying righteousness, and sanctify us by the purifying influences of his HOLY SPIRIT. SO that being *washed*, and *justified*, and *sanctified* in the name of the LORD JESUS, and by the SPIRIT of our GOD, we may have comfortable evidence that thou hast adopted us into thy family, and bestowed upon us the glorious privileges of thy children.

Gracious God! we need thy constant support and guidance. Leave us not to our own deceitful hearts. Quicken our souls which cleave to the dust. Renew them after thine own image. And may thy glory be the great object and aim of our souls. May each day be marked by a steadier faith in a Redeemer, by increasing watchfulness against temptation, by unwearied diligence in the duty which thou requirest, by more ardent zeal for thy glory, and by a more affectionate concern for the welfare of our brethren. Oh that we may be kept in holy communion and fellowship with thee, and have some foretaste of that blessedness which is to be enjoyed hereafter around the throne of the Lamb.

(Occasional Prayers.)

Into thy hands we now commend ourselves, and all our personal and relative interests this night. Thou art the keeper of Israel, who neither slumberest nor sleepest. May we lay ourselves down in peace and take our rest, remembering that it is thou alone that makest us to dwell in safety. And should we be in mercy permitted to see another day, may we grow in the grace and in the knowledge of our Lord and Savior JESUS CHRIST. Every mercy we ask for his sake, who, in compassion to our infirmities, hath taught us thus to pray:

Our Father who, &c. *Amen.*

TUESDAY MORNING

Scripture Lesson
(HEBREWS 1)

Prayer

BEHOLD us, O good and gracious God, at the footstool of thy throne this morning. We come to present our humble and sincere adorations to the Author of our life and lengthener out of our days: for it is to thee that we are indebted for our preservation during the past night; and thou alone hast caused us to see the beginning of this day. Let thy gracious presence be with us during the course of it, and all the succeeding days and nights of our earthly pilgrimage. And to the end that thou mayest hear us, notwithstanding our unworthiness and sinfulness, look upon us, O God, in the face of thine Anointed; and cause us to be partakers of all the blessed fruits of his death and resurrection. We look to the unsearchable riches of Christ, that we may see what is the fellowship of the mystery which from the beginning of the world hath been hid in God; who not only created all things by Christ, but was in him reconciling the world unto himself; and hath now exalted him to be a Prince and a Savior, to give repentance unto his people, as well as the remission of all their sins. Oh that our bodies may henceforth be the temples of God, through the Holy Spirit dwelling in us, and uniting us to Jesus Christ by a true and living faith. We would count all things but loss that we may win Christ, and be found in him, not having our own righteousness, but the righteousness which is of God by faith: we would know him and the power of his resurrection, and the fellowship of his sufferings, and be made conformable unto his death. "Forgetting those things which are behind, and reaching forth unto those things which are before, may we press towards the mark for the prize of the high calling of God, in Christ Jesus our Lord." Thou knowest, O God, and we would at the same time acknowledge and confess, the weakness and corruption of our nature, and to how many dangers and temptations we are continually exposed. Lord, give us thy strength and thy grace to preserve and keep us at all times. Let neither the world nor the flesh this day seduce us from the path of duty: but, ever thinking and acting as under God's more immediate inspection, may we keep in the love and fear of all God's holy commandments. Teach us in every circumstance to know thy will, and give us inclination and ability to do it. Continue of thy bounty to provide for all our necessities; and support and comfort us under every disappointment and trial which thou mayest see proper to bring upon us.

May we live in thy fear, that we may die in thy favor, and so be made both happy and glorious through eternity.

(Occasional Prayers.)

For thy unmerited mercy towards us, and all who are near and dear to us, we offer up our united thanksgivings; let every creature that is in heaven, and on the earth, give glory to God forever and ever. Have mercy upon us, O God, according to thy loving-kindness; and for the sake of thy Son, and our Savior, be pleased, we humbly beseech thee, to blot out all our sins, to love us freely, and receive us graciously. And now, Lord, what wait we for? our hope is in thee. Let the words of our mouths and the meditations of our hearts be acceptable in thy sight, O Lord, our Strength and our Redeemer. *Amen.*

TUESDAY EVENING

Scripture Lesson
(HEBREWS 2)

Prayer

ETERNAL and unchangeable God! we adore thee as the supreme Majesty of heaven and earth. All nations before thee are as nothing; and they are counted to thee less than nothing and vanity. Hearken unto the voice of our cry, our King and our God! for unto thee we will pray. Our sins have risen, as mountains, to separate between thee and us. We are polluted from the crown of the head to the sole of the foot; there is no soundness in us. Whither, O Lord, shall we go for cleansing? Wash us from sin and uncleanness in that fountain opened to the house of David and to the inhabitants of Jerusalem. Though our sins be as scarlet, may they be white as snow; though they be red like crimson, may they be as wool. May we abhor that which is evil, and cleave to that which is good. May we be fervent in spirit, serving the Lord, rejoicing in hope, patient in tribulation, continuing instant in prayer. Root out from our hearts all pride, and clothe us with humility, and make us partakers of the inheritance of the saints in light. We thank thee for thy written word, and that the law of the Lord is perfect, converting the soul; that the testimony of the Lord is sure, making wise the simple; more to be desired than gold, yea, than much fine gold; sweeter than honey and the honeycomb. We bless thee for the preached gospel, and that it is the wisdom of God and the power of God unto salvation to everyone that believeth. May grace be with all them that love our Lord Jesus Christ in sincerity and truth. May thy professing people be much in prayer, that they may obtain a blessing for themselves and a sinful, deluded world. Bless the ministers of religion. Make them burning and shining lights in thy golden candlesticks. Endue them with wisdom, prudence, and holy zeal. Bless the great council of our nation. Rule in the hearts of our rulers. May all who take part in civil affairs be just, ruling in thy fear. Mercifully regard all the interests of our country, domestic and foreign. Exercise compassion towards all people that dwell upon the face of the earth. Oh! let the wickedness of the wicked come to an end; but establish the just. Comfort all that are in trouble and affliction. Relieve the wants of the poor and needy, sustain those who are languishing on beds of sickness and sorrow, convert the unconverted, save the perishing, and fill the earth with thy glory.

(Occasional Prayers.)

May we be in thy fear all the day long, serve thee with pure affection, and enjoy the good things of life in innocence and with grateful hearts. In our domestic relations, may we be all of one mind, love as brethren, and live in peace; that thou, the God of peace and love, mayest be with us.

Bless our family with all needed temporal and spiritual favors. Let our lives, health, and happiness be precious in thy sight. May the return of night remind us of the night of death, and that soon we must close our eyes upon all things here below. We praise thee for the protection, the supplies, and comforts of another day. To thy merciful care we commend ourselves this night. Defend our persons, dwelling, and possessions. May we awake in the morning, and be still with God. Be pleased, O Lord! to accept this our evening service in the name of the blessed Jesus. *Amen.*

WEDNESDAY MORNING

Scripture Lesson
(HEBREWS 3)

Prayer

ALMIGHTY and everlasting God, in whom we live and move and have our being; we, thy needy creatures, render thee our humble praises, for thy preservation of us from the beginning of our lives to this day, and especially for having delivered us from the dangers of the past night. To thy watchful providence we owe it, that no disturbance hath come nigh us or our dwelling; but that we are brought in safety to the beginning of this day. For these thy mercies, we bless and magnify thy glorious name, humbly beseeching thee to accept this our morning sacrifice of praise and thanksgiving.

And since it is of thy mercy, O gracious Father, that another day is added to our lives, we here dedicate both our souls and our bodies to thee and thy service, in a sober, righteous, and godly life; in which resolution do thou, O merciful God, confirm and strengthen us; that, as we grow in age, we may grow in grace and in the knowledge of our Lord and Savior, Jesus Christ.

But O God, who knowest the weakness and corruption of our nature, and the manifold temptations which we daily meet with; we humbly beseech thee to have compassion on our infirmities, and to give us the constant assistance of thy Holy Spirit; that we may be effectually restrained from sin, and excited to our duty. Imprint upon our hearts such a dread of thy judgments, and such a grateful sense of thy goodness to us, as may make us both afraid and ashamed to offend thee. And above all, keep in our minds a lively remembrance of that great day in which we must give a strict account of our thoughts, words, and actions; and according to the works done in the body, be eternally rewarded or punished, by him whom thou hast appointed the judge of quick and dead, thy Son, Jesus Christ, our Lord.

(Occasional Prayers.)

In particular, we implore thy grace and protection for this day. Defend us from all dangers and adversities; and be graciously pleased to take us, and all things belonging to us, under thy fatherly care and protection. These things, and whatever else thou shalt see necessary and convenient to us, we humbly beg through the merits and mediation of him who is God over all, blessed for evermore. *Amen.*

WEDNESDAY EVENING

Scripture Lesson
(HEBREWS 4)

Prayer

O THOU that hearest prayer—through him who is the great Intercessor, let our prayer come before thee as incense, and the lifting up of our hands as the evening sacrifice. We praise thee for the blessings of thy providence which encompass us on every side, and are continued to us notwithstanding our unworthiness. Thou hast not only given us life and favor, but thy mercy hath preserved our spirit, and secured our personal and relative comforts.

But above all we thank thee for thine unspeakable gift. Herein is love, not that we loved God, but that he loved us, and sent his Son to be the propitiation for our sins. Oh may our souls be united to this Savior by a divine faith. May we be his disciples, and learn of him; his soldiers, and war under his banner; his beneficiaries, and live upon his fullness. When we think of our transgressions of thy law, may we remember *him* who is the end of the law for righteousness. When we feel our sins, may we think of *him* whose blood cleanseth from all sin; and when viewing our trials and duties our weakness makes us despond, may we hear the voice that cries, *my* grace is sufficient for thee.

(Occasional Prayers.)

May we be followers of him who was meek and lowly in heart, who pleased not himself, who went about doing good, who said, my meat is to do the will of him that sent me, and to finish his work. Subdue in us the selfishness that is so common to our depraved hearts, and excite in us a disposition to seek after the welfare of others.

Yet may we especially do good unto them that are of the household of faith. May all who do the will of our heavenly Father be dear to our hearts. May we prefer Jerusalem above our chief joy. Let her become a praise in the whole earth. And from the rising of the sun to the going down of the same, may thy name be great among the Gentiles, and in every place may incense be offered unto thee, and a pure offering. The harvest is truly great, but the laborers are few; command their increase, and abundantly bless those who are already employed.

And may the sincerity of our prayers appear in our exertions and sacrifices. May we honor the Lord with our substance. In our respective stations, may we adorn the doctrine of God our Savior in all things. By every kind of consistent co-operation with our ministers, may we become helpers to the truth: and carrying the effects of the sermons we hear, and dispensing them among those who refuse to hear, win them without the word. May we never hide it in a napkin, because we have only one talent; but use what we have, that more may be given; and be concerned to obtain from the Judge of all the approving sentence pronounced on Mary, she hath done what she could. May we never despise the day of small things; never grow weary in well doing; but cherish with patience as well as with diligence every serious conviction, every pious tendency, every godly impression.

And let us not labor in vain nor spend our strength for naught. May we be the honored instruments of saving some souls from death; and of producing joy in the presence of the angels of God, over one sinner that repenteth.

Above all, render us successful among those who are more fully under our instruction, influence, and authority. May we rule well our own house; and have the pleasure to see all the members of the family fellow-citizens with the saints, and of the household of Christ. Of whom, and through whom, and to whom are all things. To whom be glory for ever and ever. *Amen.*

THURSDAY MORNING

Scripture Lesson
(HEBREWS 5)

Prayer

O GOD, our heavenly Father, we bless thee for the return of this morning light. We bless thee for thy guardianship and care during the hours of darkness. Enable us, we beseech thee, to devote the first fruits of the day to thee. Accept our humble thanks for all thy mercies, and especially for the gift of thine incarnate Son. Blessed be the Lord God of Israel, that he hath redeemed us, and raised up a mighty salvation for us; that the day-spring from on high hath visited us, to give light to them that sit in darkness and in the shadow of death, and to guide our feet into the way of peace. We thank thee for that revelation, by which the power and coming of our Lord Jesus Christ are made known to us. We thank thee for the gracious offers of salvation, through his name and mediation; and for that atoning sacrifice through which our sins, though they be as scarlet, shall be as white as snow, and though they be red like crimson, shall be as wool. We thank thee especially for the sure word of prophecy, whereunto we are admonished to take heed, as unto a light that shineth in a dark place, until the day dawn, and the day-star arise in our hearts. And we beseech thee, O God, to grant us grace, that we may not receive this revelation in vain; that we may not be of the number of those who choose darkness rather than light, because their deeds are evil:—but enable us to walk as becometh the children of light.

Guide and direct us, heavenly Father, in the duties of this day. May a sense of thy continual presence abide with us, to restrain every evil passion and to support and encourage us in the discharge of our respective duties. Let thy fatherly hand be ever over us. Let thy Holy Spirit be ever with us; and so lead us in the knowledge and obedience of thy word, that in the end we may obtain everlasting life, through Jesus Christ our Lord.

(Occasional Prayers.)

We commend to thy fatherly care and protection all our friends and relatives. Give them grace as they may severally stand in need; and order all things for their present and eternal good. Show the light of thy countenance to those who are weary and heavy-laden with the burden of their sins; and comfort and sustain those who are suffering under any temporal calamity. May they receive thy chastisements as the loving correction of a kind and beneficent parent, who dost chasten them for their profit, and correct them that they may live.

And in the days of their prosperity give them a grateful sense of all thy mercies; and teach them as dutiful children, and the humble partakers of thy bounty, to ascribe all honor and glory to thee, their gracious benefactor, through Jesus Christ our Lord. *Amen.*

THURSDAY EVENING

Scripture Lesson
(HEBREWS 6)

Prayer

O THOU King of glory, we desire to approach thy divine Majesty with reverence and godly fear, and to worship thee in the beauty of holiness. The heavens are thine; the earth also is thine; the world is thine, and the fullness thereof. Thy wisdom has managed all its multiplied concerns, presiding over nations, families, and individuals, and numbering the very hairs of our head. Thy goodness is boundless; the eyes of all wait upon thee, and thou givest them their meat in due season. Thou openest thy hand, and satisfiest the desire of every living thing. Thy loving kindness is great, and the children of men put their trust under the shadow of thy wing.

Oh, teach us to place our happiness in thyself. May we never seek the living among the dead, nor ask, with the deluded many, who will show us any good? But may we prize the light of thy countenance; implore the joy of thy salvation; and passing by the attractions of creatures, be able to say, whom have I in heaven but thee, and there is none upon earth that I desire beside thee.

Thou madest man upright, and when, by voluntary transgression, we fell away from thee, thou didst not treat us with the severity we deserved. In thy love and pity thou wast pleased to provide for us a Savior, who bore our griefs and carried our sorrows, and put away sin by the sacrifice of himself.

Apply this redemption to our hearts, by the justification of our persons and the sanctification of our natures. We confess our transgressions—have mercy upon us. We are heavy laden—give us rest. We are ignorant—make us wise unto salvation. We are helpless—let thy strength be made perfect in our weakness. We are poor and needy—bless us with all the unsearchable riches of Christ.

Thus far, blessed be thy name, thou hast led us on, and we have found thee faithful to thy promises. We have had our sorrows; but thou hast been a very present help in every time of trouble. We have had our fears; but thou hast not suffered the enemy to triumph over us. Hitherto hath the Lord helped us. Thy vows are upon us, O God: we will render praises unto thee, for thou hast delivered our souls from death: wilt not thou deliver our feet from falling, that we may walk before God in the light of the living?

(Occasional Prayers.)

We would feel the connections which unite us to others, and by sympathy, and prayer, and praise, make their miseries and mercies our own. Provide support and employment for the poor. Make the widow's heart to sing for joy; and in thee may the fatherless find mercy. Visit those who are on beds of sickness, and prepare them for thy pleasure; that if they live, it may be to serve thee. Bless our nation. May every department of the nation be under the control of infinite wisdom and goodness; and let righteousness and peace be the stability of our times. Do good, in thy good pleasure, unto Zion; build thou the walls of Jerusalem: and may all our churches' like the original disciples, continue steadfastly in the apostles, doctrine, and in fellowship, and in breaking of bread, and in prayers.

Protect and refresh us through the night season, and then cause us to hear thy loving-kindness in the morning: for in thee do we trust; cause us to know the way wherein we should go, for we lift up our souls unto thee. We implore it through the intercession of thy dear Son, our Savior. *Amen.*

FRIDAY MORNING

Scripture Lesson
(ROMANS 14)

Prayer

O THOU who hearest prayer, and unto whom all flesh should come! graciously assist us to call upon thy great and holy name this morning. The Lord is good to all, and his tender mercies are over all his works. We acknowledge the grace and glory of thy gospel, and the freeness and richness of thy salvation. Oh that all would praise the Lord for his goodness, and for his wonderful works to the children of men. But, alas! we have forsaken the God who made us, and lightly esteemed the Rock of our salvation. We have been wise to do evil, but to do good we have had no knowledge. O Lord! righteousness belongeth unto thee, but unto us confusion of face. We humbly pray thee, lay not judgment to the line, nor righteousness to the plummet: for in thy sight shall no man living be justified. Forgive us, we beseech thee. Impress thine image upon us, and make us the monuments of thy mercy and the trophies of thy victorious grace.

Enkindle within us a flame of divine love, that shall never be extinguished. Oh for more love, faith, and hope!

(Occasional Prayers.)

Extend thy compassion to all men. Enlighten the Gentile world with a knowledge of the truth. May the Sun of righteousness arise upon them with healing in his wings. Let the wilderness and the solitary place be glad for them, and the desert rejoice and blossom as the rose. Let Zion share in the blessings of her Lord and Savior. We rejoice that the church lies near thy heart, and that her name is engraven on the palms of thy hands. Give unto all destitute flocks pastors after thine own heart—men of understanding and piety. May the ministers of the gospel cry aloud and spare not, lift up their voice like a trumpet, and show thy people their transgressions, and the house of Jacob their sins, and thus clear their own skirts from the blood of souls. O thou great Fountain of love! compassionate all those who are persecuted, enslaved, or in prison. Pity the sick and the afflicted, the poor and the needy, the tempted and the disconsolate, the widow and the fatherless. May thy blessings, O Lord, rest upon our family, and may all who appertain to it belong to the household of faith, and be numbered with thy jewels when thou shalt make them up. We thank thee for all thy mercies. Thou hast soothed our sorrows, healed our diseases, and richly supplied our wants. Praised be thy name for the blessings of the night, and that our repose was quiet and undisturbed. This day grant us thy presence, shield us from all dangers, and administer to our temporal and spiritual necessities. Be with us and bless us all the days we are permitted to live upon the earth: and when we drop this veil of flesh, may our souls rise to regions of eternal blessedness and glory. This our morning sacrifice we offer in the name of thy beloved Son, our great High Priest above, to whom be rendered unceasing praises. *Amen.*

FRIDAY EVENING

Scripture Lesson
(JOHN 5:1–30)

Prayer

OUR Father, who art in heaven, we desire to acknowledge thy being and agency; to adore thy perfections, and to admire the works of thy hands. Thou hast appointed the moon for seasons, and the sun knoweth his going down. The day is thine; the night also is thine: and thou makest the outgoings of the morning and the evening to rejoice. To that throne, from which none were ever sent empty away, we again approach for mercy and grace to help in time of need. Let our prayer come before thee as incense, and the lifting up of our hands as the evening sacrifice. Preserve us from formality in these exercises in which we daily engage, lest we should provoke thee to say, in vain do they worship me.

For this purpose, enable us to remember with *whom* we have to do; may we deeply feel the guilt of the sins we confess, and hunger and thirst after the blessings we implore. And while we review the numberless blessings we have received from thy hands, may we be more than ever sensible of our unworthiness, that our hearts may be unfeignedly thankful, and that we may be disposed to show forth thy praise, not only with our lips, but in our lives, by giving up ourselves to thy service, and walking before thee in holiness and righteousness all our days.

Another day has been added, by thy good providence, to the season of thy long-suffering, and the time of our preparation for eternity. We lament that in so many things we have offended, and in all come short of the glory of God. We cannot answer thee for one of a thousand of our transgressions: our only relief is, that there is forgiveness with thee; and that with thee there is plenteous redemption.

But while we hope in thy mercy, we would not abuse it. We would not sin that grace may abound; or be evil, because thou art good. But since thou art ready to forgive, we would the more sincerely grieve that ever we have offended a Being so worthy of our devotedness, and be the more concerned in future to walk so as to please thee.

Create in us a clean heart, and renew a right spirit within us. Set a watch, O God, upon our mouth; keep the door of our lips. And in simplicity and godly sincerity, not with fleshly wisdom, but by thy grace, may we have our conversation in the world, and in the church, and in the family.

(Occasional Prayers.)

We again commend ourselves to thy care. As thou hast been through the day our sun and our shield, be thou through the night our shade and our defense. Undisturbed by anxieties, unalarmed by fears, undistressed by pain or indisposition, may we retire and enjoy repose. Prepare us for the night of death, the morning of the resurrection, and the day of judgment.

And all we implore is through the mediation of Him who bore the sins of many, and made intercession for the transgressors, to whom, with the Father and the Holy Spirit, be endless prayers. *Amen.*

SATURDAY MORNING

Scripture Lesson
(JOHN 14)

Prayer

OUR voice shalt thou hear in the morning, O Lord; in the morning will we direct our prayers unto thee, and will look up. Lord! teach us to pray in faith, for he that cometh to God must believe that he is, and that he is a rewarder of them who diligently seek him. O thou eternal Father! we have sinned against heaven and before thee, and are no more worthy to be called thy children. We have gone far from our heavenly Father's house, and rioted in the vanities and follies of the world. We would repent and return; oh! have compassion upon us. Hide thy face from our sins, and blot out all our iniquities. Enable us to lay aside every weight, and the sin which doth so easily beset us, and to run with patience the race that is set before us, looking unto Jesus, the Author and Finisher of our faith. Fulfil in us all the pleasure of thy goodness, and the work of faith with power. Help us to set our affections on things above, and to withdraw them from things below, and to lay up for ourselves treasures in heaven, where neither moth nor rust doth corrupt, and where thieves do not break through nor steal. Ever may we live mindful of the day of judgment, when the Lord Jesus shall be revealed from heaven with his mighty angels in flaming fire, taking vengeance on them that know not God and obey not the gospel of our Lord Jesus Christ, and when he shall come to be glorified in his saints, and to be admired in all them that believe in that day. Bless all our dear absent friends and relatives with the same favors we ask for ourselves. Forgive our enemies, and reward our benefactors.

(Occasional Prayers.)

Do good in thy good pleasure unto Zion; build thou the walls of Jerusalem. Rectify everything which is amiss in the Christian church, in doctrine, practice, and discipline. Give unto them who mourn in Zion beauty for ashes, the oil of joy for mourning, and the garment of praise for the spirit of heaviness. Have compassion, O God! upon impenitent sinners. Show them that they stand on slippery places, and turn their feet unto thy testimonies before they are beyond the reach of mercy, where no place for repentance can be found though they seek it carefully with tears. Oh! pluck them, we beseech thee, as brands out of the burning, and save them from everlasting destruction. Bless our highly-favored country. May it ever be the residence of freedom, peace, and happiness, and a safe retreat for the persecuted and oppressed. Make all who are in places of public trust faithful to the public interest. Bless, we pray thee, the whole family of man with knowledge, righteousness, and salvation. O thou God of mercies! we thank thee for the blessings we have enjoyed. We have been fed and clothed and sustained by thee, and are under ten thousand obligations of gratitude to the Father of mercies. We praise thee that thou didst keep us during the silent watches of the night, and hast lifted upon us the light of this new day in circumstances of comfort. Be with us during this day, and all the days and nights of our earthly existence. Guide us in the path of duty and salvation, and save us eternally, through Jesus Christ our Lord. *Amen.*

SATURDAY EVENING

Scripture Lesson
(1 CORINTHIANS 1)

Prayer

O GOD, thou art the God of all the families of the earth; for they are formed by thy will, and supported by thy providence. But thou art, in a peculiar manner, the God of those families in which thy name is known and honored. Thou blessest the habitation of the just. Whatever be the disposition of others, we desire to say, as for us and our house, we will serve the Lord. Thy yoke is easy, thy burden is light; thy work is honorable and glorious; and in keeping thy commandments there is great reward.

Already thou hast laid us under infinite obligations, as the God of providence and of grace. Bless the Lord, O our souls, and all that is within us, bless his holy name! Bless the Lord, O our souls, and forget not all his benefits!

By thy good hand upon us we have been conducted through the perils, not only of another day, but another week: a period during which many have been carried down to their graves, and we have been brought so much nearer to our own. Impress us with the lapse of time, and so teach us to number our days, that we may apply our hearts unto wisdom. Many have been involved in perplexities and exposed to want; many have been confined to the house of mourning, or the bed of sickness; but we have been favored with liberty, and ease, and health, and strength; we have seen thy loving-kindness every morning, and thy faithfulness every night; and have had all things richly to enjoy.

But, O how little have we been affected by these instances of thy undeserved goodness! how imperfectly have we improved our religious privileges! how negligent have we been in seizing opportunities of doing good to the bodies and souls of our fellow-creatures—and how well does it become each of us to exclaim: behold, I am vile; what shall I answer thee? wherefore I abhor myself, repenting in dust and ashes.

Enter not into judgment with thy servants, O Lord. Our only hope is, that to the Lord our God belong mercy and forgiveness, though we have rebelled against him. Have mercy upon us, O God, according to thy loving-kindness; according to the multitude of thy tender mercies blot out our transgressions.

And may a confidence in thy goodness, instead of encouraging us to sin, that grace may abound, inspire us with that godly sorrow which worketh repentance unto life. May we be attentive to our condition, and study our character; may we bridle our tongue, and keep our heart with all diligence.

May we watch and pray in future, lest we enter into temptation. And do thou keep us by thy power; uphold us by thy free Spirit; and not only restrain us from sin, but mortify us to it.

(Occasional Prayers.)

May sleep refresh our bodies, and fit them for thy service on the ensuing day; and may thy grace prepare our minds. May we call the Sabbath a delight, and be glad when they say to us: let us go into the house of the Lord.

And, O thou God of all grace, do as thou hast said; fulfill thy word unto thy servants, upon which thou hast caused them to hope. Bless abundantly the provisions of thy house, and satisfy thy poor with bread. Clothe thy ministers with salvation, and let thy saints shout aloud for joy.

And to the God of all grace, the Father, the Word, and the Holy Ghost, be all honor and glory, both now and forever. *Amen.*

FIFTH WEEK

LORDSDAY MORNING

Scripture Lesson
(PSALM 84)

Prayer

O THOU Lord of the Sabbath, who hast set apart this day for thyself, and hast commanded us to keep it holy, look down upon a family of sinful creatures who are assembled together to acknowledge thy goodness in bringing us to see it.

We adore thee for thy forbearance in not dealing with us according to our deserts, nor rewarding us according to our iniquities. And we beseech thee to pour down upon us the abundance of thy grace, that we may rest this day according to thy commandment. So frame our minds that thy Sabbath may not be a weariness, but a delight to us. Let us honor thee by not doing our ways, nor finding our own pleasure, nor speaking our own words.

Bless us, O Lord, with all spiritual blessings in Christ Jesus. Wash us in the fountain of that blood which cleanseth from all sin. Clothe us with the robe of that righteousness which is by faith of Jesus Christ unto all and upon all them that believe. Prepare us for the various duties which are now before us.

Sanctify unto us thy appointed means of grace. Send out thy light and thy truth; let them lead us; let them bring us to thy holy hill and to thy tabernacle. May we go to thy house of prayer with the voice of joy and praise, with the multitude that keep holy-day. There may we give thee the glory which is due unto thy name, and worship thee in the beauty of holiness. May we see thy power and thy glory as thy servants see them in the sanctuary, and be satisfied with the goodness of thy house.

Grant, O Lord, that the Scriptures, which thou hast caused to be written for our learning, may be applied to our hearts in the power and demonstration of the Spirit. May we so hear them, read, mark, learn, and inwardly digest them, that we may embrace and ever hold fast the blessed hope of everlasting life, through a crucified Redeemer.

(Occasional Prayers.)

Hear our prayers, O God, for all Christian ministers, [especially for *him* whom thou hast appointed over us,] and endue them with the grace of thy Holy Spirit. Give unto them the spirit of love, and of power, and of a sound mind. Make them able ministers of the New Testament, faithful stewards of thy mysteries. Help them to take heed to themselves and to the doctrine, that, according to thy promise, they may both save themselves and those who hear them.

We beseech thee to inspire continually the universal Church with the spirit of truth, unity, and concord; and grant that all they who confess thy name may agree in the truth of thy holy word, and live in harmony and godly love. May numbers be added to it, every Lords Day, of such as shall be saved.

Look in mercy upon such as have hitherto neglected thy Sabbaths. Teach them to improve those that remain; and so to redeem the time which they have lost, that they may be numbered among thy true people.

Remember for good as many as, through sickness or any other impediment, may be prevented from attending the ordinances of thy house. Let thy presence be with them in their private meditations, even as with those who shall assemble together in the place where thy honor dwelleth. Pity and protect the widow and orphan; hear the cries of the persecuted and distressed; and be nigh unto and comfort all who are in circumstances of peril, and call upon thee for help.

We pray thee, also, to have compassion upon those who as yet belong not to thy visible church. Shine upon the nations which are sitting in darkness and in the shadow of death.

Greatly increase the number of those who shall go forth into all the world to preach the gospel to every creature. Let nation after nation be converted to the Christian faith, till the kingdoms of this world become the kingdoms of our Lord and of his Christ, and the earth be filled with the knowledge of thy glory, as the waters cover the sea.

Hear, we beseech thee, O heavenly Father, these our imperfect petitions; and answer them in the multitude of thy tender mercies, for the sake of Jesus Christ, our only Lord and Savior; to whom, with thee and the Holy Ghost, be all honor and glory, world without end. *Amen.*

LORDSDAY EVENING

Scripture Lesson
(MATTHEW 22:1–22)

Prayer

HOLY, holy, holy Lord God Almighty, who humblest thyself to listen to the adorations of the heavenly hosts above; how great is thy condescension in regarding the feeble thanksgivings and supplications of sinful mortals! But thy ways are not as our ways, neither are thy thoughts as our thoughts. Thou hast revealed thyself as delighting in mercy, and being glorified in the salvation of sinners through Jesus Christ our Lord. Enable us to take shelter in this thine appointed refuge; and finding pardon and acceptance with thee, may our evening sacrifice of prayer and praise ascend up before thee, perfumed with the incense of his merits, and be heard and answered by thee.

We bless thy name for the many seasons and means of grace which thou hast afforded us,—and especially for the opportunities we have enjoyed this day of waiting upon thee in the ordinances of thine own appointment. But alas! O Lord, the review of even this day fills us with shame and confusion of face; for what coldness of affection, what wandering of thought, what want of reverence, of love and of gratitude, have we betrayed in all our religious services! Surely, we are altogether unprofitable servants.

But we desire now to cast ourselves at thy footstool, beseeching thee, O Lord, for Christ's sake, to pardon all our iniquity, yea, the iniquity of our holy things. Wash us in the fountain of his atoning blood,—clothe us with the robe of his justifying righteousness,—and sanctify our hearts by the purifying grace of his Spirit. Oh shine upon us, and give us clearer views of the truth as it is in Jesus.

Gracious God, let not the word of thy truth which we have heard this day with our outward ears, return unto thee void. Enlighten our understandings, and open our hearts to receive it in love and in power. Grant that we may not only "read and mark," but also "learn and inwardly digest" those Holy Scriptures which are able to make us wise unto salvation, through faith which is in Christ Jesus.

(Occasional Prayers.)

Blessed Lord, hear the prayers which have been offered up this day for all sorts and conditions of men. Strengthen the weak, comfort the afflicted, instruct the ignorant, take away the heart of stone, and cause the impenitent sinner to cry for mercy. Inspire continually thy universal Church with the spirit of truth, unity, and concord. Bless the labors of thy ministering servants. May the seed which they have sown bring forth fruit to the praise and glory of thy grace. And Oh let thy ways be known upon earth, thy saving health among all nations; let both Jews and Gentiles be gathered into the Redeemer's kingdom, and let everyone that nameth the name of Christ depart from all iniquity.

We now commit ourselves into thy care and fatherly protection. Watch over us during the dark and silent hours of the night, and refresh our wearied bodies with sleep; and if it be consistent with thy good pleasure, raise us up in health and safety to enjoy the light of another day. Water our souls with the dew of thy blessing, that we may grow in grace continually, and be enabled to hold the beginning of our confidence steadfast to the end, and when our end approaches may be fully prepared, through the merits of Jesus Christ, our Lord and Savior. *Amen.*

MONDAY MORNING

Scripture Lesson
(MARK 12:28–44)

Prayer

O GOD, thou art our God; early will we seek thee. Thou art good, and doest good to all; thy mercy is over all thy works.

Unworthy as we are to offer unto thee any sacrifice, thou hast appointed unto us a great High Priest, in whose name we come boldly to the throne of grace, that we may find mercy and grace to help in time of need.

Grant that the frequency and earnestness of our prayers may be proportioned to the greatness of our wants. Make us rejoice in every opportunity of worshiping thy divine Majesty, and preserve us from the sin of drawing near to thee with our lips while our hearts are far from thee.

(Occasional Prayers.)

We humbly thank thee, O Lord, that thou hast preserved us through the night, and hast renewed unto us thy goodness this morning. Take us again into thy guidance and protection during the day; and so govern us by thy grace, that we may neither think nor speak, nor do anything this day which may displease thee or wound our own souls. Assist us to be sincere and hearty in dedicating ourselves, our souls and bodies, to thy service. Preserve us from the power of evil; from the sin that doth so easily beset us; from the lusts of the flesh, and the vanities of a wicked world.

Send thy good Spirit to direct and guide us in the ways and works of godliness: purify our affections; enliven our devotion; teach us how to pray, and how to hear, and read, and profit by thy holy word. Make us Christians, not only in name, but also in heart and in hope. Teach us the value of our souls, and the salvation which has been wrought for them by Christ Jesus. May we never be ashamed of confessing him before men; but, amidst all discouragements and difficulties, give us boldness to show ourselves his true disciples.

Let our conversation be such as becometh his gospel; and whatsoever we do in word or in deed, let us do all in his name, giving thanks to God and the Father through him. And let the words of our mouths and the meditations of our hearts be acceptable in thy sight, O Lord, our strength and our Redeemer. *Amen.*

MONDAY EVENING

Scripture Lesson
(MATTHEW 18:1–20)

Prayer

BLESSED and glorious God! Thou art the King eternal, immortal, invisible, the only wise God, the Father of mercies, and God of all grace. Thou searchest the hearts and triest the reins of all men. Oh let thy Spirit help our infirmities, and teach us how to pray. Hearken unto the voice of our cry, our King and our God, for unto thee will we pray; our voice shalt thou hear in the morning, and in the evening will we direct our prayer unto thee. We are not worthy, O Lord, of the least of thy mercies, and yet how bountifully hast thou bestowed them upon us! Open thou our lips, and our mouths shall show forth thy praise.

Lord, we would lie in the dust and cry, unclean, unclean! we were shapen in iniquity, and in sin were we conceived. And, O God, how deeply aggravated are all our sins! they have been committed against light and conviction, against promises and vows, and against manifold experiences of thy grace and love. Lord, we would abhor ourselves and repent in dust and ashes.

And as our sins are many, so, O Lord, are our necessities; we come to thee for the supply of them all. Bless us, O our God, with the pardon of all our iniquities. Let our transgressions be forgiven, and our sins covered. We have no merit to plead, but we cast ourselves upon thy mercy and grace in the Redeemer; we plead his atoning blood, which was shed for the remission of sins; we have sinned, but Christ has died, the just for the unjust, that he might bring us to God. Oh justify us freely by thy grace, through the redemption that is in Christ. Look upon us in the face of thine Anointed, and accept us in the Beloved. Create clean hearts, and renew right spirits within us; help us to crucify the flesh with its affections and lusts, that the body of sin may be destroyed. Enlighten our minds, and grant us the spirit of wisdom and revelation in the knowledge of Christ. Subdue and renew our wills. Cast down all lofty imaginations, and bring every thought into subjection to the obedience of Christ. Help us to love our enemies, and if we have aught against any man, help us to forgive, as God, for Christ's sake, forgiveth us. Enable us to bless them that curse us, and pray for them that despitefully use us.

(Occasional Prayers.)

Help us all, O Lord, duly to consider our latter end, and diligently prepare for the same. Whatsoever our hands find to do, may we do it now, without delay, and with all our might; for there is no work, nor device, nor knowledge in the grave, whither we are all hastening. O Lord, regard in mercy our absent friends and relatives; pity and relieve the poor and distressed; comfort those who mourn; bless our land and all its rulers. Pour out thy Spirit upon all flesh, and hasten the coming of thy glorious kingdom. Accept our thanks for the mercies of this day. Take us under thy protection this night; sustain us in sleep, and raise us up in the morning, and when we awake may we be still with thee. All which we beg in the name, and through the mediation of Christ our Savior. *Amen.*

TUESDAY MORNING

Scripture Lesson
(MATTHEW 25:1–30)

Prayer

ALMIGHTY God, the Father of our Lord Jesus Christ, by whom the whole family in heaven and earth were made. Dispose our hearts, by the gracious influence of thy Holy Spirit, to worship thee through one Mediator, Jesus Christ our Lord.

Thou art God, and there is none beside thee. Thou art the Creator of heaven and earth, the Lord of glory, the Lord God, merciful and gracious, long-sufferings abundant in goodness and truth, keeping mercy for thousands, forgiving iniquity and transgressions and sins, and wilt by no means clear the guilty. We bow and worship at thy footstool; we acknowledge thee to be the Lord.

We are invited to come to thee—though we be guilty and sinful, we are freely offered pardon, peace, and salvation; and thou givest us a hope full of immortality in Christ Jesus our Savior.

What shall we render unto the Lord, for all his benefits? We desire now afresh to devote ourselves to thy service. We give up ourselves, our whole selves unto thee. God of peace, sanctify us wholly. God of our life, grant that our whole spirit, and soul, and body, may be preserved blameless unto the coming of our Lord Jesus Christ.

Grant unto every one of us a saving interest in the death of Christ, full and free forgiveness of all our sins, and grace and strength to go and sin no more. Lord, help us to love thee, teach us to serve thee. Give us thy strength that we may overcome our corrupt nature. Grant that this day we may have power from on high to resist every temptation, to confess Christ before men, to labor steadfastly with a single eye to thy glory, to live in the spirit of prayer, in faith, humility, self-denial, and love, and to walk before thee in that narrow way which leads to eternal life. Fill us with love to others. Teach us to do good to all men, and to seek according to our means to visit and relieve the fatherless and the widows in their affliction; and do thou keep us unspotted from the world.

We beseech thee, according to thine infinite mercy, give us grace to serve thee constantly and unfeignedly. Herein art thou glorified, that we bear much fruit. For thine own glory, grant us thy Spirit, that we may bring forth all the fruits of righteousness.

(Occasional Prayers.)

And hear us further in behalf of our relatives and friends, our neighborhood, our ministers, and all for whom we ought to pray. Help those that are weak. Comfort those that are cast down. Heal those that are sick. Believe those that are in distress. Be merciful unto thy church. Oh bless us, and cause thy face to shine upon us, that thy way may be known upon earth, thy saving health among all nations. Bring the Gentiles to Christ. Gather thy people Israel into thy fold. Give wisdom and power to every effort of Christian love for spreading thy gospel. Bless all societies for this end, and let those who support and conduct them have thy direction and guidance. Lord, grant that the power of the cross of Christ may at length fully triumph over all error and superstition, all idolatry and delusion and sin.

Gracious Lord, not for our worthiness, but for the. name's sake of Jesus Christ alone, hear these our prayers. *Amen.*

TUESDAY EVENING

Scripture Lesson
(MATTHEW 25:31–46)

Prayer

ALMIGHTY God, Father of mercies, and God of all comfort, according to thy gracious promise give us thy Holy Spirit to help our infirmities, and enable us, in the name and through the mediation of thy Son Jesus Christ, our Lord, to call upon thee.

Great is thy goodness to us sinners, in that we, who have grievously offended thee, have such a Mediator, whoever liveth to make intercession for us. Without a Savior we can have no hope; for we have sinned against thee, and done evil in thy sight day by day.

We confess and mourn before thee our manifold sins. We daily offend thee by pride, impenitence, unbelief, forgetfulness of thee, and in many other ways: leaving undone the things which we ought to have done, and doing those things which we ought not.

We pray that we may see more of the extent of our iniquities, and feel more of their guilt. Thus may we be led to hate sin, and to feel the need and value of that Savior who came to seek and to save that which was lost. Grant that we may be partakers of his great salvation. Whatever else we lose, may we win Christ and be found in him. Lord, we are unclean; if thou wilt, thou canst make us clean. Lord, help our unbelief; Lord, make us clean.

Give us, we beseech thee, such a sense of thy mercy through the blood of Christ, that we may be constrained to present our bodies a living sacrifice unto thee. Enable us daily to crucify the lusts of the flesh. Give us such a measure of thy grace, that all the powers of our minds, all the affections of our hearts, and all the talents entrusted to us, may be unreservedly engaged for thee. Lord, incline us to spend ourselves and be spent for thee; strengthen our desire to do so, and enable us ever hereafter to bring this desire to good effect.

(Occasional Prayers.)

Let the number of thy willing and devoted servants be everywhere increased. Be thou exalted, O God, above the heavens, and thy glory above all the earth. Pour out thy Spirit upon all flesh, that all the ends of the earth may remember and turn unto the Lord, and all the kindreds of the nations may worship before thee.

Bless the land in which we dwell; its government, the ministers of Jesus Christ, and all its people. May we be a people fearing God and working righteousness. Look with especial favor on our relatives and friends, our family-connections and acquaintances. May they all be partakers of the grace of Christ here, and of his glory hereafter.

Blessed be the Lord, who daily loadeth us with benefits. All the temporal mercies granted so abundantly to us, our food, our clothing, our home, our friends, the daily provisions for our various necessities, these are from thee, who openest thy hand and fillest all things living with plenteousness. But, above all, blessed be the God and Father of our Lord Jesus Christ, who hath blessed us with all spiritual blessings in heavenly things in Christ Jesus. Thanks be unto God for his unspeakable gift.

Now unto the King eternal, immortal, invisible, the only wise God, be honor and glory forever and ever.

These prayers and praises we offer up in the name of the Lord Jesus Christ, the Savior of perishing sinners: trusting only in his mediation and merits. *Amen.*

WEDNESDAY MORNING

Scripture Lesson
(ISAIAH 59)

Prayer

O LORD God Almighty, we thank thee for having preserved us through the past night, and for granting us health and strength for our duties on this day. Blessed be the Lord for all his mercies; for giving us food to eat and raiment to put on, and for delivering us from many evils which our sins have justly deserved.

We thank thee especially, O Lord, for the gift of Jesus Christ thy Son. We confess before thee our exceeding guilt, and we pray thee, for Christ's sake, to pardon our offenses, and to receive our souls when we die.

(Occasional Prayers.)

We beseech thee also, for his sake, to grant unto us the help of thy Holy Spirit, that we may be enabled to follow our Savior's example, and to do whatsoever he hath commanded. May we be patient, humble, kind, and merciful: endeavoring to do good unto all men, and forgiving those who trespass against us, even as we hope to be forgiven. Grant us grace this day diligently to perform its duties, and to be true and just in all our dealings, doing unto others as we would they should do unto us; and help us, O Lord, to restrain our tongue, and to subdue our evil tempers, and to live in temperance, soberness, and chastity. Save us from those sins which in times past have most easily beset us; strengthen us, O Lord, for all that awaits us; carry us through all our difficulties and troubles, and help us, day by day, to grow in grace and in the knowledge of our Lord and Savior. These prayers we humbly offer up in the name of Jesus Christ. *Amen.*

WEDNESDAY EVENING

Scripture Lesson
(PSALM 53)

Prayer

O THOU, who art the God of all the families of the earth, be thou present with us now, and enable us by thy Holy Spirit, and through thy Son's intercession, to worship thee in Spirit and in truth.

We come before thee acknowledging that we were all born in sin, and have in common a corrupt nature and a continual propensity to depart from thee. And oh how often have we offended thee by actual transgressions! Even in the day that is past, by vain thoughts, by idle words, by sinful indulgences, we have grieved thy Spirit and incurred thy displeasure. Our only refuge is in thy promised mercy in Christ Jesus. We cast ourselves wholly on that mercy. Fixing all our hopes on our Savior Jesus, we confess our guilt, and earnestly pray that his blood may cleanse us from all sin.

Give us, we beseech thee, the comfortable assurance that our sins are forgiven. Let thy Holy Spirit bear witness with our spirits that we are children of God. Plentifully impart to us the gift of thy Spirit, that we may bring forth love, joy, peace, gentleness, goodness, meekness, long-suffering, forbearance, and temperance. Grant that we may so copy the example of our Savior as to be epistles of Christ, known and read of all men, and have clear evidence of our own salvation. Teach us so to live, that we may glorify thee who hast bought us with a price of such amazing value as the blood of thine own Son.

Oh that all now present may indeed obtain mercy in Christ Jesus, and love and serve thee unfeignedly. But, O Lord, how cold is our love to thee! how dead are our hearts! Help us to love thee with all our strength. Shed abroad the love of God in our hearts, and may we be taught of God to love one another. Be thou present with us in our more retired devotions; praying in our closet, to our Father which is in secret, may we find his special presence and blessing there.

(Occasional Prayers.)

Bless, O Lord, all that are near and dear to us. Give them thy grace, ever guide them here by thy counsel, and may none of them be wanting in thy heavenly kingdom.

We pray for all in authority; Lord, may their counsels be so ordered by thee as to result most for the good of our country.

Give, we beseech thee, to all the ministers of Jesus Christ, everywhere, true knowledge and understanding of thy word; and may they set it forth in their lives accordingly. Make them wise to win souls. Lord, call forth and send out many faithful laborers to the work of the ministry. Bring it to pass that the distant isles shall wait on thee, and the Gentiles come to thy light. Bless every Society established for benefiting the bodies or the souls of men, and especially those in which we are more immediately engaged and interested.

Thanks be unto thee, Holy Lord God, for all thy goodness toward us. How multiplied are thy mercies every day! We bless thee for all thy long-suffering and forbearance toward us. We bless thee for the infinite mercies of redeeming love. We bless thee for the knowledge of thy salvation, and for the light of thy truth; for protection from every danger during the night, and provision for all our wants by day. Thou hast spread our table with food, and thou givest us every needful good. Accept these our prayers and our praises, which we offer up in and through Jesus Christ, our only Mediator and Advocate. *Amen.*

THURSDAY MORNING

Scripture Lesson
(LUKE 18:1–17)

Prayer

ALMIGHTY and adorable God, permitted by thy kindness to come again into thy presence, we would begin the day with praise to thee, who hast watched over and protected us during the past night. Bless the Lord, O our souls! and all that is within us, bless his holy name!

We would sanctify all the employments and all the events of this day by placing ourselves and them in thy care, humbly and earnestly beseeching thee to overrule all things concerning us to thy glory and the good of our souls. Unto thee do we lift up our eyes, O thou that dwellest in the heavens! Oh take us into thy protection, bodily and spiritually. We are ignorant, let thy Spirit teach us; we are guilty, let us obtain pardon through the blood of thy Son; we are wandering sheep, let thy love lead us to the Savior's fold; we are in danger from enemies who lie in wait for our souls;—what then is our hope? Truly our hope is even in thee. Hold up our goings in thy paths, that our footsteps slip not; keep us as the apple of thine eye; hide us under the shadow of thy wings.

We are in the midst of an ensnaring world; O thou God of all grace, preserve us from the lust of the flesh, the lust of the eyes, and the pride of life! Teach us that the world passeth away, and the lust thereof, while only they who do thy will abide forever. Let us place thee, O our unerring director, always before us; be thou at our right hand continually, lest we make shipwreck of faith and of a good conscience. Leave us not, neither forsake us, O God of our salvation! for thy dear Son Jesus Christ's sake. *Amen.*

THURSDAY EVENING

Scripture Lesson
(ROMANS 3)

Prayer

O GOD, thy greatness is unsearchable. Thy name is most excellent in all the earth. Thou hast set thy glory above the heavens. Thousands minister unto thee, and ten thousand times ten thousand stand before thee. We feel ourselves in thy awful presence to be nothing, less than nothing, and vanity; nor do we presume to approach thee because we are deserving of thy notice—for we have sinned—we have incurred thy righteous displeasure.

But our necessities compel us, and thy promises encourage us. Thou art nigh unto them that are of a broken heart, and savest such as be of a contrite spirit. Thou hast provided and revealed a Mediator, who has not only obeyed but magnified the law and made it honorable; and thou hast made us accepted in the Beloved.

Oh look thou upon us, and be merciful unto us, as thou art unto those that love thy name! Convince us of sin both in its penalty and in its pollution; and may we mourn over it with godly sorrow. Give us faith in the Lord Jesus Christ; and believing may we have life through his name. O Lord God, for his sake we implore thy pardoning grace. Thou knowest our iniquities, for they are not hid from thee. Remember them not against us, but according to thy mercy in Christ Jesus, remember thou us, O Lord. Wash away our guilt in the fountain that is opened in his precious blood. Gracious God, we need thy support and thy guidance. Leave us not to follow the devices and desires of our own deceitful hearts.

Our souls cleave unto the dust; quicken thou us according to thy word. May we not only live in the Spirit, but walk in the Spirit. May the same mind be in us which was also in Christ Jesus; and may we feel it to be a precious privilege to go about doing good.

As he suffered for us, leaving us an example that we should tread in his steps, may we be willing to suffer like him. When reviled, may we revile not again, but commit ourselves to him that judgeth righteously. Whoever may be the instrument of our grief, may we never lose sight of an overruling agency in permitting it, but be able to say, The cup which my Father giveth me shall I not drink it? In patience may we possess our souls.

(Occasional Prayers.)

We live in a world of changes, and have here no continuing city—may we seek one to come, and have our minds kept in perfect peace, being stayed upon God. Be with us to the end of our journey; and after honoring thee by the life we have lived, may we glorify thee by the death we shall die. When heart and flesh fail, be thou the strength of our heart and our portion forever; at death may we fall asleep in Jesus; and in the morning of the resurrection, may he change our vile body, that it may be fashioned like his own glorious body; and so may we be forever with the Lord.

Who can understand his errors? Forgive, O God, the sins of the past day, in thought, word, and deed, against thy divine majesty. We bless thee for our preservation in our going out and our coming in, and in all our ways; and we bless thee for all the supplies and indulgences which thy good providence has afforded us.

And now, O thou keeper of Israel, we commit our souls and our bodies to thy all-sufficient care. Suffer no evil to befall our persons, and no plague to come nigh our dwelling. May our sleep be sweet; or if thou holdest our eyes waking, may we remember thee upon our bed, and meditate on thee in the night-watches.

And with the innumerable company who never slumber nor sleep, and who rest not day and night, we would join in ascribing blessing and honor and glory and power unto him that sitteth upon the throne, and unto the Lamb, forever and ever. *Amen.*

FRIDAY MORNING

Scripture Lesson
(ROMANS 6)

Prayer

O GOD, heavenly Father, who makest the outgoings of the morning and evening to praise thee, accept our hearty thanks for all thy mercies, and especially for the rest and refreshment of the past night. With this renewed token of thy goodness, give us newness of heart to serve thee. Look with favor upon our earnest desires, and stretch forth the right hand of thy majesty, to be our unfailing defense and protection. Turn us from all our sins, that we may keep thy statutes, and do that which is lawful and right, and save our souls alive.

O blessed Jesus, grant us grace, so to confess thee before men that thou mayest confess us before thy Father in heaven. Make us watchful and circumspect, that we fall not again into our former transgressions. Endue us with strength and fortitude, to take up our cross daily and follow thee whithersoever thy voice shall call us. May we be strong, O Lord, in the power of thy might. May we put on the whole armor of God, and fight manfully against our spiritual enemies. With the girdle of truth, the breastplate of righteousness, the shield of faith, the helmet of salvation, and the sword of the Spirit, may we be able to stand against the fiery darts of the wicked and all the wiles of the adversary.

O holy, blessed, and eternal Spirit, vouchsafe, we beseech thee, to direct, sanctify, and govern, both our hearts and bodies, in all the pursuits of this day. Quicken us to renewed diligence in our several duties, and make us just and upright in all our dealings, and charitable, kind, and compassionate in all the relations of life.

(Occasional Prayers.)

O God, whose days are without end, and whose mercies cannot be numbered, make us, at all times and under all circumstances, duly sensible of the shortness and uncertainty of human life, and of the transitory nature of all earthly things. Thou hast made our days as it were a span long; and our age is even nothing in respect of thee; and verily every man living is altogether vanity. So teach us to number our days, that we may apply our hearts unto wisdom. Guide us by thy powerful hand as we pass through this vale of misery, that so we may serve thee in holiness and righteousness all the days of our life; that when our probation shall be closed, we may be gathered in peace to our fathers, having the testimony of a good conscience and the witness of the Spirit that we are the children of God.

All which we ask through Jesus Christ our Lord, to whom, with thee, O Father, and the Holy Ghost, be all honor and glory, world without end. *Amen.*

FRIDAY EVENING

Scripture Lesson
(JOHN 19:1–18)

Prayer

O GOD, the day is thine; the night also is thine. Thou makest the outgoings of the morning and evening to rejoice. The heavens declare thy glory; the earth is full of thy riches, and so is the great and wide sea. Thou art the maker, and sustainer, and proprietor of all things. We are the creatures of thy power, and the pensioners of thy bounty. But we have sinned against heaven and before thee, and are not worthy of the least of all thy mercies, and of all the truth which thou hast shown us. We are of those that rebel against the light; for we have resisted the dictates of our consciences, the demands of thy law, the admonitions of thy providence, and the calls of the gospel of peace. We have made light of those things into which angels desire to look; we have neglected thy great salvation, and we deserve that thy wrath should come upon us as children of disobedience.

Yet we are in the land of the living, and under a dispensation of hope. We flee for refuge to that dear Savior who said, I will deliver from going down into the pit, I have found a ransom: and who himself bore our sin in his own body on the tree. Oh that we may be found in him, and know the power of his resurrection, and the fellowship of his sufferings, being made conformable unto his death. May we not only be justified by his blood, and saved from wrath through him, but may we derive from him an influence that shall subdue our iniquities and change us into his own image, from glory to glory, as by the Spirit of the Lord.

(Occasional Prayers.)

Deliver us, we pray thee, from the views and dispositions of men of the world. May we never look for that on earth which can only be found in heaven. Born from above and bound for glory, may we feel that we are but pilgrims, and pass the time of our sojourning here in fear. Reminded so often that here we have no continuing city, may we seek one to come; and in all the changing scenes of time, know in ourselves that in heaven we have a better and an enduring substance.

Cast us not away from thy presence, and take not thy Holy Spirit from us. O thou that savest by thy right hand them that put their trust in thee, keep us as the apple of thine eye, and hide us under the shadow of thy wing. Be thou our strength in weakness, and our victory in conflict. May we never deny thee. Establish our hearts with grace, and deliver our feet from falling; and may we be sincere and without offense until the day of Christ.

These are great blessings for us to ask—but we are forever undone without them—and thou hast encouraged us to hope. We plead thy command and thy promise—ask and it shall be given you, seek and ye shall find, knock and it shall be opened unto you. No suppliant, however unworthy or guilty, was ever rejected or insulted at thy footstool. And we come in the name of him who made intercession for transgressors. Him thou hearest always—and to him, with the Father, and to the Holy Spirit, be praises forever and ever. *Amen.*

SATURDAY MORNING

Scripture Lesson
(LUKE 15:1–24)

Prayer

O GOD! thou art our God, early will we seek thee; our fathers' God, and we will exalt thee. We rejoice that in everything by prayer and supplication, with thanksgiving, we are to make known our requests unto God. We acknowledge, O Lord! that we have sinned against the light of nature, and against thy written law and gospel. We have been vain in our imaginations, and our foolish hearts have been darkened. We have been lovers of pleasure more than lovers of God. And, by our iniquities, we have exposed ourselves to thine everlasting displeasure. But, O God, look upon the face of thine Anointed, and have mercy on us. May the blood of Christ, who, through the eternal Spirit, offered himself without spot to God, purge our consciences from dead works to serve the living God. Search us, O God! and know our hearts; try us, and know our thoughts, and see if there be any wicked way in us, and lead us in the way everlasting. Permit us not to spend the golden hours of time in the pursuit of vanity, but excite us to live as citizens of the spiritual Jerusalem, and to form our hearts and lives to the temper and manners of the heavenly world.

(Occasional Prayers.)

Jesus, thou Son of David! have mercy upon all men. Graciously regard those who are dead in trespasses and sin. Teach the moralist the necessity of vital godliness, and the hyprocrite the deceitfulness of his heart, that he may stand amazed. Accomplish speedily all thy predictions relative to the latter-day glory of the church. May a way be opened for the introduction of the gospel into all lands. Raise up and prepare many to obey the command of their ascended Savior: "Go ye into all the world, and preach my gospel to every creature." We bless God for the religious instructions afforded us. Ever may we take thy Word as a lamp unto our feet and a light unto our path. Glory to God in the highest, for a plan of redemption and the overtures of grace in the gospel! Oh! let us not despise the proffers of salvation, and reject a crucified Savior. We praise thee for the mercies of the night; that while many were full of tossings to and fro unto the dawning of the day, we enjoyed quiet repose. Cause us to hear thy loving-kindness in the morning, for in thee do we trust; cause us to know the way wherein we should walk, for we lift up our souls unto thee. Establish thou thy covenant with this family, for an everlasting covenant even the sure mercies of David. Prepare us for the vicissitudes of this mortal state, and when we come to die may we die in the Lord, and be blessed forever. Be pleased, gracious God! to accept our persons and services in the Beloved. Now blessing and honor, and glory and power, be unto him that sitteth upon the throne, and unto the Lamb, forever and ever. *Amen.*

SATURDAY EVENING

Scripture Lesson
(PSALM 3)

Prayer

INFINITELY powerful and glorious God! in the name of our great High-Priest, who is passed into the heavens, we draw near unto thee this evening. May we come unto thee as children unto a father who is able and ready to assist them. Indict our petitions for us, and enable us to present them before thee in faith. We rejoice, that in Christ Jesus mercy and truth are met together, righteousness and peace have embraced each other. Where sin hath abounded, grace can now much more abound. Wash away our sins in the blood of the immaculate Son of God, that we may be presented spotless before thy throne in glory. Subdue our vile passions, and make us willing captives of the Prince of peace. May the same mind be in us which was also in Christ Jesus. Let us die daily unto sin, and live unto God. May we walk circumspectly, not as fools, but as wise, redeeming the time, because the days are evil; and may we not be weary in well doing, for in due season we shall reap if we faint not.

Graciously regard, O God! all the sons and daughters of affliction. Be thou a father to the fatherless, and a judge of the widows in thy holy habitation. Give redemption to the captives, loose the bands of wickedness, undo heavy burdens, and let the oppressed go free. Pity the sick, and heal their diseases. Furnish the destitute with food and raiment. Be a guide to them who travel by sea or land. Give to all repentance, pardon, and salvation. Bless our American republic. We thank thee for all our civil, religious, and literary privileges; and that thou hast given us a good land, and crowned it with many blessings. Thou hast not dealt so with any nation. May our country continue to be under the care of thy watchful providence. May we be a holy, that we may be a happy people. May all our friends and relatives be the objects of thy favorable regard. Let them be enriched with the blessings of thy heavenly grace. May Zion awake and put on her strength; arise and shake herself from the dust, and put on her beautiful garments. Preserve the church from all dangers within and without. Extend her boundaries from sea to sea, and from the rivers to the ends of the earth. Make all the ministers of religion faithful and zealous. Let the heathen, now shrouded in the gloom of moral death, be irradiated with the light of the gospel. O Lord! how long shall darkness, ignorance, and superstition, so awfully reign? Arise, O thou most mighty! in thy strength, and convert and save a perishing world.

(Occasional Prayers.)

Now, Lord! what wait we for? Our hope is in thee. We thank thee, thou Guardian of man! for the salvation and blessings of another day and week. Watch over us for good this night. Let thy holy angels pitch their tents around our habitation, and may we dwell in security. Prepare us for the duties and services of thy holy day. May it be a season of refreshing from the presence of the Lord. Superintend all our changes in mercy, and when time with us shall be no longer, receive us to mansions of eternal blessedness. Now to the Lamb that was slain to redeem us to God by his blood, be power, and riches, and wisdom, and strength, and honor, and glory, and blessing forever. *Amen.*

SIXTH WEEK

LORDSDAY MORNING

Scripture Lesson
(PSALM 73)

Prayer

O LORD, we desire to begin the day and the week with thee. Let a solemn sense of thy presence be upon our minds; and while we offer our supplications in the name of our only Mediator, the Lord Jesus Christ, comfort our hearts by the assurance that thou art nigh unto all them that call upon thee, even all such as call upon thee faithfully.

We acknowledge before thee, O Lord, how unworthy we are to be numbered with thy children, for we have sinned against thee, and thy wrath might justly have consumed us in a moment and have sent us down to hell: but thou hast had mercy on us, and hast made known unto us by thy word how we may be saved.

We thank thee, O Lord, for the opportunities which we are invited to enjoy this day,—of hearing those blessed truths the knowledge of which is essential to the salvation of our souls. Oh, give us grace diligently to attend to thy word; enable us to understand it, and make us anxious to improve by it; that the sermons which we hear may not rise up against us at the great day.

O Lord, preserve us by thy grace from abusing and profaning thy holy Sabbaths—from wasting them in the pursuit of the unsatisfying pleasures of this world. Let us not go into the courts of thy sanctuary without consideration, but may we worship thee in spirit and truth.

Bless, O gracious God, the ministers of thy gospel, especially our own, who show unto us the way of salvation. Do thou teach them, that they may be able to teach us. O Lord, may thy word this day awaken our consciences, that we may see more evil in the nature of sin, more danger from the guilt of it, and be more earnest to secure an interest in Christ, the only Savior.

(Occasional Prayers.)

We beseech thee, O Lord, to keep us this day from all worldly thoughts and words; and may thy Spirit suggest such things to our minds as are suitable to this holy part of our time. Oh, may we keep thy Sabbath in a becoming manner, and love it as the best day of the seven, because it is a season dedicated to thy service! Preserve us, while in thy house, from a stupid and wandering frame; strengthen our memory to retain what we hear, and make this day a time of real benefit to our souls, for which we may have reason to bless thee to all eternity, for Jesus Christ's sake.

Our Father who, &c. *Amen.*

LORDSDAY EVENING

Scripture Lesson
(PSALM 63)

Prayer

ALMIGHTY and everlasting God, we adore thee for thy tender compassion and loving-kindness to us, and to the whole family of mankind. We bless thee for the gift of thy dear Son, through whose atoning sacrifice we are brought near to thee, and by whose meritorious death and passion we are redeemed from death, and from the guilt and burden of our sins. We do not presume to come before thee, O merciful Lord, trusting in our own righteousness, but in thy manifold and great mercies. We acknowledge and bewail our many and sore offenses, for which our Lord Jesus Christ humbled himself, and became obedient unto death, even the painful death of the cross; and for which thou wast pleased to bruise him and put him to grief. May we keep in lively remembrance the agonies which he endured for our sake. May we remember that he hath borne our griefs and carried our sorrows; that he was wounded for our transgressions and bruised for our iniquities; that the chastisement of our peace was upon him; that by his stripes we are healed; and that upon him was laid the iniquity of us all. May we remember the exceeding great love of our blessed Savior Jesus Christ, in dying for our sins, and the innumerable benefits which by his precious blood-shedding he hath obtained for us. And may we offer unto thee ourselves, our souls and bodies, to be a reasonable, holy, and living sacrifice; humbly beseeching thee, at all times, to accept our poor and imperfect service, not weighing our demerits, but pardoning our offenses, through Jesus Christ our Lord.

(Occasional Prayers.)

Grant, heavenly Father, that the instructive lessons which we have heard this day with our outward ears, may, through thy grace, be so grafted inwardly in our hearts that they may bring forth in us the fruits of good living; and that in all our walk and conversation we may henceforth glory in nothing else but the cross of our Lord Jesus Christ.

Unto God's gracious care and protection we now commit ourselves, and all our relatives and friends, for this night. The Lord bless us and keep us. The Lord make his face to shine upon us, and be merciful unto us. The Lord lift up his countenance upon us and give us peace, both now and evermore. *Amen.*

MONDAY MORNING

Scripture Lesson
(1 PETER 4)

Prayer

ALMIGHTY and everlasting God, in whom we live, and move, and have our being; we, thy needy creatures, render thee our humble praises for thy preservation of us from the beginning of our lives to this day, and especially for having delivered us from the dangers of the past night. To thy watchful providence we owe it, that no disturbance hath come nigh us or our dwelling, but that we are brought in safety to the beginning of this day. For these thy mercies, we bless and magnify thy glorious name, humbly beseeching thee to accept this our morning sacrifice of praise and thanksgiving, for his sake who lay down in the grave and rose again for us, thy Son, our Savior, Jesus Christ.

And since it is of thy mercy, O gracious Father, that another day is added to our lives, we here dedicate both our souls and our bodies to thee and thy service, in a sober, righteous, and godly life; in which resolution do thou, O merciful God, confirm and strengthen us; that, as we grow in age, we may grow in grace and in the knowledge of our Lord and Savior, Jesus Christ.

But, O God, who knowest the weakness and corruption of our nature, and the manifold temptations which we daily meet with, we humbly beseech thee to have compassion on our infirmities, and to give us the constant assistance of thy Holy Spirit; that we may be effectually restrained from sin, and excited to our duty. Imprint upon our hearts such a dread of thy judgments, and such a grateful sense of thy goodness to us, as may make us both afraid and ashamed to offend thee. And, above all, keep in our minds a lively remembrance of that great day in which we must give a strict account of our thoughts, words, and actions; and, according to the works done in the body, be eternally rewarded or punished by him whom thou hast appointed the judge of quick and dead, thy Son, Jesus Christ our Lord.

(Occasional Prayers.)

In particular, we implore thy grace and protection for the ensuing day. Keep us temperate in our meats and drinks, and diligent in our several callings. Grant us patience under any afflictions thou shalt see fit to lay on us, and minds always contented with our present condition. Give us grace to be just and upright in all our dealings; quiet and peaceable; full of compassion; and ready to do good to all men according to our abilities and opportunities. Direct us in all our ways, and prosper the works of our hands in the business of our several stations. Defend us from all dangers and adversities; and be graciously pleased to take us, and all things belonging to us, under thy fatherly care and protection. These things, and whatever else thou shalt see necessary and convenient to us, we humbly beg, through the merits and mediation of thy Son, Jesus Christ, our Lord and Savior. *Amen.*

MONDAY EVENING

Scripture Lesson
(JAMES 3)

Prayer

MOST merciful God, who art of purer eyes than to behold iniquity, and hast promised forgiveness to all those who confess and forsake their sins; we come before thee under an humble sense of our own unworthiness, acknowledging our manifold transgressions of thy righteous laws. But, O gracious Father, who desirest not the death of a sinner, look upon us, we beseech thee, in mercy, and forgive us all our transgressions. Make us deeply sensible of the great evil of them, and work in us a hearty contrition, that we may obtain forgiveness at thy hands, who art ever ready to receive humble and penitent sinners, for the sake of thy Son, Jesus Christ, our only Savior and Redeemer.

Vouchsafe to us, we beseech thee, the direction and assistance of thy Holy Spirit. Reform whatever is amiss in the temper and disposition of our souls; that nothing unclean may rest there. Purge our hearts from envy, hatred, and malice; that we may always go to our rest in peace, charity, and good-will, and with a conscience void of offense towards thee and towards men.

(Occasional Prayers.)

Accept, O Lord, our intercessions for all mankind. Let the light of thy gospel shine upon all nations; and may as many as have received it live as becomes it. Be gracious unto thy church; and grant that every member of the same may serve thee faithfully. Bless all in authority over us; and so rule their hearts, and strengthen their hands, that they may punish wickedness and vice, and maintain thy true religion and virtue. Send down thy blessings, temporal and spiritual, upon all our relations, friends, and neighbors. Reward all who have done us good, and pardon all those who have done or wish us evil, and give them repentance and better minds. Be merciful to all who are in any trouble; and do thou, the God of pity, administer to them according to their several necessities, for his sake who went about doing good, thy Son, our Savior, Jesus Christ.

To our prayers, O Lord, we join our unfeigned thanks for all thy mercies: for our being, our reason, and all other endowments and faculties of soul and body; for our health, friends, food and raiment, and all the other comforts and conveniences of life. Above all, we adore thy mercy in sending thine only Son into the world to redeem us from sin and eternal death, and in giving us the knowledge and sense of our duty towards thee. We bless thee for thy patience with us, notwithstanding our many and great provocations; for all the directions, assistances, and comforts of thy Holy Spirit; for thy continual care and watchful providence over us through the whole course of our lives; and particularly for the mercies and benefits of the past day.

We beseech thee to continue thy gracious protection to us this night. Defend us from all dangers and mischiefs, and from the fear of them; that we may enjoy such refreshing sleep as may fit us for the duties of the following day. Make us ever mindful of the time when we shall lie down in the dust; and grant us grace always to live in such a state, that we may never be afraid to die; so that living and dying we may be thine, through the merits and satisfaction of thy Son, Christ Jesus, in whose name we offer up these our imperfect prayers. *Amen.*

TUESDAY MORNING

Scripture Lesson
(JAMES 5)

Prayer

O LORD GOD, heavenly Father, early in the morning do we flee unto thee. Our souls do wait for thee. In thy word is our trust. Lord, what is man, that thou so regardest him? As high as the heaven is, in comparison to the earth, so great is thy mercy towards them that fear thee. But, O God, we confess our unworthiness and acknowledge our frailty. We are but dust. Thou hast made our days as it were a span long, and our age is even as nothing in respect of thee; and verily every man living is altogether vanity. At thy word all our days are gone. We must lie down in a place of darkness. But, O God, according to thy promise, thou wilt show wonders among the dead; and they shall rise up again and praise thee. Thou hast redeemed us; and thou canst restore us. Thou shalt show us the path of life: in thy presence is the fullness of joy, and at thy right hand there is pleasure for evermore.

Grant, O Lord, that as we are baptized into the death of thy beloved Son Jesus Christ, and as he was raised from the dead, even so we also may be raised from the death of sin, and walk in newness of life. Being planted together in the likeness of his death, may we also be made in the likeness of his resurrection. May our old man be crucified with him, that the body of sin may be destroyed, and that henceforth we may not serve sin. If we be dead with Christ, give us faith to believe that we shall also live with him: knowing that Christ, being raised from the dead, dieth no more; that death hath no more dominion over him. May we also ourselves be dead unto sin, but alive unto God through Jesus Christ our Lord. May we know him as our life and peace, our wisdom and righteousness, our sanctification and redemption, our refuge in every time of need, and the rock of our strength and salvation. May sin have no more dominion over us: but, being made free from sin and become servants to God, may we have our fruit unto holiness, and the end everlasting life.

(Occasional Prayers.)

Grant us grace, heavenly Father, to live this day to thy glory. In willing obedience to thy commandments; in patient and humble resignation to thy will; in unreserved confidence in thy justice, goodness, and wisdom; and under a grateful sense of all thy mercies, enable us to serve thee faithfully all the days of our life. We pray for our friends, relatives, and benefactors; and for all whom we are bound to remember in our prayers. May we all be found at last among the happy number whose names are written in the book of everlasting remembrance, and who shall be thine in that day when thou makest up thy jewels, and when thou wilt spare them, as a man spareth his own son that serveth him. May we so follow the example of our crucified and risen Savior, as to be made partakers of his blessed resurrection, through the same Jesus Christ our Lord. *Amen.*

TUESDAY EVENING

Scripture Lesson
(2 PETER 1)

Prayer

O LORD our God! help us this evening to worship thee in the beauty of holiness. Thou hast never said to the seed of Jacob, seek ye my face in vain. We would therefore call upon thy great and holy name, believing that thou art, and that thou art a rewarder of them who diligently seek thee. O Lord! we confess our sins of omission and commission. We have pursued too much the pleasures, honors, and riches of the world. How often have we offended in thought, word, and action! How stubborn have been our wills, how vain our thoughts, and how earthly our affections! Our hearts cleave to the dust. We would feel that we have offended, and that there is no help in ourselves. We would hope in the Lord, for with the Lord there is mercy, and with him is plenteous redemption. Remember not the sins of our youth and riper years; but blot out all our transgressions, and give us the peace of God which passeth all understanding. O thou Physician of souls, heal our spiritual maladies; restore us to health and soundness, and to the joy of thy salvation.

(Occasional Prayers.)

Teach transgressors thy ways, and turn the disobedient to the wisdom of the just. Suffer not those who are rich in this world to be high-minded, and to trust in uncertain riches, but in the living God, who giveth them all things richly to enjoy. May they do good, and be rich in good works, ready to distribute, willing to communicate, laying up in store for themselves a good foundation against the time to come; that they may lay hold on eternal life. Make all the poor in this world rich in faith, and heirs of the kingdom. May every Christian society flourish in knowledge, holiness, and peace. Build thou the waste places of Zion. Give unto all destitute flocks pastors after thine own heart. Let thy ministering servants be clothed with righteousness; and let thy saints shout for joy. Send forth heralds of salvation to plant churches in the region of darkness and the shadow of death. Guide the public councils of our nation; overrule all our civil affairs for thy glory. Make all our colleges nurseries of piety, as well as of useful knowledge. Cast into them the salt of grace, that from these fountains may issue streams which shall make glad the city of our God. Thanks to thy name, all gracious Father! for the blessings of thy good providence; that thou hast watched over us with paternal care, preserved us in existence, and supplied all our wants. We would rejoice that Christ has died to redeem us, and that thou hast accepted his atoning sacrifice. We thank thee for the blessings of another day; that thou hast preserved us amidst dangers, that we are still in the land of the living, and in the enjoyment of health, liberty, and safety. O thou Guardian of men! take our family and all who are near and dear to us under thy protection this night. May our dwelling-place be a safe and a quiet habitation. Sleeping or waking, living or dying, we would be thine. May the shadows of the evening remind us of the night of death, and the importance of preparing for it. Bring us to see the light of a new day, rejoicing in the loving-kindness and tender mercy of our heavenly Father. May our days on earth be happy, and our eternity joyous. And glory be to God the Father, and to the Son, and to the Holy Ghost. *Amen.*

WEDNESDAY MORNING

Scripture Lesson
(1 JOHN 1)

Prayer

ALMIGHTY and everlasting God, look in mercy upon our infirmities. We acknowledge our helplessness and dependence. Without thee we can do nothing. We are surrounded by dangers and temptations. But thou, O God, art able to sustain us. Thy hand is not shortened, that it cannot save; neither is thy ear heavy, that it cannot hear. Have pity upon us, O God of our salvation. Let not our sins cause thee to hide thy face from us. In all our necessities, stretch forth thy right hand to help and defend us. Give us such strength and protection as may support us in all dangers, and carry us in safety through all our temptations. Knowing that thou art rich in mercy to all who call upon thee in the name of thy dear Son, give us faith to believe thy word and to rely on thy promises; that our prayers may come up before thee as an acceptable offering, and that they may be heard and answered, through the merits and intercession of our blessed Savior.

(Occasional Prayers.)

O God, thou hast been found of them that sought thee not. Thou hast been made manifest to them that asked not after thee. May the sound of the everlasting gospel be spread abroad from shore to shore, until all the nations of the earth shall worship before thee. Be thou exalted among the heathen. Let them that dwell in the wilderness kneel down before thee. Let the kings of the earth fall down at thy footstool. Let all the people of the earth do thee homage.

We bless thee, O God, for having cast our lot in a land of gospel light and knowledge. May we be kept by thy grace from any mis-improvement of our great privileges. Grant that we, who profess to know thee, may walk circumspectly in all thy commandments. Enable us to fulfill our respective obligations to thee and to each other. May no occasion be given by us to the enemies of religion to blaspheme thy holy name. May we show our love to thee, by following thy precepts and living a life of purity and holiness. May we look away from the things which are seen, and are temporal, and fix our hopes and affections and desires on the things that are not seen, and are eternal. May we remember, that when our day of probation has passed away, we must all appear before the judgment-seat of Christ, that every one may receive the things done in his body, and be punished or rewarded according to what he hath done, whether it be good or whether it be evil. Direct us especially in all the duties of this day, that in all our works begun, continued, and ended in thee, we may glorify thy holy name, and finally, by thy mercy, obtain everlasting life, through Jesus Christ our Lord. *Amen.*

WEDNESDAY EVENING

Scripture Lesson
(1 JOHN 5)

Prayer

O LORD GOD Almighty, we bless thee for all the mercies of the past day, and we pray thee now to take us under thy care, and to deliver us from all the dangers of this night. Preserve us, both in body and soul, from every evil, and keep us from all sinful thoughts when we are about to close our eyes in sleep.

We confess, O Lord, that we have this day left undone many things which we ought to have done, and done many things which we ought not to have done. Pardon all our pride and vanity, our idleness and self-indulgence, our impatience, fretfulness, and discontent. Forgive, O Lord, all the rash and angry words which we have this day spoken, and all the sinful thoughts which have risen up in our minds, and which we have not been careful to resist. And especially, we pray thee to pardon our forgetfulness of thee, our God, and our want of gratitude and love to Jesus Christ. For these, and all our other sins, which from time to time we have committed, we here implore thy pardoning love, in the name of our most merciful Savior.

And since we know that our life is so short and uncertain, help us, day by day, to think of our latter end. O Lord, grant us grace so to live that we be not afraid to die; and do thou receive our souls at last into thine eternal kingdom.

Enable us this night to shake off all worldly cares and desires, and to meditate upon thee; let thy Holy Spirit be present with us to purify our hearts, to bring before us the things which concern our peace, and to inspire us with godly resolutions.

Above all things, make us rightly to understand thine infinite mercy in the redemption of mankind by Jesus Christ, and diligently to avail ourselves of all our privileges, as his disciples, and thy children by adoption and grace.

(Occasional Prayers.)

O heavenly Father, we commit ourselves to thy holy keeping this night, and desire to rest securely under the shadow of thy protection. Defend us from all perils, and especially from those which may assault and hurt the soul. Prepare us, by comfortable repose, for the duties of the morrow; and grant that we may rise disposed and strengthened for thy service, as faithful and diligent disciples of thy blessed Son. *Amen.*

THURSDAY MORNING

Scripture Lesson
(REVELATIONS 4)

Prayer

O LORD, thou art the God whose we are, and whom we ought to serve. We desire to humble ourselves here before thee, that our lives have been so unserviceable to thee, and so full of provocation against thee; that we have lived to ourselves more than to the Lord and Giver of our lives; and that we have served our own lusts and pleasures more than thy holy blessed will.

We have sinned against thee, our God, to the infinite wrong and damage of our own souls, and by our sins we have destroyed ourselves; but it is not in us to recover and save ourselves. In thee alone is all our help. Yea, thou hast laid help upon one that is mighty and able to save to the uttermost all that come to God through him: through whom thou hast encouraged us to come boldly to thy throne of grace; that we may obtain mercy, and find grace to help in every time of need. In him, therefore, we beg, O Lord, that thou wilt be reconciled to us, and at peace with us, as a Father of mercies and a God of consolation.

For his sake enable us also, we beseech thee, to demean ourselves as becomes the children of God, the redeemed of the Lord, and the followers of Jesus Christ. Oh inspire us with such principles of grace and holiness in our hearts as may make us hate all iniquity and every false way. And put thy Spirit within us, causing us to walk in thy statutes, and to keep thy judgments, and to do them. So engage our hearts to thyself, that we may make it our meat and drink to do thy will, and with increased zeal run in the way of thy commands. O thou Lamb of God, who takest away the sin of the world, cleanse us from our sins in thy most precious blood. O Lord God of our salvation, clothe us in the spotless robe of thy righteousness; that being pardoned, and justified, and accepted, through thy merits and mediation, we may have joy and peace in believing. Oh make our services acceptable to thee while we live, and our souls ready for thee when we die. And as long as we are in this world, keep us, O Lord our God, from the evil of it, and from the snares and dangers to which thou knowest we are continually exposed. Make our passage safe and sure, through all the changes, troubles, temptations, and various conditions of this mortal life, to the unchangeable glories and felicities of life everlasting.

(Occasional Prayers.)

Be merciful to us, good Lord, and bless us, and keep us this day, in all our ways and in all our lawful designs and undertakings; and may we take nothing in hand but what is warranted in thy word. Oh let us be in the fear of the Lord all the day long. And let thy love abound in our hearts, and powerfully constrain us all to faithful and cheerful obedience, acceptable in thy sight, through him that has loved and redeemed us, even the Lord our righteousness.

The blessing of God Almighty, Father Son and Holy Ghost, be with us, and all that belong to us, this day and for evermore. *Amen.*

THURSDAY EVENING

Scripture Lesson
(PSALM 139)

Prayer

IN an humble acknowledgment of our manifold sins and iniquities which we from time to time, and more especially this day, have committed against thee, in thought, word, and deed, we now prostrate ourselves before thee, O Lord of heaven and earth, beseeching thee, for the sake of Jesus Christ, our only Lord and Savior, to be merciful unto us. Forgive us, O Lord, that we have not rendered unto thee according to thy mercy and loving-kindness; that we have been forgetful and disobedient, and have sinned against heaven, and in thy sight. Let thy Holy Spirit sanctify us wholly, and give us more and more grace and strength, whereby we may be enabled to subdue all our sinful and corrupt affections; weaken our attachment to the perishing enjoyments of this world; set our affections on things above; grant that we may improve the remainder of our days with all possible care, and give all diligence to make our calling and election sure, that we may so persevere therein unto death that at last we may attain everlasting life.

(Occasional Prayers.)

Accept our praises and thanksgivings for all thy mercies vouchsafed unto us in this life, and for the hopes of a better. And now that we are going to take our rest and sleep, let us consider that thou, Lord, only makest us to dwell in safety: whether We sleep or wake, live or die, let us be found thine own, to thy eternal glory, and our everlasting salvation, through Jesus Christ. *Amen.*

FRIDAY MORNING

Scripture Lesson
(PSALM 145)

Prayer

O LORD GOD of our salvation! thou art the hope of all the ends of the earth, upon whom the eyes of all do wait: for thou givest unto all life, and breath, and all things. In thee we ever live, and move, and are; and upon thee are we dependent for all the good that we have, or hope for. Accept our thanks for thy protection during the past night, and for the blessings we enjoy this morning. Thou hast given us the assurance of thy word, that if we commit our affairs to thee, and acknowledge thee in all our ways, thou wilt establish our thoughts and direct our path. Therefore we desire, O Lord, still to put ourselves under thy gracious conduct and thy fatherly protection; and to beg thy heavenly guidance and blessing, and to dispose of us and of all that concern us, to the glory of thy name.

O Lord, withdraw not the comforts of thy presence, nor the assistance of thy Spirit, for our great contempt and manifold abuses of all such grace and goodness. Punish us not by giving us over to the love and power of our sins; but give us truly penitent hearts for all the evils committed by us, and thy merciful discharge from all the guilt that lies upon us. Grant us, O God, the comfortable sense of thy gracious acceptance of us, and thy merciful intentions towards us in the Son of thy love, that our souls may bless thee, and all that is within us may praise thy holy name.

Oh that we may find the joy of the Lord to be our strength, to enable us to contend against our sins, especially the sins to which we are most addicted, and whereof we are in greatest danger; and to make us also more ready to every good work, and better disposed for all the duties which we owe to thee our God, to our neighbor and ourselves. May we always have a conscience void of offense towards God and towards men. Oh help us to walk circumspectly, not as fools, but as wise; carefully redeeming the time that we have lost, and conscientiously improving all those seasons and means of grace which thou art pleased to give us for the profit and advantage of our souls. Do thou instruct us to avoid the temptations that may be before us, or help us to overcome them; and making it as our meat and our drink to do thy will all the day long, may we walk in the fear of the Lord, and the comfort of the Holy Ghost. While we are upon earth, oh give us all things needful and convenient for our present pilgrimage; sanctify to us all our enjoyments and all events that now befall us; till, through the merits of thy Son and the multitude of thy mercies, we are conducted safely to be ever with the Lord. Amidst all our other affairs in this world, oh let us never forget or neglect the one thing needful, but be careful so to live by faith every day, that we may be prepared for the great day of thy appearing and glory.

(Occasional Prayers.)

O gracious Father! keep us, we beseech thee, this day in thy fear and favor; and help us to live to thy honor and glory. Oh let thy good providence be our defense and security; and let thy Holy Spirit be our guide and counsellor in all our ways, through Jesus Christ, our only Savior.

Let thy grace, O Lord Jesus Christ, thy love, O heavenly Father, thy comfortable fellowship, O holy blessed Spirit, be with us, and with all for whom we ought to beg thy mercy in our prayers, this day, and for evermore. *Amen.*

FRIDAY EVENING

Scripture Lesson
(PROVERBS 8)

Prayer

O GOD, whose blessed Son came into the world to redeem us from sin and death, and was manifested, that he might destroy the works of the devil, and make us the sons of God and heirs of eternal life; grant us grace, we beseech thee, to seek with earnestness and diligence the benefits of this great salvation. May we look with humble confidence for the pardon of our sins, through the mediation of our ever-blessed Redeemer; and may we obtain that lively hope, which is as an anchor to the soul, sure and steadfast. And having this hope, may we, through the sanctifying influences of thy Holy Spirit, purify ourselves, according to the pattern and example of our blessed Savior Jesus Christ; that when he shall appear again with power and great glory, we may be made like unto him, in his eternal and glorious kingdom.

We praise thee, O God, for all the manifestations of thy goodness to a lost and ruined world. Let all the people come and worship before thee. Make bare thine holy arm in the eyes of all the nations. Let all the ends of the earth see the salvation of God. May the Redeemer, the Holy One of Israel, have the heathen for his inheritance, and the uttermost parts of the earth for his possession. Though the mountains depart and the hills be removed, let not thy kindness depart from those who fear thee; neither let the covenant of thy peace be removed. As the earth bringeth forth her bud, and as the garden causeth the things that are sown in it to spring forth; so, O Lord God, cause righteousness and praise to spring forth before all the nations.

Enable us, we pray thee, to realize the blessings of salvation, through faith in the righteousness of the Redeemer. Lord, help our unbelief; Lord, increase our faith. Open our ears to hear thy truth. Open also our lips, that our mouth may show forth thy praise. Strengthen us, we beseech thee, to fulfill the good resolutions we have made, and to serve thee truly and sincerely.

Put thy Spirit into the hearts of thy servants whom thou hast called to preach thy living word. May they go forth on this mission of mercy guided by thy truth, sustained by thy power, and animated by thy Spirit. May they go forth, preaching repentance and faith for the remission of sins. May they go forth, making disciples of all nations, baptizing them in the name of the Father, and of the Son, and of the Holy Ghost; until the kingdoms of the world become the kingdoms of Christ, and righteousness and peace cover the face of the earth as the waters cover the sea.

(Occasional Prayers.)

We bless thee, heavenly Father, for the mercies bestowed upon us this day. We humble ourselves before thee as unworthy sinners, beseeching thee to watch over us this night, and to protect us from all the evils to which we may be exposed. Above all, keep us from sin, and from all the wiles of the adversary. Let us repose under the shadow of thy wing till every danger be over, and we are brought again before thee to renew our prayers and praises, and to enter again upon our respective duties.

We ask for all, in the name and for the sake of Jesus Christ our Lord, to whom, with thee, O Father, and thee, O Holy Ghost, be all honor and glory, world without end. *Amen.*

SATURDAY MORNING

Scripture Lesson
(ACTS 26:1–29)

Prayer

O ETERNAL and unchangeable Jehovah, who dwellest in light which no mortal eye can behold, and dost from thy sanctuary look down on the things that are in heaven and earth;—we adore thee that thou hast, in the riches of thy grace, opened a new and living way, whereby sinners may draw nigh to thee, and find thee to be a just God, and yet a Savior, able and willing to save to the uttermost all who come unto thee through thy incarnate Son.

O God, we have reason to loathe ourselves, and to repent in dust and ashes. We mourn over and bewail at thy footstool those sins which we, from time to time, have committed by thought, word, and deed, against thy divine majesty.

But to thee belong mercies and forgiveness, though we have sinned and rebelled against thee. We bless thee, that the blood of Jesus Christ cleanseth from all sins; that he has made reconciliation for iniquity, and has brought in everlasting righteousness; and that thy word, which cannot err, declares, that "whosoever believeth in him shall not perish, but have everlasting life;" that "though our sins be as scarlet, they shall be made as white as snow; though they be red like crimson, they shall be as wool!"

O Lamb of God, who takest away the sin of the world, cleanse us from our sins by thy most precious blood, and clothe us in the spotless robe of thy righteousness, that, being justified and accepted by thy merits, we may have joy and peace in believing.

O holy and eternal Spirit, enable us, by our life and conversation, to adorn the doctrine of God our Savior in all things. May we prove to those around us that we are the children of light; that we have received Christ's precepts, are influenced by his grace, are following his example, and are pressing forward to his kingdom. Suffer us not to place our security in an arm of flesh, but teach us ever to look for it where alone it is to be found, in the Lord Jesus Christ. Grant that, being united to him by a living faith, we may obtain victory over the corruption of our hearts, the temptations of Satan, and the sinful cares and allurements of the world. Let the language of our hearts ever be— "Behold, God is our salvation, we will trust and not be afraid, for the Lord Jehovah is our strength and our song, he is also become our salvation!"

(Occasional Prayers.)

Into thy hands we commend ourselves, and all that belong to us, this day. Keep us under the shadow of thine almighty wings. Guide and direct us continually by thy counsel, until thou hast brought us to thy glory.

O Lord, we now lift up our voices with thanksgivings to thee, for the multiplied favors, both of providence and grace, which thou hast heaped on our undeserving heads. We bless thee for our creation, preservation, and all the other blessings of this life; but above all, we praise thee for the gift of thy Son,—for the word of thy gospel,—for the promise of thy Spirit,—for the means of grace,—and for the hope of glory. O Lord, help us to show forth our gratitude, not merely with our lips, but in our lives, by giving up ourselves to thy service, and by bringing forth the fruits of righteousness and holiness, which are by Jesus Christ, to the praise of the glory of thy grace. Hear us, heavenly Father, and whilst thou hearest have mercy on us. Pardon the iniquity of our holy offerings, and in all things enable us with the Psalmist to say,—"Not unto us, O Lord, not unto us, but unto thy name, give glory, for thy loving-mercy and thy truth's sake."

Now to God the Father, God the Son, and God the Holy Ghost, the glorious, unchangeable, and eternal Jehovah, be ascribed everlasting praise. *Amen.*

SATURDAY EVENING

Scripture Lesson
(REVELATIONS 22)

Prayer

O OUR GOD, another week has just passed away, and we are still in the land of the living, while so many of our fellow-creatures have passed from time into eternity. Blessed be God for the continuance of life and health, and for prolonged opportunities of preparing for death and judgment!

O gracious God, let not this continuance of mercy increase our condemnation, by encouraging us to commit sin because hitherto thine anger has been withheld from falling upon us. Let us not treasure up wrath unto ourselves against the day of wrath; but teach us to number our days, that we may apply our hearts unto wisdom.

(Occasional Prayers.)

Prepare us, most blessed God, by sleep and rest, to take our part in the duties of the Lords Day tomorrow. Give us that sense of sin which leads to a full confession of its guilt, and to faith in the atonement of Christ for its pardon. Give us that adoring gratitude for all thy mercies, more especially for the great mercy of a Savior, which may incline us to praise thee with joyful lips. Give us that sense of the value of our souls, and of the greatness of thy salvation, which may lead us to seek life and mercy with all our hearts. Oh let not the coming Lords-day be defectively used, like those which are passed; but let it be so improved, by public and private means of grace, as to advance our meetness for the service of that eternal Sabbath that remaineth for the people of God: through the merit and mediation of Jesus Christ. *Amen.*

SEVENTH WEEK

LORDSDAY MORNING

Scripture Lesson
(ISAIAH 40)

Prayer

O MERCIFUL LORD, from whom alone every good and perfect gift cometh, pour upon us, we humbly beseech thee, the Spirit of thy grace, that we may approach thy mercy-seat through Jesus Christ our Divine Redeemer, and make known our requests unto thee by prayer and supplication with thanksgiving.

We come before thee, this morning, to pray that we may be enabled to see and confess our real state and character in thy sight. We would pour out our hearts before thee, and make the Most High our refuge. We would seek thee while thou art to be found, and call upon thee while thou art near. We would forsake every wicked way, and every unrighteous thought, and return to the Lord for mercy and abundant pardon. Draw nigh to us most merciful Father, and forgive us our numerous offenses.

We praise thee for the great encouragement which thou hast given us, to worship, and bow down, and kneel before thee. We confess that we have erred and strayed from thy ways like lost sheep, and are unworthy to come into thy presence; but we would draw near unto thee, because thou hast graciously opened for us a door of access, through faith in thy beloved Son, our Savior, and hast revealed thyself as our merciful Father in him. We bless thee, that through him thou hast sent unto thy people a full, free, and everlasting redemption, and that in thy blessed gospel thou hast promised pardon and peace to all who believe in his name. Enable us by faith to look unto Jesus as the Lord our Righteousness, and to receive out of his fullness grace to supply our wants, to conform our souls to his divine image, and to enrich us with all the blessings of his salvation.

Blessed Lord, we praise thy name for having appointed this day to be kept holy; for this is the holy day of the Lord, which thou hast set apart to thyself, as a memorial of the accomplishment of the work of creation, and of the still more glorious work of redemption.

O Lord, preserve us by thy grace from abusing and profaning thy holy Sabbaths. Let us not rush into the courts of thy sanctuary without consideration, but may we worship thee in spirit and in truth. Let us not be satisfied to approach thee with our lips whilst our hearts are unhumbled and unclean in thy sight. Create in us clean hearts, and renew right spirits within us. Pardon all our multiplied offenses, and give us thy grace, that we may glorify thee by the sanctification of thy Sabbaths, not only outwardly in our actions, but inwardly in our thoughts and affections.

Gracious God, meet and bless us in all our religious services this day; and whether we are engaged in secret, in family, or in public worship, impart to us a holy solemnity of mind. May thy word be profitable to us, being mixed with faith in our hearts, and may it be as good seed springing up and yielding the fruits of righteousness and true holiness, to thy honor and glory.

O God of the spirits of all flesh, we beseech thee to bless all that wait upon thee in thy house this day, and suit thy mercies to their several wants. Clothe thy word with power, and make it effectual to the subduing of many hearts to the obedience of Christ. Awaken the careless,—humble the proud,—comfort the afflicted,—strengthen the weak,—give to them that mourn in Zion beauty for ashes, the oil of joy for mourning, and the garment of praise for the spirit of heaviness.

Bless all thy ministering servants, and especially those who labor amongst us in the word and doctrine which thou hast revealed for our instruction. May they go forth in the fullness of the blessing of the gospel of peace; and, being sensible of the important charge committed to them, may they be instant in season and out of season, showing the people their transgressions, and making known the mystery of the glorious gospel of God our Savior. Oh let thine almighty power be manifested, and let thy truth have free course and be glorified.

(Occasional Prayers.)

Accept these our prayers and supplications, we humbly beseech thee, through Jesus Christ our Mediator and Advocate, to whom, with thee, O Heavenly Father, and thee, O Eternal Spirit, the Comforter and Sanctifier of the church of God, we desire to unite with angels and the spirits of just men made perfect, in ascribing all glory, honor, and praise, forever and ever. *Amen.*

LORDSDAY EVENING

Scripture Lesson
(PSALMS 8, 9.)

Prayer

HOLY, holy, holy, Lord God Almighty! who humblest thyself to listen to the adoration of the heavenly hosts above: how infinitely great is thy condescension in regarding the feeble thanksgivings and supplications of sinful mortals! Thou hast revealed thyself as delighting in mercy, and as being glorified in the salvation of sinners through Jesus Christ our Lord. Enable us to take shelter in this thine appointed refuge; that we may find pardon and acceptance with thee, and that our evening sacrifice of prayer and praise may ascend up before thee perfumed with the incense of his merits, and be heard, and accepted, and obtain an answer of peace.

We bless thy name for the many seasons and means of grace which thou hast afforded us. We bless thee especially for the opportunities we have enjoyed this day of waiting upon thee in the ordinances of thine own appointment. But, O Lord our God, the review of even this day fills us with shame and confusion of face; for, alas! what coldness of affection, what wandering of thought, what want of reverence, of love, and of gratitude, have we betrayed in all our religious services! Surely we are altogether unprofitable servants.

But we desire now humbly to cast ourselves at thy footstool, beseeching thee, O Lord, for Christ's sake, to pardon all our iniquity, yea, the iniquity of our holy things. Wash us in the fountain of his atoning blood, clothe us with the robe of his justifying righteousness, and sanctify our hearts by the purifying grace of his Spirit. Oh shine upon our souls, and give us clearer views of the truth as it is in Jesus. And may it influence our tempers and dispositions, our life and conduct, that in all things we may adorn the doctrine of God our Savior.

Gracious Lord, let not the word of thy truth, which we have heard this day with our outward ears, return unto thee void. Enlighten our understandings, and open our hearts to receive it in love and in power. Grant that we may not only read and mark, but also learn and inwardly digest, those holy Scriptures which are able to make us wise unto salvation through faith which is in Christ Jesus.

Blessed Lord, hear the prayers which have been offered up this day for all sorts and conditions of men. Strengthen those who are weak in faith; comfort the afflicted in body or in mind; instruct the ignorant; take away the heart of stone, and cause the impenitent sinner to cry unto thee for mercy. Inspire continually thy universal church with the spirit of truth, unity, and concord. Bless the labors of all thy ministering servants. May the seed which they have sown bring forth fruit to the praise and glory of thy grace. And, O God, let thy ways be known upon earth, thy saving health among all nations; let both Jews and Gentiles be gathered into the Redeemer's kingdom;

and let everyone that nameth the name of Christ depart from all iniquity.

We now commit ourselves into thy care and fatherly protection. Watch over us during the night season, and refresh our wearied bodies with sleep; and if it be consistent with thy good pleasure, raise us up in health and safety to enjoy the light of another day.

Blessed be the Lord our God, the God of Israel, who only doeth wondrous things; and blessed be thy glorious name forever, and let the whole earth be filled with thy glory. *Amen.*

MONDAY MORNING

Scripture Lesson
(EXODUS 15:1–19)

Prayer

O ALMIGHTY and most merciful God! thou art the inexhaustible Fountain of wisdom, of truth, and of mercy; grant us thy Holy Spirit, that we may draw nigh unto thee, through Jesus Christ our Lord, to worship at thy footstool, and to praise thee for thy goodness and mercy vouchsafed to us.

We have been protected by thee during the past night: we have been refreshed with comfortable sleep, and are now permitted, with the renewed gift of life and health, to behold the light of another morning, and to spread before thy mercy-seat all our wants and desires. Bless the Lord, O our souls, and all that is within us bless his holy name!

But how should we venture into thine awful presence, O Lord God Almighty, or take thy sacred name within our lips? We are guilty, corrupt, and helpless creatures. Our souls cleave unto the dust, and even our secret sins, which are unknown to others, and which our own deceitful hearts excuse or make light of, are all seen by thee, and expose us to thine anger and condemnation.

O Lord God, our heavenly Father, enable us to flee for refuge to the hope that is set before us in Christ Jesus; help us to feel our need of him, and to discern the all-sufficiency of his salvation. And as thou hast, with thy holy arm, exalted thy beloved Son to be a Prince and a Savior, to give repentance and forgiveness of sins, we would implore from his grace that repentance which is not to be repented of—that true conviction of sin, that genuine sorrow and contrition of heart, which proceeds from a sense of redeeming love—and that pardon which he bestows, that we may forsake sin and everything that is contrary to thy holy word. Oh give us humbled and contrite hearts, and come and dwell in us according to thy promise. Oh help us to sincerely repent of our numerous transgressions; have compassion upon us, we beseech thee. Hide thy face from our sins, and blot out all our iniquities, and guide us in the path of duty and salvation. Enable us to fight the good fight of faith, and to resist all our spiritual enemies, to overcome our numerous temptations, to mortify our sinful habits, and to abound in all the graces of the Christian life.

We now commend to thy protection and mercy our dear relatives and friends. Bless all who love our Lord Jesus Christ in sincerity. Strengthen the weak in faith. Comfort those who are afflicted in body or mind. Enable them to look unto Him who bore our griefs and carried our sorrows. Bring home to thy fold such as still wander from thy ways, that they may attend to the things which belong to their peace, before they be forever hidden from their eyes. O Lord, enlarge thy church and purify it by thy grace, that it may be unto thee a praise in the whole earth. May false religion, superstition, and self-righteousness perish at thy feet, and may the knowledge of thy name and of thy salvation cover the earth, as the waters cover the depths of the sea.

Accept in mercy, O heavenly Father, these our supplications and prayers. Send down an answer of peace, and do for us exceeding abundantly above all that we can ask or think, through Jesus Christ our High-Priest and Advocate; to whom, with thee, O heavenly Father, and thee, O eternal Spirit, one God in three Persons, the God of our salvation, be glory and honor from all creatures in heaven and on earth, now and for evermore. *Amen.*

MONDAY EVENING

Scripture Lesson
(MARK 4:21–41)

Prayer

O THOU infinitely glorious and merciful Lord God! thou art worthy to receive glory, honor, and power from all thy creatures, for thou hast created all things, and for thy pleasure they are and were created. Help us, we beseech thee, to close this day with that self-abasement and humiliation of soul at thy footstool which becomes us as sinful creatures.

We confess that we are sinners both by nature and by practice. We have erred and strayed from thy ways like lost sheep, and have preferred the vanities and follies of this transitory world to thy favor. Yea, even since the blessings of salvation, through our crucified Redeemer, have been set before us, how often have we given way to an evil heart of unbelief! how often have we abused the mercy which we still implore, and forsaken the fountain of living waters, in order to seek happiness from the broken cisterns of earthly enjoyments and possessions!

Surely it is of thy mercies that we are not consumed, and because thy compassions fail not! Thou dost magnify the freeness and fullness of thy grace, by never despising the contrite sighs, nor rejecting the humble petitions, of those who call upon thee through the merits of thy dear Son. O Lord God, for his sake we again implore thy pardoning grace. Wash away our guilt in the fountain that is opened in his precious blood. Cover us with the robe of his justifying righteousness, and sanctify us by the purifying influences of his Holy Spirit; so that, being washed, and justified, and sanctified in the name of the Lord Jesus, and by the Spirit of our God, we may have comfortable evidence that thou hast adopted us into thy family, and bestowed upon us the glorious privileges of thy children.

Gracious God! we have, from sad experience, great cause to lament our departure from thee, and our insufficiency to help ourselves. We need thy support and thy guidance in all time of our wealth and prosperity, as well as in every hour of sorrow and temptation. Leave us not to follow the devices and desires of our own deceitful hearts. Quicken our souls, which cleave to the dust. Renew them after thine own image. And may thy glory be our great object, aim, and end.

Into thy hands, O Lord, our heavenly Father, we commend ourselves, and all that belongs to us, this night. Thou art the keeper of Israel, who neither slumberest nor sleepest. May we lay ourselves down in peace and take our rest, remembering that it is thou alone who makest us to dwell in safety. And should we be in mercy permitted to see another day, may we be thankful for thy continued goodness to us, and may we grow in grace and in knowledge through our Lord and Savior Jesus Christ. *Amen.*

TUESDAY MORNING

Scripture Lesson
(PROVERBS 11)

Prayer

MOST holy, blessed, and glorious Lord God! in whom we live, and move, and have our being: enable us to approach thee with unfeigned humility and contrition of heart, pleading the atoning sacrifice of the Lord Jesus Christ, which alone can speak mercy, pardon, and peace to our guilty souls.

O Lord, thou knowest our wants and our miseries. Show us thy mercy and grant us thy salvation. Turn thou us, and so shall we be turned. Exhibit before us the grace and the glory which are in the Lord Jesus Christ, and which are communicated through him to all that believe on his name. Oh grant that, confiding in him as the Lord our Righteousness, we may find real peace and joy of soul, even that joy which is unspeakable and full of glory.

And as by the sacrifice of thy beloved Son on the cross thou hast manifested thine utter hatred of sin, and thy love of holiness, help us to abhor that which is evil, and to cleave to that which is good. Subdue every rebellious thought that exists within us. Mortify in us every sinful inclination. Shed abroad in our hearts the love of Christ by thy Holy Spirit, and clothe us with the spirit of humility, love, and self-denial. Suffer us not, O Lord, to set our affections inordinately upon any created good. May we always recollect that every earthly enjoyment is transitory and unsatisfying,—that this is not our place of rest,—and that we are seeking a city which is eternal in the heavens, whose builder and maker is God; and, having our hope fixed on the Lord Jesus Christ, may we purify ourselves even as he is pure.

O God of the spirits of all flesh, hear our prayers in behalf of all sorts and conditions of men, from our chief magistrate to the poorest and humblest citizen. Endue him whom thy providence hath set over us as our President, with the grace of thy Holy Spirit, that he may always incline to thy will, and walk in thy way. Instruct all our governors, senators, and legislative representatives, and direct their measures to the advancement of thy glory and the promotion of true religion in the world. Take under thy fatherly care all who are afflicted in mind, body, or estate. Speak peace to their souls, and lead them to the consideration of those things that belong to their everlasting peace.

O thou great Head of the Church, enlarge the borders of thy kingdom in this world. Make thy ways known upon earth, thy saving health among all nations. Be gracious to thy people Israel. Cause them to look unto him whom their fathers have pierced, and to mourn with godly sorrow. Hasten the time when heathen abominations shall cease, and when the fullness of the gentiles shall be brought in. Vouchsafe thy special blessing to that part of the Church of Christ which has been planted in this country. Water it with the dew of thy heavenly grace, that those who bear thy name may not be unfruitful in the knowledge of our Lord and Savior Jesus Christ. Enable thy people to walk in wisdom and prudence towards them that are without, and to be kindly affectioned one to another.

But while we are imploring these blessings upon the church at large, O Lord, let none of us deceive ourselves. Enable us sincerely to examine ourselves, whether we be in the faith, and whether our faith worketh by love to thee and all mankind, and overcometh the world. Let thy Holy Spirit establish us in the faith and love of thy name, and carry on the work of grace in our souls. May we thus be living members of the Church militant on earth, and be trained up for the Church triumphant in heaven.

(Occasional Prayers.)

Hear these our prayers and supplications, for thy mercy's sake; and enable us to begin on earth our eternal song, by ascribing blessing, and honor, and glory, and power, unto him that sitteth upon the throne, and unto the Lamb, forever and ever. *Amen.*

TUESDAY EVENING

Scripture Lesson
(MARK 9:1–29)

Prayer

O THOU incomprehensible Lord God! in whose sight all things are naked and open; let not any of us approach thee with our lips, or in form only, while our hearts are estranged from thy grace and love; but enable us, under a deep conviction of our own guilt and helplessness, to draw nigh unto thee in faith and hope, pleading the meritorious name and perfect righteousness of Jesus Christ our Lord, who ever liveth to make intercession for us.

Without this way of access into thy presence, we could not presume to lift up our eyes unto thee. But, gracious God, encouraged by the revelation of thy mercy in Christ, we desire now to humble ourselves at thy footstool with contrition and self-abasement, and to take shelter in Him, acknowledging that there is salvation in no other.

O thou Holy Spirit, whose office it is to glorify the Lord Jesus, by taking the things which are his and revealing them to the hearts of thy people; help us not only to discern his personal glory, and to confess before men that he is our Lord and our God; but likewise to know his mediatorial fullness; that he was made sin for us, that we might be made the righteousness of God in him. Enable us to make him the sole object of our faith and hope,—of our love and joy, yielding ourselves to the guidance of his word and providence. May he be the first object of our thoughts in the morning, and the last at night; that so by looking unto Jesus from day to day, and by walking in his footsteps, we may be changed into the same image, from glory to glory, as by the Spirit of the Lord.

Blessed be thy name, O God, for the rich treasures of thy word, and for the exceeding great and precious promises with which it abounds. Enable us to believe them, and to wait with patience for their accomplishment through Christ Jesus, in whom they are all Yea and Amen. And, O God the Spirit, by whose divine inspiration the holy Scriptures were written, teach us to know thy mind therein, and to have a right judgment of every part of thy blessed word. Gladden our hearts with a full discovery of the grace which it reveals; and grant that we may daily become more obedient to its sacred precepts,—more humble, more heavenly-minded, more self-denying; till in heart and life we are altogether conformed to thy holy mind and will.

Look down, O Lord, in mercy upon thy whole church. Carry on the work of thy grace among the children of men. Let there be added daily to thy church such as shall be saved. Send forth the glad tidings of great joy to heathen and Mohammedan lands. Regard in mercy thine own ancient people Israel. And hasten the time when the wilderness shall be turned into the garden of the Lord, and when all flesh shall see the salvation of our God.

(Occasional Prayers.)

And now, O heavenly Father, while we bless thee for all the mercies of the past day, we beseech thee to renew thy mercies to us, and to spread thy protecting wing over us during the dark and silent hours of the night. And should it please thee to raise us up in health and safety to see the light of another day, lift up also the light of thy countenance upon us; that we may walk before the Lord in the light of the living. Hear these our imperfect petitions, which we offer through the prevailing merits of Jesus Christ our Redeemer. *Amen.*

WEDNESDAY MORNING

Scripture Lesson
(ISAIAH 64)

Prayer

O LORD GOD Almighty, who art, and wast, and art to come! thy name is most holy, and thy glory reacheth above the heavens. We adore thee, that through thy beloved Son thou hast opened the way to the throne of grace, and hast declared thyself to be rich in mercy to all that call upon thee. We rejoice that thou hast proclaimed thyself the Lord God, merciful and gracious, long-suffering and abundant in goodness and truth, keeping mercy for thousands, forgiving iniquity, and transgression and sin, and that will by no means clear the guilty. O Lord! what is man, that thou art mindful of him? and the son of man, that thou visitest him?

Great and glorious God, we are individually and unitedly bound to give thee our fervent thanks, because thy hands have made us, thy power preserves us, and thou givest us all things richly to enjoy. It is of thy goodness that we have not spent a wearisome night, full of tossings to and fro until the dawning of the day; yea, it is because thou hast sustained us, that we have not slept the sleep of death. We adore thee that in times of danger thou hast been our shield and our defense against the multiplied evils and calamities in which many others have been involved. But in an especial manner we adore thee for thine unspeakable mercy and everlasting love, displayed in sending thy beloved Son to be the propitiation for our sins; and that thou hast made peace through the blood of his cross, by him to reconcile sinners unto thyself.

Merciful Father, make us sensible that we are not worthy of the least of all thy mercies, and grateful that thy loving-kindness is ever more and more towards us. Help us to own thy providence in all our concerns, and to bless the hand that overrules to our good all the afflictions and trials of this mortal life. And may we trace up all our streams of earthly and spiritual comfort to the fountain of eternal love in Christ Jesus.

O thou Holy Spirit, whose office it is to take of the things of Christ and show them with power to our souls, discover to us more and more of the all-sufficiency of the Lord Jesus, and of the endearing offices and relations which he sustains towards his people. May we know him as our life and peace, our wisdom and righteousness, our sanctification and redemption, our refuge, and the rock of our strength.

Blessed Lord, put thy fear into our hearts. Give us an understanding to know thy will in all things, and grace to perform the same. Enable us to gain the victory over our besetting sins. Wean our affections from the things of time and sense. Put the world, the flesh, and the devil, under our feet. And enable us to glorify thee with our bodies, our souls, and our spirits, which are thine.

We now make our supplications unto thee, O Lord, in behalf of our relations and friends. May they all be dear to thee. Have mercy on those who are ignorant of themselves and of thee; who neither see nor feel the guilt and corruption of their nature, and are therefore unhumbled before thee, and alienated from thee. Enlighten their dark minds by thy word and Spirit, and make them wise unto salvation through faith in Jesus Christ. Be gracious, also, to those who have received a good hope through thy grace. Establish their faith, animate their hope, increase their love, and fix their affections where true joys are to be found. And while the door of mercy is yet open, cause sinners of every description to flee to him who delivereth from the wrath to come. O Lord, let the word of thy truth have free course and be glorified; let the borders of thy church be enlarged; and let every tongue, and kindred, and people, unite in praising the God of their salvation.

Hear us, O heavenly Father, for the sake of him who hath loved and redeemed us, even the Lord our righteousness; to whom, with thee, and the Holy Spirit, our Guide and Comforter, be ascribed the kingdom, the power, and the glory, both now and for evermore. *Amen.*

WEDNESDAY EVENING

Scripture Lesson
(JOHN 6:1–40)

Prayer

O BLESSED God! who lookest down with compassion and tender mercy on sinners who prostrate themselves before the footstool of thy grace, in the name of Jesus Christ our Savior, dispose us to direct our prayer unto thee, and to look up for thy blessing.

Praised be thy name for all the dispensations of thy providence towards us, and for the suitable provision which thou makest, day after day, for the supply of all our temporal wants. But above all, praised be thy name that, though we are guilty and miserable creatures, thou hast not shut us up in despair; but hast sent to us that glorious gospel in which thou hast brought life and immortality to light, and hast encouraged us to enter into thine immediate presence by the blood of Jesus, by a new and living way which he has consecrated for us, through the rent vail of his crucified body.

We come before thee, pleading his merits and righteousness for our acceptance at the throne of grace; and we pray that the life which we now live in the flesh may be by the faith of the Son of God, who loved us and gave himself for us. May we be conformed to his divine image; and as he who hath called us is holy, so may we be holy in all manner of conversation. Create in us clean hearts, O God; and give to each of us the ornament of a meek and quiet spirit, which in thy sight is of great price. Deliver us from the love of this present evil world, and make us ever to remember the awful declaration, that "if any man love the world, the love of the Father is not in him." Cast down every high imagination within us that exalteth itself against the knowledge of God, and bring into captivity every thought to the obedience of Christ. May we prove to all around us that we are the followers of the Lamb; that we have partaken of his Spirit; and that the genuine fruits of it are manifested in our tempers, our actions, and our whole conversation.

Enable us, O our God, in whatsoever state we are placed, therewith to be content. In every trouble cause us to look to him who for our sakes became poor, that we, through his poverty, might be rich. And in every condition of life, keep us looking unto Jesus, our compassionate High-Priest, who is ever touched with a feeling of the infirmities of his people, and will not suffer them to be tempted above what they are able to bear.

Gracious God, we bless thee for the mercies of the day past. How many comforts and advantages do we enjoy which are denied to others! Not only have we health, and strength, and all things needful for the support of our bodies, but thou dost exercise the tenderest forbearance towards us, in still sparing us, and setting before us the rich blessings of thy grace. O Lord, what shall we render unto thee for all thy benefits to us? We will rejoice in thy salvation, and call upon the name of the Lord.

We commend to thy merciful protection our bodies and souls this night. Sleeping or waking, living or dying, we would be thine. Lord, keep us, and all who are near and dear to us, from every danger, and surround us by thy power, that no evil may happen to us. Impart all those blessings which we have been asking for ourselves, to our friends and relations also; and may they and we receive, from time to time, all needful direction, strength, and consolation, out of the fullness of that grace which is treasured up in Christ Jesus, in whose name and words we sum up all our petitions. Our Father, &c. *Amen.*

THURSDAY MORNING

Scripture Lesson
(PROVERBS 3)

Prayer

O THOU eternal and unchangeable Jehovah! who dwellest in light which no mortal eye can behold, and dost from thy sanctuary look down on the things that are in heaven and earth: we adore thee that thou hast, in the riches of thy grace, opened a new and living way whereby sinners may draw nigh to thee, and find thee to be a just God and yet a Savior, able and willing to save to the uttermost all who come unto thee through thine Incarnate Son.

O Lord, our heavenly Father, we mourn over and bewail at thy footstool the sins which we from time to time have most grievously committed, by thought, word, and deed, against thy Divine Majesty.

But unto thee, O Lord, belong mercies and forgivenesses, though we have sinned and rebelled against thee. We bless thee that the blood of Jesus Christ cleanseth from all sin; that he has made reconciliation for iniquity, and has brought in everlasting righteousness. O thou Lamb of God, who takest away the sin of the world, cleanse us from our sins in thy most precious blood. O Lord God of our salvation, clothe us with the spotless robe of thy righteousness; that being pardoned, and justified, and accepted, through thy merits and mediation, we may have joy and peace in believing.

And do thou, O Holy and Eternal Spirit, enable us, by our life and conversation, to adorn the doctrine of God our Savior in all things. May we prove to those around us that we are the children of light; that we are sitting for instruction at the feet of the Lord Jesus; that we have received his precepts, are influenced by his grace, are following his example, and are pressing forward to his kingdom. Suffer us not to place our security in an arm of flesh; but teach us ever to look for help where alone it is to be found—in the Lord Jesus Christ. Grant that, being united to him by a living faith, we may obtain victory over the corruptions of our hearts, the temptations of Satan, and the sinful cares and allurements of the world.

Into thy hands we commend ourselves, and all that belongs to us, this day. We are short-sighted creatures, and know not what a day may bring forth. Keep us under the shelter of thine Almighty wings. Guide and direct us continually by thy counsel, until thou hast brought us to thy glory.

O Lord, we thank thee for thy protection during the night-season; and for the multiplied favors, both of providence and grace, which thy bounty continually heaps upon us. But, above all, we praise thee for the gift of thy Son; for the word of thy gospel; for the promise of thy Spirit; for the means of grace, and for the hope of glory. O Lord, help us to show forth our gratitude, not merely with our lips, but in our lives, by giving up ourselves to thy service, and by bringing forth the fruits of righteousness and holiness, which are by Jesus Christ, to the praise of the glory of thy name.

Hear us, O Heavenly Father, and whilst thou hearest, have mercy upon us. Pardon the iniquity of our holy offerings, and accept us in Christ our Righteousness.

Now to God the Father, God the Son, and God the Holy Ghost, the glorious, unchangeable, and eternal Jehovah, be ascribed by us on earth, as by angels and glorified saints in heaven, everlasting praise. *Amen.*

THURSDAY EVENING

Scripture Lesson
(MARK 10:1–27)

Prayer

O BLESSED Lord! thou art slow to anger, abundant in goodness and truth, and thy mercy endureth forever: enable us, by thy Holy Spirit, to draw nigh to thy mercy-seat with humility and reverence, through Jesus Christ our Mediator.

Great God, thou art the eternal Jehovah, who art of purer eyes than to look upon iniquity; whereas we are sinful dust and ashes. If thou shouldest enter into judgment with us, either for our thoughts, our words, or our actions, we could not answer thee, but must lay our hands upon our mouths, and cry out, "Woe unto us, for we are undone; because we are men of unclean lips, and we dwell in the midst of a people of unclean lips."

But thou art God, and not man; thou changest not, therefore are we not consumed. Great as our sins and provocations have been, greater, far greater is thy mercy in Christ Jesus. Thou art a reconciled Father and Friend to the very chief of sinners that come unto thee with faith in his name, who has satisfied the righteous demands of thy justice, and has died to redeem us to God by his blood.

Merciful Lord, remove from us all ignorance, hardness of heart, and unbelief of the truth as it is in Jesus. Enlighten our understandings, and influence our hearts, that we may behold and admire the freeness and the perfection of his great salvation. Clothe us in the garments of the Redeemer's righteousness; and enable us, with thine adopted children, to call thee our Father and our God. And grant that a constraining view of his boundless love, and of the invaluable price that has purchased our salvation, may cause us to surrender our hearts, our souls, our bodies, our all, to the service of the Lord. May it be seen that we are Christians, not only in name, but in reality; that we have not only the form of godliness, but its power also; and that we have not only received the doctrines, but are endeavoring to follow in the footsteps of the blessed Jesus. Enable us to carry religion into every relation of life; that wherever our sphere of duty extends, we may adorn the doctrine of God our Savior in all things.

O God of the spirits of all flesh, we supplicate thy mercy in behalf of all mankind. Be graciously pleased to bless and preserve the President whom thy providence has set over us. Grant to him, and to all who are put in authority over us, grace, to rule with wisdom and justice, and to set an example of godliness and virtue to thy people. Look down in mercy upon the whole state of thy holy church militant on earth. May the standard of the cross be erected in all lands, and may all nations and tongues flow unto it. May sinners everywhere lay down the arms of their rebellion, and become good soldiers of Christ Jesus; and may all who name the name of Christ depart from iniquity. Oh let there be a genuine revival of religion in this place. May thy ministering servant amongst us be greatly blessed as an ambassador of Christ. Touch his heart as with a live coal from off thine altar, and and enable him to dispense the oracles of God with faithfulness and success. And may many persons who are now dead in trespasses and sins, be quickened and made spiritually alive, and be among those who shall finally be saved. Heal the divisions of thy people; kindle within them a lively zeal for thy glory; and grant that they may unite with one heart, as well as in one faith, to hasten the kingdom of our blessed Redeemer.

(Occasional Prayers.)

Almighty God, into thy protecting arms we commit ourselves, and all that we have, this night. Grant us quiet and refreshing repose, and let no harm come nigh our dwelling. Oh may our sleep remind us of the last sleep of death, and our beds of the awful bed of the grave, to which we are hastening. May we be always ready, since we know not the day nor the hour in which the Son of Man cometh. O Lord, may we be taught by the Holy Spirit to know the things that belong to our everlasting peace, that when the hour of death arrives, we may, with a firm confidence in thy promises, fall asleep in Jesus.

Hear us, gracious Father, for the sake of thy beloved Son Jesus Christ; whom, with thee and the eternal Spirit, we adore as the God of our salvation, both now and for evermore. *Amen.*

FRIDAY MORNING

Scripture Lesson
(ISAIAH 51:1–16)

Prayer

MOST blessed Lord! thou hast declared in thy holy word that where two or three are gathered together in thy name, there thou art in the midst of them. We plead this promise, and beseech thee to prepare our hearts by thy Holy Spirit to worship at thy footstool.

We presume not to come before thee, O Lord, trusting in our own strength or righteousness. We are full of weakness and sin; our hearts are prone to evil, and our very best actions are stained with imperfection. But, merciful God! guilty, weak, and helpless as we are, it is our comfort, that with thee there is plenteous redemption, and that thine arms are widely extended to receive every returning penitent who seeks for mercy in thine appointed way. May a view of the Cross fill our souls with hope and consolation; and may we count all things but loss for the excellency of the knowledge of Christ Jesus our Lord. May we, beholding by faith the sufferings of the Lamb of God, mourn over and abhor those sins which pierced him; and, reflecting upon his amazing love in dying for the guilty, may we love him in sincerity, and be enabled with truth to say, as thy penitent Apostle did, "Lord, thou knowest all things, thou knowest that we love thee!" May we be conformed to the image of our Redeemer in all things; in his purity and self-denial, his meekness and humility, his love to man, and his submission to thy will. O Lord, thou alone canst give us ability for these things; let thy strength be made perfect in our weakness; and, being upheld by thy Spirit, may we glorify thy holy name in all our life and conversation.

O Father of mercies, we have abundant cause to praise thee for the many temporal as well as spiritual blessings which we enjoy. In thee we live, and move, and have our being. Thou hast brought us through unseen dangers, and preserved us to this day under the shadow of thine Almighty wings. And while some of our fellow-creatures are languishing on the bed of sickness, and afflicted with pain and want, we enjoy health, and ease, and plenty:—While others are breathing their last, perhaps in the depths of despair, or in fatal ignorance of thy blessed gospel, we are the monuments of thy forbearing mercy, and thou dost continue to bless us with spiritual blessings in Christ Jesus. O Lord, what shall we render unto thee for all thy benefits? Enable us to show forth our gratitude to thee, by bringing forth the fruits of righteousness, which are by Jesus Christ, to the praise and glory of thy grace.

O Lord, prepare us by every dispensation of thy providence, and by thy heavenly grace, for that awful day when we must all stand before the judgment-seat of Christ. Enable us to realize the scene when the heavens shall be dissolved, and the elements shall melt with fervent heat, and when the secrets of all hearts shall be revealed; and seeing that these things will assuredly come to pass, let us consider what manner of persons we ought to be, in all holy conversation and godliness! May we give diligence to make our calling and election sure; and may our conversation be in heaven, from whence also we look for the Savior, the Lord Jesus Christ; who shall change our vile body, that it may be fashioned like unto his glorious body, according to the working whereby he is able to subdue all things unto himself.

Hear us, O Lord God of our salvation, and do for us above all that we can ask or think, for Christ's sake. *Amen.*

FRIDAY EVENING

Scripture Lesson
(MARK 10:28–52)

Prayer

O THOU God of all grace and mercy! enable us, through Christ our Redeemer, to draw nigh unto thy mercy-seat with humble hope and filial confidence; that we may obtain the supply of all our wants out of that infinite fullness of grace which is treasured up in him.

O Almighty God, who resisteth the proud, but givest grace to the humble, we beseech thee to humble us in our own sight. Strip us of every thought that would exalt itself against thy rich and sovereign grace. Discover to us our utter helplessness, and our innumerable acts of rebellion against thee. Oh let us never try to dissemble or palliate our guilt; but do thou bow down our hearts in the deepest self-abasement; that we may with true humility, and not with feigned lips, confess, "against thee, thee only, have we sinned, and done evil in thy sight. Have mercy upon us, O God, according to thy loving-kindness; and, according to the multitude of thy tender mercies, blot out our transgressions."

Most gracious God, we adore thee, that though we are cut off from all hope of acceptance with thee on account of anything we have done or ever can do, yet that thou wast in Christ reconciling the world unto thyself, not imputing unto mankind their trespasses. Therefore, on the Crucified Jesus—that tried corner-stone—that sure foundation laid in Sion—we build all our hopes of acceptance with thee; for he is our merciful High-Priest, who has presented the perfect sacrifice of himself upon the altar of the cross; he is our all-sufficient Advocate, who perpetually appears before thy throne on high, to make intercession for us; he is the propitiation for our sins, and his blood speaketh mercy, pardon, and peace to the believing soul. O Lord, let a sense of thine unspeakable love be shed abroad in our hearts by the Holy Ghost; let it call forth our gratitude and praise to thee; and may it constrain us to employ our time and talents in thy service and to thy glory.

Enable us to exercise unfeigned love to the brethren, and forbearance and patience under injuries towards all. Set before us continually the example of the meek and lowly Jesus; who was holy, harmless, undefiled, and separate from sinners. May it be our constant endeavor to walk even as he walked; and thus may we go on from strength to strength, till, with all the ransomed of the Lord, we at length appear before our God in the heavenly Sion.

And now, gracious Father, we commend to thy mercy all who are united to us by the ties of kindred or friendship. Be favorable to them; protect them from all evil, surround them with the mercies of thy providence; and enrich them with the blessings of thy covenant love in Christ Jesus. Look on the face of thine Anointed, and for his sake visit them with thy salvation; and, O God, in tender compassion stretch out thine arm to save those whom thou knowest to be under the power of their spiritual enemies. Lead them into the way of peace; and enable them to fly for refuge to the Savior of sinners, that they may obtain pardoning mercy through him. We pray thee to diffuse the light of thy glorious gospel among the children of men throughout the whole world. O Lord, hasten the time when all shall know thee, from the least even to the greatest: when the kingdoms of this world shall become the kingdoms of our Lord and of his Christ, and when thou, O Jehovah, shalt reign as the Most High over all the earth.

Take us under thy protection this night. Refresh our wearied bodies with comfortable sleep; and if thou permitest us to see the light of another day, may we rise in the morning with grateful hearts for thy goodness to us; and may we live day by day to the glory of thy name. We ask all for the sake of him who is God over all, blessed for evermore. *Amen.*

SATURDAY MORNING

Scripture Lesson
(ROMANS 4)

Prayer

O EVER-BLESSED God! we draw near to thy mercy-seat this morning in prayer and supplication, with thanksgiving. We beseech thee to pour down thy Holy Spirit upon us, and to behold us in thy beloved Son; that we may approach thy throne of grace with humble confidence in his merits, and may obtain mercy for the past, and grace to help us in this and every future time of need.

Heavenly Father! it becomes us to draw near to thee with the deepest self-abasement and contrition of heart; for, alas! how often have we broken thy precepts, in thought, word, and deed; how often have we abused our privileges; yea, how often have we requited thy richest favors with the basest ingratitude! Surely the whole head is sick, and the whole heart faint. But thou art long-suffering and plenteous in goodness, and thy mercy is very great. We beseech thee, O Lord our God, for the sake of thy Beloved Son, not to remember against us our sins and our iniquities; but to write thy laws on our hearts, and to enable us to walk worthy of the high vocation wherewith we are called. Conscious of our own weakness, we come to thee for grace and strength; that we may obtain the victory over our corruptions, and may withstand the various temptations, and bear up under the many trials, to which we are exposed. If thou be for us, who can be against us? Oh strengthen us with might by thy Spirit in the inner man. Mortify all our evil desires and inclinations. Weaken our attachment to the perishing enjoyments of this world. Set our affections on things above. Endue us with humility; and in every state wherein we may be placed, teach us therewith to be content.

Take under thy protection and guidance those for whom we are in duty bound to pray. If any among them are weak in faith, do thou strengthen and settle them; if any are afflicted and poor, do thou comfort and enrich them with the unsearchable riches of Christ; if any are at a distance from thee, or halting between two opinions, bring them nigh through the blood of the Cross, and enable them to choose that good part which shall never be taken away from them. And, O Lord, add daily to thy church such as shall be saved. Send thy gospel to the dark places of the earth. Clothe it with power; and hasten the time when Jews and Gentiles shall be gathered into one fold, under one Shepherd, Jesus Christ the Lord.

And now, blessed Lord, we would not rise from our knees without offering to thee our tribute of praise for all thy mercies and loving-kindness to us. If our houses have been filled with plenty, and our lives preserved in time of danger, surely it is thy goodness that holdeth up our souls in life, and suffereth not our feet to slip. If we know the truth as it is in Jesus, and have found acceptance in the Beloved; if we have been enabled to renounce the world, the flesh, and the devil, it is thy Almighty grace which has obtained for us the victory. Bless the Lord, O our souls, and all that is within us bless his holy Name. Bless the Lord, O our souls, and forget not all his benefits.

Vouchsafe to us, we pray thee, a continuance of thy mercies. Carry on the good work which we trust thou hast begun in our hearts, until the day of the Lord Jesus. Then may we appear arrayed in white robes, even in the garments of our Redeemer's righteousness, and find an abundant entrance into thy heavenly kingdom. Now unto him that is able to do exceeding abundantly above all that we can ask or think, according to the power that worketh in us; unto him be glory in the church by Christ Jesus, world without end. *Amen.*

SATURDAY EVENING

Scripture Lesson
(MARK 7:14–37)

Prayer

O ALMIGHTY God! who art exalted far above the praises even of the heavenly hosts; how great is thy mercy in opening a way for lost sinners to approach thee, and to spread their wants before thy footstool!

Great God! we might justly have been left under thy wrath for our ingratitude and rebellion, having no way to escape, had not thine own arm brought salvation. Thou hast sent thine Incarnate Son to seek and to save the guilty, and hast revealed thyself in him as a just God, and yet the Savior of sinners. O Lord, save us, we beseech thee. We fall as guilty sinners at the footstool of thy mercy, loathing ourselves in our own sight on account of our iniquities. We renounce all dependence on any merits of our own, for in us dwelleth no good thing. We plead thy promises, and offer before thee no other sacrifice or righteousness but the all-sufficient sacrifice and spotless righteousness of thy beloved Son, in whom thou art ever well-pleased. May we come unto thee, as children unto a father who is able and ready to assist them. Indict our petitions for us, and enable us to present them before thee in true faith.

O thou Holy Spirit! who dost convince the world of sin, and of righteousness, and of judgment; discover to us the pride of our nature, and the alienation of our hearts from God. Cause us to renounce our own wisdom and righteousness, and to be willing to receive pardon, and the hope of eternal life, as the gift of free unmerited mercy, through Jesus Christ our Lord. Create in us clean hearts, O God; and renew right spirits within us. Subdue our corrupt desires, and set our affections on heavenly things.

We have often erred and strayed from thy fold; yet now again we return unto thee, hungry and thirsty, weak and defenseless, diseased and perishing. Oh may we hear thy voice and follow thee; may we feed on thy precious promises; may we drink of the waters of life; may we be supported by thy grace, and enjoy thy favor. And if thou, O Lord, seest it necessary to visit us with diseases, disappointments, or crosses of any kind, give us resignation and submission to thy blessed will. Enable us to examine ourselves whether we be in the faith; and may we know that all things work together for good to them who love thy name, to them who are the called according to thy purpose.

Bless our dearly-cherished American republic. We thank thee for all our civil, religious, and literary privileges; and that thou hast given us a good land, and crowned it with many blessings. Thou hast not dealt so with any other nation. May our country continue to be under thy care and watchful providence. May we be a holy, that we may be a happy people.

(Occasional Prayers.)

With humble and heartfelt thanks for the mercies of the day and week that is past, we implore thy gracious protection during the dark and silent watches of the night. O thou keeper of Israel, who never slumberest nor sleepest, be thou about our path and about our bed. Defend us from all dangers; refresh our wearied bodies with sleep; and if it should please thee to raise us up to behold the light of the returning sun, let us arise with thankful hearts, remembering that the day is the Sabbath of the Lord. Be with all thy ministering servants on the morrow, and especially with him who ministers unto us thy holy word. May they go forth in the fullness of the blessing of the gospel of peace, preaching peace through the blood of the cross; and may the word of thy grace be as the rain that watereth the earth, and maketh it to bring forth and bud; may it accomplish thy good pleasure, and prosper in the thing whereto thou shalt send it. All these things we ask for the sake and through the intercession of our Lord and Savior Jesus Christ; to whom, in the unity of the Father and the Holy Spirit, be ascribed all honor and glory, now and for evermore. *Amen.*

EIGHTH WEEK

LORDSDAY MORNING

Scripture Lesson
(PSALMS 28 AND 29)

Prayer

O BLESSED Lord, who art the God of our salvation, and who daily loadest us with thy benefits, we again draw nigh unto thee in the name of Jesus Christ, our Mediator and Redeemer. We thank thee for thy merciful care over us through the night past, and for thy preservation of us to the return of another Sabbath-day. We thank thee, O Father of mercies, that thou hast fixed our habitation in a country where the light of the glorious gospel shineth, where thy Sabbaths are observed, and thine ordinances kept; and where, without interruption, we may hear thy word, and worship thee with prayer and praise in the assemblies of thy people.

But, O God, the remembrance of these great mercies, while it calls forth our thankfulness to thee, should fill our hearts with shame and sorrow for our unprofitableness under them. We confess that we have awfully neglected thy command,—"Remember the Sabbath-day to keep it holy." Instead of considering thy service as our highest privilege and glory, our hearts have been too full of the world and of sin, to seek after communion with thee and with our Lord Jesus Christ. Instead of treasuring up thy word in our minds, that it might be the power of God unto our salvation, we have been impenitent and unbelieving; we have disregarded its doctrines; we have disobeyed its precepts; we have lightly regarded its precious promises.

But we now again implore thy pardoning mercy for the sake of thy beloved Son, who is the Lord our peace and our righteousness. Oh look upon us in the face of thy beloved Son; and forgive us all our past iniquities, and our neglect of thy Sabbaths, thy worship, and thy word. And, O gracious God, let thy peace and love shine from henceforth upon our hearts; and let the remembrance of our past neglect make us the more earnest to improve this and every future opportunity, for the benefit of our souls and for the glory of thy name.

O Lord God, forasmuch as without thee we are not able to please thee, mercifully grant that thy Holy Spirit may in all things direct and rule our hearts. May his quickening power raise our thoughts and desires to thee in every part of thy holy worship; and may he testify of Christ to us, and comfort us with a view of the fullness of his grace and of his salvation.

When we enter thy house of prayer to-day, may we realize thy gracious promise, that "where two or three are met together in thy name, there thou art in the midst of them." From the beginning to the conclusion of the services of thy sanctuary, may we feel thy presence with us, and may all the means of grace be blest to our souls. When we confess our sins, may we be humbled with a deep sense of our unworthiness, and deeply feel our need of thy pardoning mercy. When we offer up our thanksgivings to thee, or sing thy praises, may we pour forth our whole soul before thee in a lively remembrance of all thy mercies. When we present our intercessions to thee for our Church, our President, and our country, and for all who are afflicted or distressed, may we be actuated by a fervent desire that thou wouldst appear on their behalf. When we hear thy word read or preached, may thy Holy Spirit open our hearts to understand the Scriptures. And may we not be forgetful hearers, but doers of thy word. May it dwell in us richly in all wisdom, and may the fruits of it abound in us, in our hearts and lives, to thy praise and glory.

And now, O Lord, hear our prayers for thy universal Church—for all who in every place call upon the name of Jesus Christ our Lord, both theirs and ours. Show thy power and thy glory in the sanctuary. Let thy blessing rest upon all thy servants who are employed in making known to their fellow-sinners thy glorious gospel. May thy Holy Spirit so teach them that they may speak the things that become sound doctrine: and whilst they show unto men the way of salvation, do thou give success to the word of thy grace; and enable them to ascribe the excellency of the power unto thee. May sinners be converted from the error of their ways, and the penitent and believing be comforted and edified. Oh let not thy word return unto thee void this day, but let it prosper wheresoever thou shalt send it.

And we beseech thee, O Lord, let not the effectual preaching of the blessed gospel be confined to our own shores. Prosper every attempt to make known the way of salvation to the nations who sit in darkness and the shadow of death; and regard with compassion thine ancient people Israel, that they may look unto him whom their fathers have pierced, and mourn with godly sorrow. Oh let thy way be made known upon the earth, thy saving health among all nations. Let the people praise thee, O God, let all the people praise thee. And let the glorious day soon arrive when all flesh shall see thy salvation.

Hear and accept these our imperfect supplications, for thy dear Son's sake. *Amen.*

LORDSDAY EVENING

Scripture Lesson
(PSALM 31)

Prayer

MOST glorious and holy Lord God, who hast set thyself above the heavens and thy glory above all the earth, and yet art pleased in mercy to regard even sinners who call upon thee through thy beloved Son; we desire to exalt thy name, and to bless thee for thy continued mercies vouchsafed unto us. Help us, O Lord, to praise thee for the opportunities and privileges which we have enjoyed on this thy holy day; for the ordinances of thy house, the instructions of thy word, and the many spiritual mercies of a personal and family nature with which thou hast favored us.

Almighty Spirit of grace, open our eyes, that we may spiritually discern those things which belong to our peace; and open our hearts, that we may more fully believe the blessed truths of thy holy word. Oh may the word of Christ dwell in us richly, in all wisdom and spiritual understanding.

Gracious God, forgive whatever thy pure and all-seeing eyes have seen amiss in us this day. Deal not with us according to our deservings, but according to thy mercy in Christ Jesus. And though we have profited so inadequately by what we have heard and seen this day, though our prayers have been attended with frequent wanderings and distractions, and our hearts and affections have been full of coldness and formality—yet, we beseech thee, let the blessings which we have enjoyed on this thy holy day serve to increase our hungering and thirsting after righteousness. Cherish in us whatever holy desires thy word and ordinances may have produced in our minds, and make us to grow in grace and in the knowledge of our Lord and Savior.

Gracious Lord, enable us constantly to look at the things which are not seen, and which are eternal. In the enjoyment of those seasons of rest which thy Sabbaths on earth afford, and in all our intercourse with thee, may we contemplate in faith that everlasting Sabbath, that season of perpetual rest and peace, which remaineth for all thy people. In these memorials of our blessed Redeemer's resurrection, may we be filled with joyful anticipations of his second coming, and of the resurrection of his saints to a blessed immortality; when we shall no longer behold thee through ordinances, darkly, but face to face; when we shall see the blessed Jesus as he is, and unite in the song of the redeemed, "Worthy is the Lamb that was slain, to receive power, and riches, and wisdom, and strength, and honor, and glory, and blessing."

We now commend to thy mercy all our beloved friends and relations. We beseech thee to bless them not only outwardly in their bodies, but also inwardly in their souls. Let not the word of thy grace be a savor of death to any of them. Take from them all vain hopes, all hardness and unbelief of heart. Lead them in faith to the crucified Savior, and may they and we be enabled to rejoice in a well-founded hope of being the children of God, members of Christ, and inheritors of the kingdom of heaven.

Finally, wherever the glad tidings of mercy and salvation have been preached this day in simplicity and godly sincerity, there, O thou Holy Spirit, thou gracious Author of light and life, do thou grant thy blessing. Make it effectual to the enlargement of thy church, by the conversion of sinners; and to the comfort, and peace, and holiness of those who are already gathered into that church, and are training up for the church triumphant in heaven. O Lord, regard with thy special mercy our country; and though our iniquities testify against us, and we deserve thy wrath, yet in the midst of judgment remember mercy, and continue to us the blessed light of thy gospel, and the means of grace, and the ordinances of our holy religion. And may the Sun of righteousness arise upon the nations which are now in darkness and in the shadow of death, to guide their feet into the way of peace.

Take us under thy protection this night. May our sleep be refreshing. And if we are permitted to see another day, may we live as it becometh those who are washed, and justified, and sanctified in the name of the Lord Jesus, and by the Spirit of our God. Hear us, O Lord God; hear and answer these our imperfect supplications, for thy Name's sake. *Amen.*

SECOND MORNING

Scripture Lesson
(PSALM 38)

Prayer
For Conviction of Sin, and Humiliation before God.

O THOU great and glorious Lord God, unto whom all hearts are open, and before whom nothing that is unrighteous shall stand, impress us with a due sense of thy holiness and thy majesty. Enable us, by the influence of thy Holy Spirit, to commence this day with a solemn review of our guilt and helplessness, that our souls may be truly humbled, and that we may mourn over our sins with a godly sorrow.

O merciful God, thou hast assured us that thou hast no pleasure in the death of a sinner, but rather that he should turn from his evil ways, and live; and thou hast not spared thy beloved Son, but hast sent him to seek by his grace, and to save by his death, that which was lost. For his sake, be pleased to look in mercy upon us. Suffer us not to dissemble our sins before thee, nor to attempt to excuse our guilt or palliate our disobedience. But, oh thou who resistest the proud and givest grace to the humble, subdue that proud and self-righteous spirit within us which is ever ready to turn from the sight of our natural corruption, and cannot endure the charge that our minds are alienated from thee, and that we desire not the knowledge of thy ways.

O God the Holy Spirit, who alone canst show to them that are in error the light of truth, shine upon our souls; and as it is thy special office, in bringing souls to Christ, to convince them of sin, discover to each of us, we beseech thee, its defiling and destructive nature. Teach us that the evil of sin is manifest in the departure of the heart from thee, and in the proneness which we so often feel to rest in the creature and to find our satisfaction in earthly things; and that it is the transgression of thy holy law, and exposes our guilty souls to thy deserved displeasure and condemnation.

Oh may we be taught by thy grace to examine ourselves, and compare our thoughts, our desires, and our practices, with the righteous demands of thy pure and holy law. May we reflect on all our sins of omission, as well as those of commission, of heart as well as of life. May we be convinced of sin, and truly humbled on account of our unbelief, and pride, and impenitence of heart; on account of our worldliness of spirit, our neglect of the offers of mercy, and our disregard to the honor of thy name and the temporal and eternal happiness of our fellow-creatures. Oh may we remember with self-abasement the many evil passions which have gained the ascendency over us; the many over-anxious and worldly cares which we have indulged; our ingratitude and want of thankfulness for all the mercies we have received, while we deserved not the least of them; and our want of submission under thy chastisements, when we might justly have been cut down as cumberers of the ground. In these and other respects, surely, our own hearts condemn us; how much more then, thou who art greater than our hearts, and knowest all things. We are verily guilty before thee, and have incurred thy righteous displeasure. But turn thou us, merciful Lord, and so shall we be turned. Wound our hearts, that thou mayest afterwards heal them. Bruise them under thy rod and power, if thou wilt but at length condescend to bind them up.

Merciful God, may every fresh remembrance of our sin and misery not only affect our hearts with godly sorrow and true repentance, but may it cause us to apply to the all-sufficient remedy which thy gospel reveals for the comfort and salvation of the humbled and penitent soul. Oh may our mourning for sin, and our fervent longings of heart to be delivered from the love and dominion of it, be always accompanied by a lively faith in the Lamb of God, who taketh away the sin of the world; that, believing with the heart on him, we may make him the foundation of our hope, and enjoy in and through him all the blessings of pardon, peace, and glory. Lord, hear and mercifully answer us: remember not our sins and offenses, but, according to thy mercy, think thou upon us, for thy goodness' sake. We ask these blessings in the all-prevailing name and through the mediation of Jesus Christ, our Advocate and Intercessor. *Amen.*

SECOND EVENING

Scripture Lesson
(PSALM 102)
A Family Confession of Sin, and Prayer for Contrition and Repentance.

O LORD GOD, gracious and long-suffering, we desire with humiliation and sincere repentance to acknowledge thy tender forbearance and goodness towards us, and to mourn over our own unworthiness and ingratitude to thee.

Though we can plead no righteousness of our own, thou hast laid help upon one who is mighty to save, even on thine own dear Son, and hast graciously promised that in and through him thou wilt hear the sighings of the captive, and wilt not despise the broken and contrite heart. O merciful Father, look upon us in thy beloved Son, and behold us as suppliants at the throne of thy grace; hearken unto the voice of our cry, for unto thee do we look up.

We have sinned and done very wickedly, O Lord, in thought, word, and deed. We have sinned against the rebukes and warnings of our own consciences; against the spirit and letter of thy righteous laws; against the tender and merciful declarations and promises of thy blessed gospel; against the admonitions of thy Holy Spirit; against our own most solemn vows and resolutions.

We have sinned against thee, our God, against our neighbor, and against ourselves. Instead of esteeming thy service to be perfect freedom, and communion with thee our highest delight, we must with shame and confusion of face acknowledge that we have too often dared to set up our own will against thine, and, by our impenitence and unbelief, by our forgetfulness and contempt of thy word, we have too often manifested the natural enmity and ingratitude of our hearts to thee, our Benefactor and gracious Redeemer. Instead of fulfilling the duties which we owe to our neighbor with a tender regard to his happiness and best interests, we have been grievously defective both in motive and in action; we have been backward in showing love without dissimulation towards all men; and our attempts have been few and feeble to promote amongst our fellow-creatures the kingdom of God and his righteousness. And when we look to ourselves, we must indeed confess our shame, our sin and misery; we have all of us destroyed ourselves by fulfilling the lusts of the flesh and of the mind: our hearts have been full of pride, of self-indulgence, and of the love of the world.

But, O Lord, return and deliver our souls, save us for thy mercy's sake. Save us from the guilt and punishment, save us from the power and pollution, of all our sins. It is thy blessed work not only to accept, but also first to bestow, the broken and contrite spirit. Spare us, good Lord, spare thy people, whom thou hast redeemed with thy most precious blood, and be not angry with us forever. Magnify thy name in our deliverance. And cause it to be seen by thy work of grace upon our souls, that where sin hath abounded, thy grace can much more abound.

Let thy Holy Spirit impart to us true contrition for all our sins, and that genuine repentance which needeth not to be repented of. May every fresh view of our own sinfulness make the Savior more precious to our souls, and cause us to apply unceasingly to him who is alone able to heal the broken in heart, and to bind up all their wounds.

And oh may we be watchful over all our ways, and live continually to the glory of his name who hath loved us, and given himself for us.

We would now, most merciful Father, commend ourselves to thy care and protection: watch over us in thy providence, and give us peaceful and refreshing sleep; and if it please thee to spare us to see the light of another day, may we rise with renewed resolutions to dedicate ourselves unto thee.

Pour down upon our absent relatives and friends thy richest streams of mercy. Quicken in their hearts a lively sense of sin, and a due apprehension of their great and eternal concerns; and show thyself to them as a pardoning God in Christ Jesus, ready to forgive and willing to save. Oh may we be a family living under the saving influence of thy grace; and be thou our God and guide, our hope and help, our joy and portion, this night and for evermore. *Amen.*

THIRD MORNING

Scripture Lesson
(PSALM 143)

Prayer
For Pardoning Mercy.

O THOU high and lofty One, who inhabitest eternity, whose name is Holy, and who deignest to dwell with those who are of a contrite and humble spirit, to revive the spirit of the humble, and to revive the heart of the contrite ones; we desire to approach thy footstool with unfeigned repentance and godly sorrow for all our sins, praying for the fulfillment of thy gracious promise to our souls.

We adore thy grace, that though in ourselves as sinners we are hopeless and helpless, yet that thou hast revealed thyself in thy holy word as the Lord God, merciful and gracious, long-suffering, and abundant in goodness and truth. We bless thee, O Father of mercies, that to us has been sent the ministry of reconciliation, making known to us the glorious truth that God was in Christ reconciling the world unto himself, not imputing unto them their trespasses. Enable us with gratitude and joy to accept thy offered grace—to look to the Lamb of God that taketh away the sins of the world,—and to build all our hopes for time and for eternity upon the only sure foundation, Jesus Christ the Lord.

O blessed Savior, thou art the way, and the truth, and the life. Grant us to have a deep and lasting impression on our minds that no man can come unto the Father but by thee. Thou art full of grace and truth, the same as when thou didst say to the woman that was a sinner, and sought thy mercy, "Go in peace, thy sins are forgiven thee." May we rejoice in knowing that we need no advocacy with our heavenly Father but thine,—that thy all-prevailing merit is our only plea at the throne of mercy,—and that thy grace is sufficient for us, to deliver us from the dominion of Satan, and from the love of sin and of this present evil world; and to bring us into the enjoyment of all the blessings and privileges of the children of God.

And, O God the Holy Spirit, thou glorifier of Jesus and Comforter of the church of God, enlighten our minds in the knowledge of Christ. Make known to us the grace and the glory of the salvation effected by his obedience unto death; and may we have a deep and humbling sense of our need of all those blessings which his gospel reveals. May holiness to the Lord be inscribed upon all our conversation, whether in the church, in the family, or in the world,—that we may be, in our day and generation, a people fearing God and working righteousness.

And oh prepare us by thy grace for the heavenly world, and enable each of us, in joyful expectation of the glory of God, to say—"To me to live is Christ, and to die is gain."

We now desire to bless thee, O heavenly Father, for thy protection of us during the last night, and for the rest and refreshment which thou hast given us therein. We desire to bless thee for the mercies of the day, and for the health and safety and many comforts with which thou art continually following us; and we beseech thee to preserve in our minds such a grateful sense of thy loving-kindness towards us, that we may employ all our blessings according to thy will, and to thy glory.

Extend, we beseech thee, the blessings we have been imploring for ourselves, to our relations, our friends, and our neighbors. May Christ be formed in their souls, as the hope of glory; and put thy fear into their hearts, that they may faithfully serve thee in the present world, as a people redeemed from their vain conversation and made zealous of good works. Regard, O Lord, with thy special mercy, the land in which we dwell. Preserve us from public calamity; put an end to the rebellions of ungodly men; stop the progress of infidelity and apostasy; and let sinners of all descriptions be turned from the error of their ways. Bless the ministry of thy word; and let great grace accompany thy preached gospel. Have mercy on the afflicted in mind, body, or estate. And regard with peculiar favor the rising generation. Oh that our children and our children's children may early seek the Lord, and find that Christ's yoke is indeed easy, and his burden light. Finally, give peace in our days, O Lord. Overrule all changes in kingdoms and nations to the furtherance of thy blessed gospel and the establishment of thy kingdom over all the earth. Hear us in these our humble supplications, for the sake of Jesus Christ, our only Lord and Savior. *Amen.*

THIRD EVENING

Scripture Lesson
(JOHN 1:1–12, or COL. 1:1–19)

Prayer
Adoration of Christ.

O LORD Jesus Christ, enable us at this time to contemplate with adoration and thankfulness the revelation of thy glory and of thy grace. Regard us, we humbly beseech thee, for thine own name's sake, with the favor that thou bearest to thy people; and show us thy salvation. Endue us with thy Holy Spirit, the glorifier of thee; that we may have a right judgment and discernment of thine infinite love to our sinful souls, and be filled with joy and peace in believing.

We adore thee, O Lord, in thy revealed character as God over all, blessed forever. Thou art indeed exalted far above all blessing and praise; yet, help us with humility and sincerity to confess thee before men as "our Lord and our God," and to give thee thanks for thy great glory; for thou only art the Lord of heaven and earth, thou only, O Christ, with the Holy Ghost, art most high in the glory of God the Father.

We adore thee, O Lord Jesus, as the eternal Word, by whom all things were made, and without whom there was not anything made that was made; and we bless thee that in the fullness of time thou didst condescend to assume our nature, and to dwell among us and become Jesus, the Savior, that thou mightest save thy people from their sins. We bless thee that thou, who wast alone able to pay the price of human redemption, didst in thine infinite love redeem us to God by thy blood, and, by the willing sacrifice of thyself upon the cross, didst bear the sin of many, and become the propitiation for our sins. We bless thee that by thy holy and perfect obedience to the law for us, thou didst manifest thyself to be Jehovah our Righteousness; that those who were lost and ruined sinners in themselves might, by believing in thy name, be made righteous in the sight of the holy God. Oh let that holy oil, the grace of the Spirit, which was poured out without measure upon thee, the Head, run down upon all, even the meanest and weakest of thy members; that partaking of the unction of the Holy One, we may bring forth fruit unto God, and may seek thy glory, and acknowledge thee as the supreme Lord of our affections.

O Lord, we would now praise thee for all the temporal favors which through thy bounty are bestowed upon us; for in thee we live and move and have our being. Oh enable us to look unto thee to be the finisher as well as the author of our faith; the keeper and preserver of our souls, as well as the bright and morning star to guide us into the way of peace.

Regard with thine especial mercy the land of our nativity. O thou Prince of peace, give peace in our time. O Lord, let not our country be destroyed by unhappy divisions. May sinners of all descriptions be turned to the Lord. And, O Savior of the world, who art a light to lighten the Gentiles, and the glory of thy people Israel, make known thy salvation to the ends of the earth. Hasten the coming of that blessed day when thou shalt possess the earth for thine inheritance, and when both Jew and Gentile shall be gathered into one fold, under thee, their one gracious and glorious Shepherd. O Lord, let thy kingdom come. Let thy name, thy salvation, and thy glory, be universally known and adored.

To thy protection, O thou who neither slumberest nor sleepest, we commit ourselves, and all our dear relations and friends, this night. Bless us with quiet and refreshing sleep; and if we are spared to see another day, do thou, O Sun of Righteousness, arise upon us with healing in thy wings. And when thou shalt come in thy divine glory, with all thy holy angels, to judge the world, may we be found an acceptable people in thy sight, who livest and reignest with the Father and the Holy Spirit, ever one God, world without end. *Amen.*

FOURTH MORNING

Scripture Lesson
(PSALM 32)

Prayer
For the renewed Dedication of our Hearts to God.

O GOD the Father of heaven, have mercy upon us, miserable sinners. O God the Son, Redeemer of the world, have mercy upon us, miserable sinners. O God the Holy Ghost, proceeding from the Father and the Son, have mercy upon us, miserable sinners. O holy, blessed, and glorious Trinity, three persons and one God, have mercy upon us, miserable sinners. We confess, O Lord God, that we have forfeited thy favor, and are utterly unworthy of any blessing from thee. But, adored be thy Name, thou hast graciously provided for all who truly repent and believe the gospel, that the guilt of their sins should be removed through the blood of Christ, and their power should be subdued by the grace of the Holy Spirit. O Lord, we desire to cast ourselves anew from day to day upon thy mercy, imploring thee to give us true repentance and a lively faith; that we may be numbered among those who are washed, and justified, and sanctified, in the name of the Lord Jesus, and by the Spirit of our God.

O merciful God, our Creator, Redeemer, and Sanctifier, who hast renewed to us this morning the blessings of life and health, may we now, with humble and grateful hearts, renew the unreserved surrender of ourselves to thee, the Giver of all good. We would commit our bodies, and all our worldly affairs, to the conduct of thy wise and merciful providence; and our souls, with all their concerns, to the government of thy spirit and grace. Search us, O God, and try our hearts, and help us to see if there be any way of wickedness in us; and lead us in the way everlasting. May we ever consider it our highest honor to be called by thy Name, and to be employed in thy service.

Suffer us not to rest in the outward form of godliness, nor in a mere assent of the mind to the doctrines of thy blessed gospel; but let the reality of our repentance and faith be made manifest by a change, not only of our views and apprehensions, but also of our principles and conduct. O merciful God, grant that all carnal affections may die in us, and that all things belonging to the Spirit may live and grow in us. And grant that we may have power and strength to withstand and to triumph over the world, the flesh, and the devil.

We live, O Lord, greatly below our privileges. Our souls cleave unto the dust: raise us, we beseech thee, from this low and groveling state of mind. May we watch and strive against the first risings of sin in our souls. May we rejoice in Christ Jesus, and have no confidence in the flesh; and may all the blessed fruits of the Spirit abound more and more in our hearts and in our lives. May a holy fear of offending thee be ever present with us; and in all our works, begun, continued, and ended in thee, may thy glory be our never-ceasing object and aim. If we have been turned from darkness to light, if thy peace rules in our hearts, if we bring forth any fruits of righteousness, to thee be all the praise.

Be gracious, O God, to our country. We are indeed a sinful people; and it is of thy mercies that we have not been consumed. Continue, we pray thee, to spare and to bless us; and may thy goodness towards us lead us to repentance. Bless the President, and all that are in authority over us. Direct the public councils of the nation to the furtherance of thy glory. Supply the wants of all thy people. Comfort and relieve the afflicted. Dwell in the families of all who fear and love thee. Remember with thine especial mercy all our dear relations and friends. May the blessings we have been imploring for ourselves be also bestowed upon them, and may they and we be enabled by thy grace to serve thee faithfully in this life, and finally be admitted to see thy glory in the life everlasting, world without end. *Amen.*

FOURTH EVENING

Scripture Lesson
(ROMANS 12)

A General Family Prayer.

O ALMIGHTY God, enable us to approach thy mercy-seat with holy reverence and godly fear; and be pleased to pour upon us the Spirit of grace and of supplication, that we may spread before thee our wants, and may praise thee for the numerous favors which thou art bestowing upon us from day to day.

Gracious God, we desire to acknowledge with thankfulness all the mercies, both temporal and spiritual, which we have received from thee in the whole course of our lives. We bless thee for thy watchful care and kind providence over us this day, for the preservation of our health and strength, and for the continued use of our reason; but we more particularly bless thee for the source and fountain of all these blessings, Christ Jesus, remembering that by his incarnation, his cross and passion, his resurrection and ascension, we receive every present means of grace, and our hope of future glory.

But, O heavenly Father, it is with shame and sorrow that we recall to mind our multiplied offenses against thee. Too long have we wasted our time, our talents, and our thoughts, upon the unsatisfying pleasures of this transitory world, and said unto thee in our hearts, Depart from us, for we desire not the knowledge of thy ways. But, O Lord, gracious and merciful, we desire now to humble ourselves at the footstool of thy mercy, acknowledging our sinfulness, and bewailing our depravity, and pleading before thee the atoning blood and perfect righteousness of our Lord Jesus Christ, as the only ground of our hope for pardon and acceptance with thee. Oh look upon us in thy beloved Son, our Redeemer and Mediator; give us that repentance which is not to be repented of, and that faith which lays hold of thy gracious promises of mercy and pardon; and send forth the Spirit of thy Son into our hearts, that we may be enabled, with humble confidence, to call thee Abba, Father.

And grant, O Lord God, that, having Christ formed in our souls as the hope of glory, it may be our constant endeavor to be more and more conformed, both inwardly and outwardly, to him; that we may show forth, in our measure, all those heavenly dispositions which were manifest in him. Make us kind and tender-hearted in our family and among our acquaintances, forbearing and forgiving to all, even as we hope, for Christ's sake, to obtain forgiveness from thee. May we aim to be instrumental in promoting the knowledge of thy truth, conducting ourselves with meekness towards those that oppose themselves. If reviled, may we bless; if persecuted for righteousness' sake, may we patiently endure; if defamed, may we look unto him who, though the brightness of his Father's glory, and the express image of his person, yet endured the contradiction of sinners against himself. O God, establish within us thy kingdom of righteousness, peace, and joy in the Holy Ghost; and carry us on from strength to strength, until we receive the end of our faith, even the salvation of our souls.

Let thy heavenly benediction rest upon us, O Lord, in all our personal and relative concerns. May each member of this family conscientiously perform the duty of his proper station. Bless those whom thou hast placed at the head of it with wisdom and increasing grace.

[Defend, O Lord, these children with thy heavenly grace; let thy fatherly hand ever be over them; let thy Holy Spirit ever be with them; and so lead them into the knowledge and obedience of thy word, that finally they may obtain everlasting life, through our Lord Jesus Christ.]

Let thy blessing also rest upon the domestics of this family; may they endeavor to approve themselves as the servants of God, by giving up their hearts unto thee, and by acting with truth and faithfulness. And remember for good, gracious Lord, all those who are more immediately related to us, and those who need or desire our prayers. Be gracious to all that are afflicted in mind, body, or estate; and support and comfort them. Heavenly Father, we now commit ourselves to thy care for this night. We pray thee to guard us from all evils and dangers; and if it be thy good pleasure to preserve us until the morning, may we anew devote ourselves to thy service, and continue to live in thy fear and favor. And when our days are brought to a final close, may our souls be received, through thy mercy, to eternal glory. We ask all through the prevailing merits of Jesus Christ, our merciful Lord and Redeemer. *Amen.*

FIFTH MORNING

Scripture Lesson
(PSALM 19)

Prayer
For a Blessing upon the Word of God.

FATHER of mercies, and God of all consolation, help us by thy Holy Spirit to draw nigh unto thy throne of grace this morning, and to make known our requests unto thee by prayer and supplication with thanksgiving. We bless thee for our creation, our preservation, and all the blessings of this life. To thee we are indebted for all our personal and family mercies; for the health, and peace, and safety, and the many comforts and blessings which we severally enjoy. But, above all, we especially adore and praise thee for thine inestimable love in the redemption of the world by our Lord Jesus Christ, and for all the present and everlasting benefits which flow to us through the kindness and love of God our Savior. May we receive into our hearts that great mystery of godliness, that God was manifest in the flesh; and that in Christ crucified there is plenteous redemption through his blood, even the forgiveness of sins, according to the riches of thy grace.

We thank thee, O Lord, for the instructions of thy holy word. May we ever reckon it amongst our chiefest blessings that our lot has been cast in an age and country in which thou dost continue to bless us with the gospel of our salvation. May we acknowledge this thy goodness to us, and know the day of our merciful visitation; and may we imitate the example of the Bereans of old, in receiving the word with all readiness of mind, and in searching the Scriptures daily, and examining whether what we hear be according to the testimony thereof. But, O Lord, who is sufficient for these things? Thou knowest that we are weak and helpless. We lament our slowness of heart to believe all that is written in the law and the prophets; and that we take so little heed to the things which we have heard, that we oftentimes let them slip from our minds, and thus become forgetful hearers, and not doers of the word. We are taught, O blessed Lord, that, though Paul may plant, and Apollos may water, thou alone canst give the increase. Pour down upon each of us the graces of thy Holy Spirit; that we may have a right understanding of those Scriptures which holy men of God spoke as they were moved by him. Grant unto each of us the Spirit of wisdom and of revelation in the knowledge of thyself. Enlighten the eyes of our understanding; give us a spiritual discernment of the things of the Spirit, that we may have a right judgment in all things, and know what the will of the Lord is. And help us so to do thy will, that we may be assured of the truth of the holy Scriptures, that they were given by inspiration of God, while we perceive the power and efficacy of thy word in our hearts and lives.

Enable us to follow on to know the Lord; and continually to mix faith with what we read and hear of thy word, that we may profit and grow thereby. May its doctrines be the constant rule of our faith, its precepts the constant rule of our practice; and may all its promises be fulfilled in our experience; so that we may abound more and more in all joy and peace in believing. Oh give thy gospel a free and effectual passage throughout the world, that it may be further propagated where it has not yet reached, and the joyful sound be heard even where Christ is not yet named; and give such good success to it where it shines already, that all who have received it may sincerely obey it, and everyone who names the name of Christ may depart from iniquity: and let their light shine before men to the glory of our heavenly Father, and to the adorning of thy doctrine, and advancing the gospel and religion of God our Savior.

O Holy Spirit, thou glorifier of the Savior, and Comforter of the Church of God, vouchsafe to bring the words of Christ continually to our remembrance. May our sentiments, our tempers, and our whole lives, be conformed to thy revealed will. May we cast all our care upon the Lord; taking up our cross daily, and following him, until at last we behold his face in glory, and partake of his promised salvation.

O gracious and long-suffering God, though we live in an age when iniquity abounds, and when the love of many towards thee waxeth cold, we thank thee that thy word is widely disseminated, and that thy gospel is faithfully and extensively proclaimed. Oh clothe it with thy mighty power, and cause it to reach the hearts of young and old, rich and poor, magistrates and subjects. Show unto them the light of thy truth, that they may be made wise unto salvation, through faith, which is in Christ Jesus. Especially may all our dear friends be brought under the influence of thy blessed word, and be supported and comforted with the hope of the glory of God. Hear and answer us, O God of our salvation, through Jesus Christ our Lord. *Amen.*

FIFTH EVENING

Scripture Lesson
(JER. 31:1–14)

Prayer
Family Supplication and Intercession.

MOST gracious God, our heavenly Father in Jesus Christ our Lord, who art continually doing us good, though we are evil and unthankful, we come into thy presence, encouraged by the merciful promises of thy word, to implore thy protection and thy grace, without which we can neither be safe nor happy.

We confess, O Lord, with sorrow and shame, that, from the youngest to the eldest amongst us, we have, by our sins and guilt, forfeited thy favor, and justly incurred thine anger and condemnation. But, O Lord, it is thy work to have mercy and to forgive. Have mercy upon us, miserable sinners. Spare thou them, O God, who confess their faults; restore thou them that are penitent; according to thy promises declared unto mankind in Christ Jesus our Lord. And grant, O most merciful Father, for his sake, that we may hereafter live a godly, righteous, and sober life, to the glory of thy holy name.

O thou Lord and giver of all spiritual life, help us to renounce every false hope, and all dependence upon ourselves, and to come unto thee, repenting truly of our sins, and seeking for mercy and salvation in the name of our only and our all-sufficient Redeemer and Mediator. O thou eternal and almighty Spirit, let there not be one in all this house who is unconcerned about the great truths which relate to our everlasting welfare. Impress our minds at all times with a firm persuasion that "thou God seest us;"—that to thee our respective characters and wants, yea, all our thoughts and motives, are fully known. Convince each of us of our individual sins,—the sins of our hearts and of our lives, the sins of our youth, and the sins which have increased with our riper years; and grant unto us the blessedness of those whose transgression is forgiven, and whose sin is covered; and unto whom the Lord imputeth not iniquity. May we feel our need of a personal interest in the all-sufficient atonement and perfect righteousness of the Son of God. Lord, increase our faith; and may the fruits of it—love to God, and love to man, and victory over the world, the flesh, and the devil—be daily exhibited by us in our lives. Help us not only to receive Christ Jesus the Lord, but also to walk in him, in a sense of constant dependence upon his grace, and an unceasing endeavor to follow his pure and perfect example.

Heavenly Father, accept our humble thanks for all our social and domestic mercies; for the many comforts of this life; and for the far richer mercies set before us in the life eternal. Thou hast been with us and helped us in all our troubles. Often thou hast healed our diseases, removed our sorrows, and renewed our strength. Whilst many have been cut off and passed into an awful eternity, we are yet, by thy mercy, numbered with the living. God of compassion, take not thy Spirit from us. Continue to us thy heavenly blessings. We acknowledge thee in all, and we desire to ascribe unto thee the whole praise and glory. Let thy blessing rest upon this house, that it may be the habitation of peace, and love, and holiness. May those who are set over this family resolve, through grace, "As for us and our house, we will serve the Lord." May they guide and instruct those who are under their care with wisdom and in the spirit of kindness; teaching them the fear of the Lord, and setting before them a holy example: that all the members of the household may follow them, as they themselves follow Christ.

O Lord, renew the hearts of the younger members of this family; that they may seek thee early, and find thee to be their reconciled God and Father in Christ Jesus. May they know from their childhood those holy Scriptures which are able to make them wise unto salvation; and as they advance in years, may they grow in grace and in the knowledge of our Lord Jesus Christ. May they be dutiful and obedient to their parents and teachers; kindly affectioned one towards another; and in all things desirous to live to thy praise and glory.

And may the domestics of this household be the servants of the Most High God; may they be patterns of industry and obedience; faithful to their trust; doing their work with singleness of heart, as unto the Lord.

Finally, O Lord, bless all who are united to us by the ties of kindred or friendship. May they all be dear to thee, and be possessed of that wisdom which cometh down from above. May they and we obtain more of thy grace from day to day.

Take us this night under thy merciful care and protection. Whether we sleep or wake, live or die, may we be thine. May every evening remind us of the solemn close of our earthly existence; and every morning extend our view to the final resurrection of the blessed to eternal glory. We supplicate every mercy for the sake of Jesus Christ, our only Redeemer and Advocate. *Amen.*

SIXTH MORNING

Scripture Lesson
(PSALM 72)

Prayer
For the Advancement of true Religion in our own Country.

O EVER blessed and most gracious God, we would thank thee that thou hast preserved us through the past night, and hast raised us up this morning, and given us another opportunity of meeting together before thy throne of grace.

O thou Lord and Giver of life, shine upon our souls; incline our hearts to follow Him who is the light of the world, that we may not abide in darkness, but have the light of life. May we by the grace of thy Holy Spirit obtain from day to day a deeper conviction of our own guilty and corrupt state, and a more lively faith in the abundant mercy and exceeding riches of the grace of our God in Christ Jesus. And, O blessed Spirit, the Comforter of the church of God, fill our souls with all joy and peace in believing; and grant that our love to thee may abound more and more in knowledge and in all judgment.

Look down in mercy upon our native land. We bless thee that thou hast vouchsafed unto us the light of thy glorious gospel. We praise thee for all the national mercies and privileges which we enjoy. But, alas! we would remember before thee, with shame and confusion of face, the rebellion and ingratitude which we have continually betrayed towards thee, who art ever loading us with thy benefits. Send throughout the land, O Lord, an universal spirit of repentance, that we may turn every man from his evil ways, and may amend our doings. Turn us, O God of our salvation, and so shall we be turned. Pour out the influence of thine illuminating Spirit upon us; that we may still be a favored nation, fearing thee, and working righteousness.

We beseech thee, Almighty God, whose kingdom is everlasting, and power infinite, to save and defend all Christian nations and Christian rulers and governors, and especially thy servant, our President, that under him we may be godly and be quietly governed. Let his administration be established in righteousness; and so rule his heart that he may above all things seek thy honor and glory. Instruct all his counsellors, and direct their measures to the preservation of domestic concord, the maintenance of peace among the nations, and the furtherance of the Redeemer's kingdom.

May the continual dew of thy blessing be sent down upon all the ministers of thy gospel, and on all congregations committed to their charge. May they all rightly divide the word of truth, and direct sinners to the Lamb of God who taketh away the sin of the world. Make thy ministers mighty in the Scriptures. Open to them an effectual door of usefulness. Let thy hand be with them, and let thy word be accompanied with thine own almighty power in the hearts of sinners, that many in our day may believe it and be turned unto thee. O Lord, we lament, among other national sins, the neglect with which thy blessed gospel hath been treated by many in our country. Oh that the true and blessed religion of our Lord Jesus may prevail powerfully; and gain more converts daily of such as shall be saved, throughout the world; that Jerusalem may be the joy and praise of the whole earth, and that we may see the good of it all the days of our life.

We humbly beseech thee to bless the rising generation; may the youth of our land be brought up in the nurture and admonition of the Lord; may the principles of faith and love, and of the fear of thy name, be early implanted in their hearts; and as they advance in years, may they grow in grace and in the knowledge of our Lord and Savior Jesus Christ. And let thy blessing rest upon all the instructors of youth in our colleges and seminaries, in our public schools and Sunday-schools, and in private families. More especially bless those who bestow their time in teaching the children of the poor. May they themselves be taught of thee, and may their labor not be in vain in the Lord.

Bless all our fellow-citizens throughout the land. Multiply grace, mercy, and peace upon all who love our Lord Jesus Christ in sincerity. Heal all our unhappy divisions. Deliver us from all sedition and violence. Put to silence the deceitful lips of infidelity, and show to them that are in error the light of thy truth. Bless and preserve the fruits of the earth. Satisfy our poor with bread. Prosper their endeavors to provide things honest in the sight of all men; make them poor in spirit, and partakers of the unsearchable riches of Christ. Visit with thy mercy the sons and daughters of affliction, and overrule the dispensations of thy providence for their good. Strengthen the weak in faith; comfort those that mourn; subdue the enmity of the hardened heart; and cause sinners of every description to flee to thee while the door of mercy is still open.

Finally, O Lord, we implore thy protection and mercy for our dear relatives and friends. May their names be written in the book of life. May they be members of thy family while on earth, and heirs of thy glory in heaven.

We offer up these our supplications and intercessions at the throne of grace, in the name of Jesus Christ, our most blessed Savior and Redeemer. *Amen.*

SIXTH EVENING

Scripture Lesson
(PSALM 2)

Prayer
*For the promotion of Christ's kingdom amongst the Jews and the
Heathen.*

MERCIFUL God, and our heavenly Father in Christ Jesus, we desire
this evening to pray that thou wouldst send the light of thy truth to
the dark parts of the earth; and be pleased to make thy ways known
unto them, thy saving health unto all nations.

We adore thee for the blessed privileges which thou hast
bestowed upon our highly favored though ungrateful country; and
especially that unto us hath been sent the word of salvation, the
message of reconciliation through our Lord Jesus Christ. Gracious
God, let not our unbelief and our impenitence cause thee to remove
our lamp out of its place, as thou hast removed that of other churches;
but pour down a spirit of contrition upon our nation, that we may
break off from our iniquities, and turn to thee with full purpose of
heart. Help us to believe and to value the glad tidings of grace which
thy word hath brought to our ears. And may the love of Christ be so
shed abroad in our hearts by the Holy Ghost, that we may not only
ourselves rejoice in hope of the glory of God, but be earnestly
desirous that the heathen and the unbelieving Israelites may be made
partakers of the common salvation.

O thou almighty God, the God of the spirits of all flesh, whose is
the earth and the fullness thereof, and whose power alone can change
and renovate the hearts of sinful men, look down in compassion, from
the habitation of thy holiness, upon a world lying in ignorance and
iniquity. We bless thee that thou hast taught us to pray, "thy kingdom
come," and that we are encouraged to plead before thee thy gracious
promise that "all the ends of the earth shall see the salvation of our
God." We therefore beseech thee to hasten the fulfillment of thy
promises; to send forth thy light and thy truth into the most
benighted corners of the earth; to enlighten the millions who sit in
darkness and in the shadow of death, and to turn them from the
power of Satan unto thyself, the living God.

O thou glorious Head of the church, who hast obtained the
heathen for thine inheritance, and the uttermost parts of the earth for
thy possession; raise up, we beseech thee, many messengers of thy
mercy, and endue them abundantly with wisdom and grace, that thy
gospel may be preached by them to every creature. May the pagan

nations of the earth forsake their idols and their refuges of lies, and hear and receive thy holy word. May thy Holy Spirit prepare their hearts to welcome the sound of the glorious gospel of God our Savior; and may they be taught effectually by his grace that there is none other name under heaven given amongst men whereby they can be saved, but thine, O thou blessed Lord Jesus, thou only deliverer from the wrath to come.

And, O God of Abraham, of Isaac, and of Jacob, pour down upon thine ancient people Israel the Spirit of grace and of supplication, that they may look unto Him whom their fathers pierced, and mourn. Let the deliverer come out of Sion, and turn away ungodliness from Jacob. Remove the vail that is upon their hearts; and hasten the time when they shall acknowledge the Lord Jesus to be their Messiah, and be gathered into his fold; that thus both Jews and Gentiles may become one fold under one Shepherd, and unite in one triumphant song of praise to thee, their God and Savior.

Finally, O Lord, let thy blessing rest upon every association formed amongst thy people for the purpose of promoting thy glory and the salvation of man. May love to thy name, and zeal in the furtherance of the work of missions, be spread throughout the church of Christ; and may that day of blessing which thou hast promised to thy church soon arrive. Hasten, O Lord, thy coming; hasten the period when all the kingdoms of the world shall become the kingdoms of our God and of his Christ.

And now, O Lord, we would pray for ourselves. We beseech thee to bless us, even us also. Protect and refresh us this night with quiet and comfortable sleep; and if thou art pleased to bring us to see the light of another day, renew, O Lord, the grace and teaching of thy blessed Spirit to our souls. Search and try our hearts, that we may not be under any self-deception concerning the things which belong to our eternal peace. May we be determined to know nothing as our ground of hope or source of comfort, save Jesus Christ and him crucified, in whose name and for whose sake we earnestly supplicate these blessings. *Amen.*

SEVENTH MORNING

Scripture Lesson
(JOHN 3:1–22)

A General Family Prayer.

O THOU great and gracious Lord God, whose tender mercies are over all thy works, and whose compassions fail not; we beseech thee favorably to regard the unworthy family now assembled before thee.

We desire to approach thy mercy-seat this morning, deeply humbled under a sense of our guilt. Blessed be thy name forever,—in the midst of wrath thou rememberest mercy; thou hast laid help upon one that is mighty; and, in the riches of thy free grace, thou hast invited weary and heavy-laden sinners to come boldly to the throne of grace, through thy well-beloved Son, Jesus Christ the righteous, in whom there is redemption through his blood, even the forgiveness of our sins. In his name alone do we now venture to present ourselves before thee; for his sake we beseech thee to blot out our sins as a cloud, and our iniquities as a thick cloud; heal all our backslidings, and let thine anger be turned away from us forever.

Thou hast encouraged us in thy word to spread before thee our manifold wants, and to plead thine exceeding great and precious promises. Oh do thou supply all our need out of the riches of thy mercy by Christ Jesus. Separated from an ungodly world, and delivered from the power of our spiritual enemies, may we walk, as the ransomed of the Lord, in holiness and righteousness before thee, all the days of our life. Establish thy kingdom of grace within us; give unto us the earnest of thy blessed Spirit; may he subdue in us every rebellious feeling, cast down every lofty imagination, and bring every thought of our mind into subjection to the obedience of thy blessed will. And grant, O merciful God, that, under his divine teaching and influence, we may, in true penitence of heart, be kept continually at the foot of the cross, and be enabled to rest in a blessed assurance of our personal interest in the redeeming love and finished work of Jesus.

We look up to thee, O heavenly Father, under a sense of our own weakness, for grace and strength to support us every moment. Enable us to walk as it becometh those who are called by thy name; and preserve us from the sins and infirmities which do so easily beset us. May we never be ashamed to confess the faith of Christ crucified, and manfully to fight under his banner against sin, the world, and the devil.

Direct us in the way wherein we ought to go. Hold up our goings in thy paths, that our footsteps slip not. In whatsoever we do, may thy love constrain us to act according to thy holy will, and may thy glory be the end we have in view; and grant that we may walk as children of light, and adorn the doctrine of God our Savior in all things.

We desire now, O Lord, to offer up our praises and thanksgivings for thy manifold and great mercies. May we trace thy fatherly love in all thy dealings with us ever since we were born; may the remembrance of them fill us with gratitude and love; and may we learn to cast all our cares upon thee, and to live in the daily exercise of faith and confidence in our God. Dispose, we beseech thee, of all our earthly concerns as it seemeth best to thy unerring wisdom, and let the dispensations of thy providence respecting us be ever accompanied with the sanctifying influence of thy Spirit; that, whether in adversity or prosperity, in sickness or in health, in life or in death, we may be enabled to glorify thy holy name in all things.

We commend unto thee all those to whom we are bound by the ties of affection and friendship. Bless our dear relatives and friends; bring them nigh unto thyself through the blood of Jesus; remember them with the favor that thou bearest unto thy people, and make them partakers of all the blessings of thy salvation.

Look in mercy, O God, upon our beloved country. Bless our President, the Cabinet, both houses of Congress, our courts of justice, state legislatures, and every officer of government. May their rule be established in righteousness. Give peace in our time, we beseech thee. Bless thy church and people. Support, strengthen, and encourage the ministers of the gospel. We ask every blessing in the name of our adorable Mediator and Advocate, whoever liveth to make intercession for us; to whom, with thee and the Holy Ghost, we ascribe all honor and glory, now and forever. *Amen.*

SEVENTH EVENING

Scripture Lesson
(PSALM 103)

Thanksgivings for Mercies received, and Supplications at the close of a Week.

MOST blessed Lord God, we would give thanks unto thy name, for thou art gracious, and thy mercy endureth forever.

We thankfully acknowledge that thy loving-kindness has been ever more and more towards us. By thee we were formed, and by thee have we been holden up ever since we were born. We bless thee for our health and strength, peace and safety; for the supply of our bodily wants, for thy watchful care and kind providence over us from day to day, and for every temporal favor shown to our family, our kindred, and our country. But, above all, we adore thee for the richer blessings of redemption, and especially for the source and fountain of them all, Jesus Christ our Savior; for all the invaluable benefits resulting to our fallen world from his incarnation and death, his resurrection and ascension; for the means of grace and for the hope of glory. O heavenly Father, thou God of all grace, we can never sufficiently magnify thy mercy and thy goodness towards us, in causing us to hear of that name at which every knee shall bow, whether of things in earth, or things in heaven; and besides which there is none other name given among men whereby we may be saved.

But, O Lord, to us belong shame and confusion of face. We have sinned, and have grievously departed from thee. We have abused thy patience amidst all the blessings which we have daily received at thy hands. Gracious Lord, may thy goodness and long-suffering lead us to repentance. Make us deeply sensible of the pride and the unbelief of our hearts, and enable us, in penitence and faith, to flee to the cross of our divine Redeemer. Be graciously pleased for his sake to forgive us our sins, and to cleanse us from all unrighteousness. O Lord Jesus Christ, our most merciful Savior, we beseech thee to intercede for us. By thy cross and passion, by thy precious death and burial, by thy glorious resurrection and ascension, and by the coming of the Holy Ghost, good Lord, deliver us. In all time of our tribulation, in all time of our wealth, in the hour of death, and in the day of judgment, good Lord, deliver us.

O thou heart-searching God, who knowest our inmost thoughts, we pray thee to suit thy mercies to our wants. Help us to place our confidence in thee alone; and not to be led away by every wind of doctrine, nor to build our hopes on any false foundation, or on any device of man, but solely on the death and righteousness of our incarnate Lord. While reviewing the past week, make us sincerely penitent for all the offenses which we have committed against thee in thought, word, or deed. And if any among us are still walking in darkness, or are unconcerned about their eternal interests, we beseech thee to enlighten their understandings and to fix their attention on spiritual and everlasting objects. If any are halting betwixt two opinions, cause them to remember that "one thing is needful" for their happiness and salvation; and may they choose that good part which shall never be taken from them. May we all be more deeply impressed with the shortness and uncertainty of life. May we remember that our last week, our last hour, will soon come; and may neither domestic cares nor worldly occupations prevent us from seeking our life and happiness in thee. Give us grace to look up to thee, in the time of health, as our reconciled Father in Christ, that so in trouble we may find thee our friend, in death our support, and in eternity our portion.

To thy merciful care we commit our souls and bodies this night. To thee alone do we look for our preservation, and for a continuance of the blessings of health, and peace, and safety. May we ever rejoice in the return of thy holy day, and endeavor to profit by all the opportunities and means of grace which thou dost afford us. Be present with us tomorrow in public and in private; pour into our hearts the Spirit of grace and of supplication. If permitted to attend at thy house, make us more sincere and devout in our confessions, and prayers, and praises, and more attentive to the word of thy salvation.

Bless the ministers of thy gospel; assist them in their preparation for the services of the approaching Sabbath; and wherever thy word is faithfully preached, there let the power and energy of thy Spirit be felt, that sinners may be converted, and thy faithful people refreshed and comforted. Let the bright beams of thy light be shed upon thy church; let thy ways be made known upon earth, thy saving health among all nations. We ask these mercies in the all-prevailing name of Jesus Christ our Lord. *Amen.*

PARTICULAR DAYS AND SEASONS
LAST EVENING OF THE OLD YEAR

Scripture Lesson
(PSALM 90)

ALMIGHTY and eternal Lord of heaven and earth, with whom is no variableness, neither shadow of turning, who art the same yesterday, and to-day, and forever, and whose years fail not—from everlasting to everlasting thou art God.

Accept, we beseech thee, our sacrifice of praise and thanksgiving for thy goodness and mercy, which have followed us all our days. We especially bless thee for delivering us from the dangers of the year that is now drawing to a close. Not by our own strength, nor for our righteousness, have we been spared. But because thy compassions fail not, and for thy mercy's sake, we have not been consumed. We humble ourselves before thee, confessing and bewailing all that we have done amiss. According to the multitude of thy tender mercies, blot out our offenses. Pardon and accept us, for the sake of thy only begotten Son, whom thou didst send into the world, to take our nature upon him, that he might redeem us unto thee by his blood. Turn us from our iniquities, and cleanse us from our sins, and let them all be buried with the closing year, to rise up against us no more forever.

Keep us mindful, O Lord, as the years of our life pass away, that the end of all things is at hand; and make us sober and watchful unto prayer. May we never forget that we are strangers and pilgrims upon earth, and that here we have no continuing city; and may we learn diligently to seek one to come. Lord, teach us to number our days, that we may apply our hearts unto wisdom. Make us to know our end, and the measure of our days, that we may consider how frail we are, and may be admonished to redeem the time that remains. Give us grace to watch and pray, since we know neither the day nor the hour, when the Son of man cometh. Above all we beseech thee to preserve in our minds a lively remembrance that we shall, every one, receive the things done in the body according to that we have done, whether it be good or whether it be evil. May we, by the assistance of thy grace, so believe in Christ and live in thy presence, that when we die, we may die the death of the righteous, and our last end be like his. Help us to fight the good fight, to finish our course, and to keep the faith, that there may be laid up for us a crown of righteousness, which thou, the righteous and merciful Judge, wilt give unto us in that day.

(Occasional Prayers.)

Hear our intercession, O Lord, for all who are partakers of the same frail nature with ourselves. Take the little children into the arms of thy mercy, and bless and preserve them. Look in tender compassion upon those who are in the morning of their years. May they remember their Creator in the days of their youth, before the evil days come, and the years draw nigh of which they shall say, There is no pleasure in them. May they grow in wisdom, as they grow in years, and in favor with thee and man. Mercifully regard, also, such as are in the strength and vigor of life; and dispose them to give unto thee the best of their days. We pray thee also to remember those whose strength is now but labor and sorrow. Enable them to bring forth fruit in their old age to thy praise and glory. May they come to their graves at last as a shock of corn cometh in his season. When their flesh and their heart fail them, be thou the strength of their heart, and their portion forever. Grant all this, for the sake of Jesus Christ our Lord.

Unto God's gracious mercy and protection we commit ourselves, and all for whom we are bound to pray. The Lord bless us and keep us. The Lord make his face to shine upon us, and be gracious unto us. The Lord lift up his countenance upon us, and give us peace, both now and evermore. *Amen.*

NEW YEAR MORNING

Scripture Lesson
(ECCLESIASTES 12)

OF old thou hast laid the foundation of the earth: and the heavens are the work of thy hands. They shall perish, but thou shalt endure; as a vesture shalt thou change them, and they shall be changed: but thou art the same, and thy years shall have no end.

May we rejoice, that, while men die, the Lord liveth; that, while all creatures are found broken reeds and broken cisterns, he is the rock of ages, and the fountain of living waters. Oh that we may turn away our hearts from vanity, and, among all the dissatisfactions and uncertainties of the present state, look after an interest in that everlasting covenant which is ordered in all things and sure.

We thank thee that thou hast revealed to us that Jesus is the way, the truth, and the life. In his name we come. Oh receive us graciously. Justify us freely from all things. Renew us in the spirit of our minds, and bless us with all the spiritual blessings in heavenly places in Christ.

Suffer us not to neglect the claims of eternity in the pursuit of the trifles of time; but, knowing how frail we are, may we be wise to choose that good part which shall not be taken away from us. May thoughts of death and eternity so impress our minds, as to put seriousness into our prayers and vigor into our resolutions; may they loosen us from an undue attachment to things seen and temporal; so that we may weep as though we wept not, and rejoice as though we rejoiced not.

Remembering that the present life—so short, so uncertain, and so much of which is already vanished—is the only opportunity we shall ever have for usefulness, may we be concerned to redeem the time. May we be alive and awake at every call of charity and piety. May we feed the hungry and clothe the naked; may we instruct the ignorant, reclaim the vicious, forgive the offending, diffuse the gospel.

As we have entered on a new period of life, may we faithfully examine ourselves, to see what has been amiss in our former temper or conduct; and in thy strength may we resolve to correct it.

Prepare us for all the duties of the ensuing year. All the wisdom and strength necessary for the performance of them must come from thyself: may we therefore live a life of self-distrust and of prayer; may we ask and receive, that our joy be full; may we live in the Spirit and walk in the Spirit.

If we are indulged with prosperity, let not our prosperity destroy us or injure us. If our relative comforts are continued to us, may we love them without idolatry, and hold them at thy disposal; and if they are taken from us, may we be enabled to say, The Lord gave, and the Lord hath taken away; blessed be the name of the Lord.

Fit us for all events. Nothing can befall us by chance. Thou hast been thus far our helper; thou hast engaged to make all things work together for our good; all thy ways are mercy and truth. May we therefore be careful for nothing, but in everything, by prayer and supplication with thanksgiving, may we make known our requests unto God; and may the peace of God, that passeth all understanding, keep our hearts and minds through Christ Jesus.

Bless, oh bless the young! May each of them, this day, hear thee saying, My son, give me thy heart; and from this day may they cry unto thee as the guide of their youth. Regard those who have reached the years wherein they say, We have no pleasure in them. If old in sin, may they be urged to embrace, before it be forever too late, the things that belong to their peace; and if old in grace, uphold them with thy free Spirit, and help them to remember that now is their salvation nearer than when they believed.

Bless all the dear connections attached to us by nature, friendship, or religion. Grace be to them, and peace be multiplied.

Let our country share thy protection and smiles. Bless all our rulers and magistrates.

Bless all our churches and congregations. Bless all thy ministers; may thine ordinances in their hands be enlivening and refreshing, and thy word effectual to wound and to heal.

May this be a year remarkable for the conversion of souls and the extension of the gospel. Bless all missionary societies; and let the circling months see the banner of the Redeemer carried forward, till all nations are subdued to the obedience of faith. And to thee shall be all glory forever. *Amen.*

NEW YEAR EVENING

Scripture Lesson
(PSALM 103:1–22)

GREAT and eternal God! we bow before thee at the close of this first day of the new year with the deepest reverence and with unfeigned thanksgiving. Surrounded by every temporal and spiritual blessing, how could we be otherwise than joyful in the God of all our mercies? What shall we render to the Lord for all his benefits? Oh that thy goodness may lead us all to true repentance and a life of sincere obedience and piety. Lord, we know that our responsibilities are great; for of him to whom much is given, much will be required. Thou hast given us much; may we so use thy gifts, that, when called to render up an account of our stewardship, we may do it with joy, and not with grief. Blessed with health and happiness, we have entered upon this new year; but we do not know that we shall live to see its close. We cannot tell what a day or night, yea, a single hour, may bring forth; how much less what may occur in a whole year! We commit our ways to the Lord, assured that he will bring it to pass. This year some of us, perhaps all of us, may die. Before another new year's day dawns upon the earth, we may be numbered with the pale nations of the dead. Grant, O Lord, that we may lay to heart those solemn admonitions: "Set thy house in order, for thou shalt die and not live!" "Watch, therefore, for ye know not the day nor the hour wherein the Son of man cometh." May we take warning by the example of the foolish virgins, and never be satisfied with having simply the lamp of a profession, without the oil of grace in our hearts.

Our time is precious. May not a day nor an hour of this year be misspent or sinfully squandered away. Help us to be diligent in business, fervent in spirit, serving the Lord. Whatsoever our hands find to do, may we do it with our might, knowing that there is no knowledge nor wisdom, work nor device, in the grave whither we are going. Lay us out for usefulness. May we in our several spheres accomplish a great work for God and souls this year.

Bless the land in which we live. Make it Immanuel's land. Fill it with thy glory. Continue to us our precious civil and religious privileges, and make us and all the citizens of this country sensible of our responsibilities to thee in view of them. May peace and prosperity, health and plenty, be our happy lot this year. Bless our civil rulers, and all that are in authority among us. May they rule in thy fear, and remember that they are accountable unto thee for the manner in which they discharge their duties. May all our people "be subject to the powers that be," and love law and order.

In mercy remember thy church and all the ministers of thy holy religion. Say to Zion, "Arise, shine; for thy light is come, and the glory of the Lord is risen upon thee." May the church be greatly prospered this year in all parts of the earth. May genuine revivals be multiplied everywhere, and tens of thousands be savingly converted to thee. May thy ministers all be men after thine own heart, and be abundantly successful in accomplishing the work which thou hast given them. Bless our dear minister. Encourage his heart and strengthen his hands. May our congregation be richly blessed this year, and may we all act our parts well. And now we beseech thee to pardon the sins of this day—to fill our hearts with love, joy, peace, and hope, in believing—and in great mercy do thou watch over us for good this night. With this new year we would commence a new life, and live more devotedly to thee than we have ever done. And at last, when all our years and days on earth are ended, take us, one and all, to thyself in heaven, and we will praise thee, the Father, Son, and Holy Ghost, forever and ever. *Amen.*

CHRISTMAS MORNING

Scripture Lesson
(MATTHEW 2:1–23)

ALMIGHTY God, the Father of our Lord Jesus Christ, we humbly beseech thee to accept our hearty thanks for the manifold mercies which thou hast poured upon us.

We bless thee, especially, for sending thy well-beloved Son, to take our nature upon him and to be made in the likeness of sinful flesh.

We rejoice that unto us a child is born; that unto us a Son is given. And we would join the multitude of the heavenly host, in ascribing glory to thee in the highest; peace on earth; good-will towards men. We praise thee for revealing to us the way in which mercy and truth have met together, in which righteousness and peace have kissed each other. And we account it a faithful saying, and worthy of all acceptation, that Christ Jesus came into the world to save sinners.

Help us, O Lord, to employ this day in meditating on this great mystery of godliness, God manifest in the flesh, which thy holy angels desire to look into.

O thou great and glorious Redeemer, who art Wonderful, Counsellor, the Mighty God, the Everlasting Father, the Prince of peace, we praise thee, we bless thee, we worship thee, we glorify thee, we give thanks to thee for thy great glory, O Lord God, Lamb of God, the only begotten Son, Jesus Christ, King of kings, and Lord of lords, Immanuel, God with us.

But chiefly at this time we adore thee for leaving the glory which thou hadst with the Father before the world began. We know thy grace, O Lord Jesus Christ, that, though thou wast rich, yet for our sakes thou didst become poor, that we through thy poverty might be made rich. O thou Son of David, have mercy upon us. Thou, who didst come that we might have life, and might have it more abundantly, be gracious unto us.

Thou who wast called Jesus, that thou mightest save thy people from their sins, save us, and help us, we humbly beseech thee, O Lord. Give unto us grace, Almighty God, that we may cast away the works of darkness, and put upon us the armor of light, now in the time of this mortal life, in which thy Son, Jesus Christ, came to visit us in great humility.

May we rejoice to take his yoke upon us, and to learn of him who was meek and lowly in heart, that we may find rest unto our souls. Grant that we, being regenerate and made thy children by adoption and grace, may daily be renewed by thy Holy Spirit, and follow the blessed steps of his most holy life, ever remembering that he gave himself for us to redeem us from all iniquity, and to purify us unto himself a peculiar people, zealous of good works.

Have compassion, also, on those who have never heard of the coming of our blessed Lord in the flesh. In him who hath arisen to rule over the Gentiles, let the Gentiles trust, and find his rest to be glorious.

Mercifully with thy favor look upon the whole Christian world. May all that name the name of Christ depart from iniquity. Especially preserve them from turning this season into an occasion of reveling and unholy mirth. Let them rejoice, as Christians, in Christ their Savior; and let thy grace teach them to deny all ungodliness and worldly lusts, and to live soberly, righteously, and godly, in this present world.

And as at thy first coming, O Lord Jesus Christ, thou didst send thy messenger to prepare thy way before thee, we beseech thee, finally, to grant that the ministers and stewards of thy mysteries may likewise so prepare and make ready thy way, by turning the hearts of the disobedient to the wisdom of the just, that, at thy second coming to judge the world, we may be found an acceptable people in thy sight, through Jesus Christ, our Lord, in whose name we further pray, Our Father, who art, &c. *Amen.*

CHRISTMAS EVENING

Scripture Lesson
(1 JOHN 4)

O HOLY and merciful God, who art of purer eyes than to behold iniquity, and yet long-suffering towards sinners, we approach thy throne acknowledging our unworthiness, and putting our whole trust and confidence in the promises which thou hast made unto us in Christ Jesus our Lord.

We have greatly provoked thee to anger by our manifold offenses; and, were not judgment thy strange work, we should long since have received at thy hands the just reward of our evil-doings. But thou declarest thy almighty power chiefly in showing mercy and pity. Thou hast not stretched forth the right hand of thy majesty to avenge thee of thine enemies; but with thine own arm thou hast wrought out redemption for us. Thou hast not sent thy Son into the world to condemn the world, but that the world through him might be saved.

We bless thee for revealing to us this great mystery, which was hid for generations, but is now made manifest unto the sons of men. We rejoice that unto us was born a Savior, which is Christ the Lord. Our souls do magnify the Lord, and our spirits do rejoice in God our Savior.

Blessed be thou, the God of Israel, for visiting and redeeming thy people, and raising up a horn of salvation for them; for performing the promise made unto their fathers, and for remembering thy holy covenant. Praised be thy name, for sending forth, in the fullness of time, thy only begotten Son, made of a woman, made under the law, that we might receive the adoption of sons.

O thou, who wast in Christ reconciling the world unto thyself, forgive us all our trespasses. Through him who was made in the likeness of sinful flesh, and came to seek and to save that which was lost, have mercy upon us.

And, since thy blessed Son was manifested that he might destroy the works of the devil, to make us the children of God and heirs of eternal life, grant, we beseech thee, that, having this hope, we may purify ourselves, even as he is pure; and that, when he shall come again, in power and great glory, we may be made like unto him, in his eternal and glorious kingdom.

Let the same mind also be in us which was in Christ Jesus; who, being in the form of God, and thinking it not robbery to be equal with God, yet made himself of no reputation, and took upon him the form of a servant, and was found in fashion as a man, a man of sorrows and acquainted with grief.

Help us continually to follow his example. In lowliness of mind may we esteem others better than ourselves. And give us grace so to walk in faith and all holiness of living, that we may not be ashamed before him at his coming.

We pray likewise, O heavenly Father, that, through thy tender mercies, the Day-Spring from on high, which hath visited us, may arise and shine upon the nations that are sitting in darkness and in the shadow of death, to guide their feet into the way of peace. Let thy way be made known upon earth, thy saving health among all nations. Blessed and holy Lord Jesus! at thy name shall every knee be made to bow, of things in heaven, and things in earth, and things under the earth; and every tongue shall confess that thou art Lord, to the glory of God the Father. Hasten, O Lord, thy coming and thy kingdom; hasten the time when all flesh shall see thy salvation.

Raise up faithful and able ministers of the New Testament, to go before the face of the Lord, to prepare his ways, to give knowledge of salvation to his people, by the remission of their sins. O Lord, thine is the kingdom, and the power, and the glory; do thou add to thy church daily such as shall be saved.

Pour down thy grace and heavenly benediction upon all who are called Christians. May the children of Zion be joyful in their King! And may they so truly follow the blessed steps of their Lord and Master, that they may be saved by him in the great day of his appearing and glory. Grant this for Jesus Christ's sake, our only Lord and Savior. *Amen.*

GOOD FRIDAY MORNING

Scripture Lesson
(JOHN 19:31–42)

O THOU King eternal, immortal, and invisible! We bless thee for the revelation which thou hast given us, and that in thy word we can view thee as the Father of mercies and the God of all grace. We praise thee for the displays of thy goodness in the productions of nature and the bounties of thy providence; but above all, for thine inestimable love in the redemption of the world by our Lord Jesus Christ, for the means of grace, and for the hope of glory. Herein thou hast commended thy love towards us, in that, while we were yet sinners, Christ died for us.

We find ourselves this morning at the foot of his cross, where angels are desiring to look into these things; and if they who need no repentance study the sufferings of Christ and the glory that should follow, how much more should we, to whom they are not only true, and wonderful, and sublime, but all-important and infinitely interesting! Help us, O Lord, to turn aside and see this great sight, and not suffer a dying Savior to address us in vain. Behold and see if ever there was sorrow like unto my sorrow.

Here may we see the value of our souls in the price paid for their deliverance. Here may we contemplate the evil of sin, and abhor it; here look upon him whom we have pierced, and mourn. Yet, remembering that he was not only slain by us, but for us, may we rejoice in our tears, and, by believing, enter into rest.

With humble and holy confidence may we be enabled to say, Surely he hath borne our griefs and carried our sorrows; the chastisement of our peace was upon him, and with his stripes we are healed.

May we never degrade his death, by fearing that it will not be available for guilt so great and aggravated as ours, even if we depend upon it, and plead it before God; but be fully persuaded that his blood cleanseth from all sin, and that by once offering up himself he hath perfected forever them that are sanctified.

Yet, O God, never suffer us to sin that grace may abound. May we never crucify the Savior afresh, and put him to an open shame. May he never be wounded in the house of his professing friends. Rather may we live only and wholly for him who died for us, and adorn the doctrine of God our Savior in all things.

May our old man be crucified with him, and the body of sin be destroyed, that henceforth we may not serve sin. As he suffered for us, leaving us an example that we should follow his steps, may we learn of him submission, and meekness, and forgiveness of injuries: when reviled, may we revile not again; when suffering, may we threaten not, but commit ourselves to him that judgeth righteously.

As thou hast made his soul an offering for sin, may he see his seed, and prolong his days, and the pleasure of the Lord prosper in his hand. May he see of the travail of his soul and be satisfied; and by his knowledge may he justify many, having borne their iniquities.

Yea, having been lifted up from the earth, may he draw all men unto him. May all kings fall down before him, and all nations serve him; and in all the earth which he has purchased with his own blood, may there be one Lord, and his name one.

And when he who made himself of no reputation, but took upon him the form of a servant and became obedient unto death, even the death of the cross, shall come in his glory, with all the holy angels, may we be enabled to say, Even so, come Lord Jesus, and unite with those who will be eternally employed in saying—

Unto him that loved us, and washed us from our sins in his own blood, and hath made us kings and priests unto God, and to his Father, be glory and dominion forever and ever. *Amen.*

GOOD FRIDAY EVENING

Scripture Lesson
(ISAIAH 53)

O THOU, whose name alone is Jehovah, the most high over all the earth: thou art the only wise God. Thou art holy in all thy ways; even the heavens are not clean in thy sight.

How shall we come before the Lord, or bow before the high God? Blessed be thy name, thou hast shown us what is good; we behold the Lamb of God, who is the propitiation for our sins, and not for ours only, but also for the sins of the whole world.

Here a foundation is laid for our hope, in connection with the highest glory of all thy perfections; and we rejoice to think that, while pleading for salvation by the blood of the cross, we ask thee not to deny thyself, or to trample on thy holy law: for here thy law is magnified and made honorable; here all thy attributes are developed and harmonized: mercy and truth meet together, righteousness and peace kiss each other.

Here, weary and heavy-laden, may we come for relief and find rest unto our souls. May we take fresh views of this adorable sacrifice under a sense of our constant unworthiness and ill-desert; and in all our approaches to thee may we have boldness and access with confidence by the faith of him.

May we not only rely upon his cross, but glory in it. Yea, may we joy in God through our Lord Jesus Christ, by whom we have now received the atonement. And may we be able individually to say, I am crucified with Christ; nevertheless I live, yet not I, but Christ liveth in me; and the life that I now live in the flesh, I live by the faith of the Son of God, who loved me and gave himself for me.

We are thankful that as he atoned for our guilt, so he procured for us the grace of life. May we prove that he gave himself not only for our sins, but that he might deliver us from this present evil world; yea, that he might redeem us from all iniquity, and purify unto himself a peculiar people, zealous of good works.

And oh that in every future moment of our existence we may be constrained to live not to ourselves, but to him that died for us and rose again. As he so loved us, may we also love one another, and never deem anything too great to do or to suffer while endeavoring to seek and to save that which is lost.

Smile upon our rulers and our country. Let all the churches of the faithful be edified and multiplied. Bless all the ministers of the everlasting gospel, and may they increasingly determine to know nothing save Jesus Christ and him crucified.

Increase the number of those who love his salvation; and as he gave himself a ransom for all, may it be testified in due time; that he may have the heathen for his inheritance, and the uttermost parts of the earth for his possession, and reign King of kings, and Lord of lords.

Hear us, O Lord, in mercy, and save us forever, through Jesus Christ, our only hope. *Amen.*

EASTER SUNDAY MORNING

Scripture Lesson
(JOHN 20:1–18)

ALMIGHTY God and heavenly Father: we praise thee for the glorious resurrection of thy blessed Son, our Savior Jesus Christ, whom we acknowledge as the very Paschal Lamb foreshadowed in the Scriptures, and offered on the cross as a propitiation for the sins of the world; who, by the shedding of his own precious blood, has overcome death, and, by rising from the grave, is made the first-fruits of them that sleep, and has opened unto us the gate of everlasting life.

We confess that we are by nature dead in trespasses and sins, and cannot, by our own power, raise ourselves to newness of life. But blessed be thy name that thou hast, of thy abundant mercy, begotten us again to a lively hope, through the resurrection of Jesus Christ, to an inheritance incorruptible, undefiled, and that fadeth not away, reserved in heaven for all those who are kept by thy power through faith unto salvation.

Give us grace, heavenly Father, so to bewail our sinfulness, and so to meditate on thy wondrous love, that we may find our hearts dead indeed unto sin, and alive unto thee, through Jesus Christ our Lord.

We beseech thee, gracious God, to grant us thy special blessing this day. May the Spirit of him that raised up Jesus from the dead dwell in us, and direct us in all our duties. Raise our thoughts from the things of this world, and fix them upon those things which are above, where Christ sitteth at thy right hand.

Since Christ our Passover has been sacrificed for us, therefore let us keep the feast: not with the old leaven, neither with the leaven of malice and wickedness, but with the unleavened bread of sincerity and truth. May we fervently join in the prayers and praises of thy people in the courts of thy sanctuary.

Grant also to all those who shall assemble with us in thy house of prayer, that they may be plenteously endued with thy heavenly grace, and be prepared, with meek heart and due reverence, to hear and receive thy holy word, and to be meet partakers of thy holy mysteries.

(Occasional Prayers.)

Pour down thy Spirit from on high on the ministers of thy blessed gospel: and, while they preach Jesus and the resurrection, let thy word, in their mouth, be as life from the dead; that so they who are sleeping in their sins may awake, and arise from the dead, that Christ may give them light.

And now may the God of peace, who brought again from the dead our Lord Jesus Christ, the great Shepherd of the sheep, through the blood of the everlasting covenant, make us perfect in every good work to do his will, working in us that which is well-pleasing in his sight, through Jesus Christ our Lord, to whom be glory forever and ever. *Amen.*

EASTER SUNDAY EVENING

Scripture Lesson
(JOHN 20:19–31)

MOST merciful God and Father, receive, we beseech thee, our hearty thanks for thy great goodness; and especially for the blessings and mercies bestowed upon us this day. We bless thee for the preaching of thy word, and for the administration of thy holy sacraments. We bless thee for thy gracious condescension, in having thy habitation among the sons of men, and in dwelling in the midst of the assemblies of thy people. Let thy blessing rest, we beseech thee, upon those whom thou hast called to minister in holy things; let them be clothed with righteousness; and let thy people rejoice in thy salvation. Grant that the words spoken in thy name may not be spoken in vain. Grant us grace so to hear and receive the godly counsel and instruction of those who are set over us in the Lord, that in all our words and deeds we may seek thy glory and the increase of thy kingdom.

We bless thee, heavenly Father, for the revelation of our Lord Jesus Christ as the resurrection and the life, and for the gracious declaration, that whosoever liveth and believeth in him shall never die. Grant us grace to humble ourselves before thee, knowing that thou art able to exalt us in due time. May we follow the example of thy dearly-beloved Son, in patience, meekness, and humility. And as he died and rose again for us, so may we, who are baptized into his death, die from sin, and rise again unto righteousness, continually mortifying all our evil and corrupt affections, and daily proceeding in all virtue and godliness of living.

We commend to thy rich mercies in Christ Jesus, all the nations that are sitting in darkness and in the shadow of death. May the Sun of Righteousness rise upon them, and the light of the everlasting gospel shine into their hearts, to give them the knowledge of the glory of God in the face of Jesus Christ.

Have mercy on the house of Israel, and teach them by thy Spirit to know that thou hast made that same Jesus, whom their forefathers crucified, both Lord and Christ.

Awaken the impenitent to a sense of their danger, by putting them in remembrance that thou hast appointed a day in which thou wilt judge the world in righteousness, by him whom thou hast ordained, whereof thou hast given assurance unto all men, in that thou hast raised him from the dead.

(Occasional Prayers.)

And now, O God, we commit ourselves, and all who are near and dear to us, to thy holy keeping. Let us go to our rest in humble trust and confidence in thy unfailing mercy. And let us remember, as we close our eyes in sleep, that the hour is coming in the which all that are in the graves shall hear the voice of the Son of man, and shall come forth—they that have done good, to the resurrection of life, and they that have done evil, to the resurrection of condemnation. And may we be so prepared by thy grace for this event, that, when our mortal bodies shall be committed to the ground, they may rest in sure and certain hope of a joyful resurrection to eternal life, through Jesus Christ our Lord, to whom, with thee, O Father, and the Holy Ghost, be all honor and glory, world without end. *Amen.*

ASCENSION DAY MORNING

Scripture Lesson
(ACTS 1:1–14)

O GOD, the King of glory, who hast exalted thine only Son, Jesus Christ, with great triumph unto thy kingdom in heaven, permit us, we beseech thee, to draw near to thee in his all-prevailing name, knowing that he ever liveth to make intercession for us miserable sinners. May this great High-Priest, who has passed into the heavens, ever be our advocate with thee. Accept, we implore thee, his mediation in our behalf; and when thou hearest, have mercy upon us. May our sins, though many, be forgiven us, through the riches of thy grace. Excite in us that godly sorrow for sin which worketh repentance unto salvation, not to be repented of. Give us that living faith which worketh by love, purifying the heart, overcoming the world, and bringing forth the abundant fruits of righteousness.

And, O thou, who hast ascended up on high, and hast led captivity captive, and hast received gifts for men, and hast given us apostles, and prophets, and evangelists, and pastors, and teachers, for the perfecting of thy saints and for the edification of thy church; grant, we beseech thee, to all the ministers and stewards of thy word, the abundance of thy grace, that they may evermore be ready to spread abroad thy gospel and to preach the glad tidings of salvation; until all men shall come, in the unity of the faith and of the knowledge of the Son of God, unto the perfect stature of the fullness of Christ.

We bless thee, heavenly Father, for all thy various and great mercies, for the wonderful work of redemption, and for the hope set before us in the gospel. We bless thee for the privilege of meeting together for prayer and praise on this memorable morning. Give us grace to celebrate, with grateful hearts, the exaltation of thy blessed Son to his eternal throne. May our thoughts also thither ascend, drawing up our affections and desires to heavenly things, and fitting and preparing us for the final enjoyment of thy presence in the mansions of glory.

(Occasional Prayers.)

We intercede with thee, gracious God, for all who are near and dear to us. Look with pity upon those who have hitherto placed their hopes and affections on the objects of this world, and have neglected the things which belong to their eternal peace. Quicken them from the death of sin, unto a new and holy life. Make them wise unto salvation; and enable them hereafter to seek those things which are above, where Christ sitteth at the right hand of God. And to those who have known the power of thy word, and have turned their hearts from serving the vain idols of this world, to serve thee, the living God, give the abundance of thy grace. Keep them through thine own name from the evils and temptations of this present life. Sanctify them through thy truth; and grant that, with them and all others who shall believe in thy Son Jesus Christ, we may have our perfect consummation and bliss in thy eternal and everlasting glory, through Jesus Christ our Lord, to whom, with thee, O Father, and the Holy Ghost, be all honor and glory, world without end. *Amen.*

ASCENSION DAY EVENING

Scripture Lesson
(HEBREWS 10:1–29)

THOU art the King of Glory, O Christ; thou hast ascended on high, "leading captivity captive and giving gifts to man." Thou art exalted far above all principalities and powers, and enthroned in the highest glory in thy heavenly kingdom, where saints and angels, and all the hosts of heaven, admire and adore thee. Be thou exalted, Lord, and reign in the greatness of thy power and majesty, till thou hast brought all enemies in subjection under thy feet. But, Lord, remember us, now that thou art in thy kingdom, where thou rulest and reignest on high. Oh regard the supplications and relieve the necessities of thy poor subjects and servants here below. Save, Lord, and let the King of heaven hear us when we call. And oh that we may feel the powerful attraction of thy grace and Holy Spirit, to draw up our minds and desires from the poor enjoyments here below to those most glorious and everlasting attainments above, where thou sittest at the right hand of God. Oh let us lay up our treasure and have our conversation with thee in heaven; and so love thy appearing, and desire to be dissolved and to be with Christ, that when Christ, who is our life, shall appear, we may also appear with him in glory; and after our ascending and dwelling above in heart and spirit, we may at last personally ascend, in soul and body, to be ever with the Lord; there, with thy whole triumphant church, to see and admire, and love and bless, and praise and glorify thee throughout eternal ages.

Blessed Jesus, thou art an High-Priest forever exalted to the right hand of God to give repentance and remission of sins. Thou canst be touched with a feeling of our infirmities, for thou knowest that we are dust and ashes. Therefore we come boldly to thy throne of grace, that we may find mercy and obtain grace to help in time of need. Oh give us true repentance and remission of all our sins. Make us thine indeed. Help us to lay aside every weight and the sin that doth so easily beset us, and to run with patience the race set before us. Unto thee we would commit and commend ourselves this night. May we repose in perfect peace and safety beneath the shadow of thy wings. Remember all the sick and afflicted, the poor and needy, and such as are in any way in danger or distress. Let thine ears be open to their cries and thy hands to supply all their want. Have mercy upon our world, which lieth in sin and wickedness. May thy gospel soon be preached to all men, and let the knowledge of the Lord soon cover the whole earth. Be our God and guide through life, and afterwards receive us to thy glory for our blessed Redeemer's sake. *Amen.*

WHITSUNDAY MORNING

Scripture Lesson
(JOHN 14:15–31)

O GOD, merciful Father, we give thanks to thee, for all the bounties of thy providence and grace; and especially for thy great goodness, in sending down the Holy Ghost, the blessed Comforter, to abide with thy church forever, and to direct, sanctify, and govern the hearts of thy people.

We wait this morning at thy footstool for new supplies of thy grace, to help our infirmities, to purify our thoughts, and to endue us with a spirit of prayer and supplication. Grant, we beseech thee, that thy Holy Spirit may now rest upon us, as a Spirit of wisdom and understanding; a Spirit of counsel and strength; a Spirit of knowledge and true godliness; a Spirit of holy fear and reverence; a Spirit of truth, and love, and unity; a Spirit of everlasting consolation.

(Occasional Prayers.)

O blessed Jesus, who, after thou hadst ascended up on high, didst shed upon thy holy apostles many excellent gifts, and who hast graciously promised to be with the ministers of thy church to the end of the world, we commend to thy heavenly grace all those whom thou hast appointed and commanded to feed thy flock. Make them diligent in preaching thy word and in dispensing thy holy sacraments; that they may teach the truth in love, and administer the wholesome discipline of the church in thy fear and to thy glory.

And to all thy people extend the riches of thy grace. Pour out thy Spirit upon all flesh. Send out thy light and thy truth to the nations who have never heard thy name. Look with pity on thy ancient people Israel. Give them a new heart, and revive a right spirit within them, that they may hereafter confess thy name, and keep thy statutes, and follow and obey thy ordinances. And shed abroad thy spiritual blessings on all the churches of thy saints throughout the world. May they be edified by thy truth; and, walking in thy fear and in the comfort of the Holy Ghost, may they enjoy on earth an earnest and foretaste of the joys and consolations of thy church triumphant in heaven.

In thy all-prevailing name, O blessed Savior, we offer these our prayers and supplications; ascribing to thee, with the Father and the Holy Ghost, equal adoration and praise, now and evermore. *Amen.*

WHITSUNDAY EVENING

Scripture Lesson
(ACTS 10:34–44)

O GOD, the Father of our Lord Jesus Christ, through whom we have access by one Spirit unto thee, hear, we beseech thee, the voice of praise and thanksgiving with which we close this day. We bless thee for all the benefits bestowed upon us, and especially for the spiritual blessings sealed to us by the coming of the Holy Ghost. We bless thee for thy holy word, for thy ministry and ordinances, and for all the means of grace which we have been permitted to enjoy this day.

[Thanksgiving for Communion-day.]

We praise thee, O God, for opening unto us a fountain for sin and uncleanness, and for purifying the humble and contrite soul by the washing of regeneration and the renewing of the Holy Ghost. Make us all partakers of this heavenly gift. Grant that all sinful affections may die in us, and that all things belonging to the Spirit may live and grow in us.

Give us grace to put off, concerning the former conversation, the old man, which is corrupt, according to the deceitful lusts; and to put on the new man, which, after thy image, is created in righteousness and true holiness. Cleanse the thoughts of our hearts by thy holy inspiration, that we may perfectly love thee and worthily magnify thy holy name. Grant, we beseech thee, that as thou didst teach the hearts of thy faithful people, by sending to them the light of thy Holy Spirit, so we, by the same Spirit, may have a right judgment in all things, and may evermore rejoice in his holy comfort.

O Lord God, inasmuch as the manifestation of the Spirit is given to every man to profit withal, let none receive his grace in vain. Have compassion on those who deny his eternal power and godhead, and show unto them who are thus in error the light of thy truth, that they may return into the way of righteousness. Be merciful unto such as profess to believe in him, and yet in works deny him, and are doing despite unto his grace. Let them no longer grieve that Holy Spirit by which they are sealed unto the day of redemption, but give them strength ever hereafter to obey his godly motions in righteousness and true holiness.

Be gracious unto those whom the Holy Ghost hath made overseers to feed the church, and may they be faithful dispensers of thy holy word and sacraments, through the grace of our dear Redeemer, Jesus Christ.

O God, Holy Ghost, sanctifier of the faithful, visit us, we pray thee, as a family and household, with thy love and favor. Enlighten our minds more and more with the light of the everlasting gospel; graft in our hearts a love of the truth; increase in us true religion; nourish us with all goodness; and of thy great mercy keep us steadfast in the faith, O blessed Spirit, whom, with the Father and the Son, we worship and glorify as one God, world without end. *Amen.*

FAST-DAY MORNING

Scripture Lesson
(ISAIAH 58)

O THOU justly-offended Sovereign; we desire to bow before thee, on this day of fasting, humiliation, and prayer, with the deepest self-abasement. May we offer unto thee the sacrifice of a broken and contrite heart, which thou wilt not despise. O our God! we are ashamed, and blush to lift up our faces to thee; for our iniquities are increased over our heads, and our trespasses are grown up into the heavens. We confess that we are by nature children of wrath even as others, and are under the curse of a broken law. We have wickedly and ungratefully departed from thee, the living God, and practically said, Depart from us, we desire not the knowledge of thy ways. We have hated and despised reproof, and disregarded thy warnings and instructions, abused thy goodness, and slighted thy mercies. Thou hast nourished and brought us up as children, but we have rebelled against thee. It is of the Lord's mercies that we are not consumed, because thy compassions fail not. Look down, O God! in mercy upon us miserable sinners. Pardon us through the mediation of Christ. Blot out all our transgressions, and be at peace with us. Wash us, and we shall be clean; purify us, and we shall be whiter than snow. Help us to keep such a fast-day as thou hast chosen, and to rend our hearts, and not our garments; and turn unto the Lord our God, for he is gracious and merciful, slow to anger, and of great kindness, and repenteth him of the evil. We acknowledge, O Lord, that iniquity abounds, and the love of many waxes cold. We lament the profanation of thy holy name and thy holy day; the disregard of thine authority, and the disobedience of thy sacred laws, and that such multitudes cast off fear, and restrain prayer before thee. Pour, we beseech thee, upon thy people a spirit of repentance and reformation. Let the wickedness of the wicked come to an end; but establish the just. May temperance and sobriety, industry and good habits, universally prevail. Behold thy people prostrate at the throne of grace, and hear their prayers, whether offered in the sanctuary, in the family, or in the closet. Spare thy people, O Lord! and give not thine heritage to reproach. We deserve all thy rebukes and chastisements. Return, O Lord! how long? and let it repent thee concerning us thy servants. Oh satisfy us early with thy mercy, that we may rejoice and be glad all our days. Preserve us from the pestilence that walketh in darkness, and the destruction that wasteth at noon-day. Save us from the ravages of tempests and earthquakes, fire and water, persecution and the sword. Continue the health and happiness of thy people. Bless the people of this nation in all their interests and concerns. Ever may we remember that righteousness exalteth a nation, but sin is a reproach to any people. Propitiously regard the President of the United States, all heads of department, and all in subordinate authority. Give them that wisdom which is from above, and is first pure, then peaceable, and easy to be entreated, full of mercy and good fruits, without partiality and without hypocrisy. May they ever desire to promote the glory of God, and the highest interest of this people. Bless the Governor of this State, and the legislative, judicial, and executive branches of the government. Smile mercifully upon all the ministers of religion. May they not shun to declare all the counsel of God, whether men will hear, or whether they will forbear. Make them burning and shining lights in thy golden candlesticks, and instrumental of great good to Zion. May all our colleges, academies, and schools of learning, be nurseries of useful knowledge and of piety. Bless all the institutions of true religion, humanity, and benevolence. Graciously prosper all efforts to spread a knowledge of the gospel of Christ among the great family of man. Compassionate the circumstances of all people, and fill the earth with thy glory. Now unto him that is able to do exceeding abundantly above all that we ask or think, according to the power that worketh in us, unto him be glory in the church, by Christ Jesus, throughout all ages, world without end. *Amen.*

FAST-DAY EVENING

Scripture Lesson
(JEREMIAH 9)

O GOD, thou hast established thy throne in the heavens, and thy kingdom extendeth over all. We prostrate ourselves before thee, deeply impressed with a sense of the vastness of thy agency and dominion. Thou changest the times and the seasons. Empires rise and fall, and fade and flourish, at thy bidding; and all nations are in thy hand but as clay in the hand of the potter.

But none of thy dispensations are arbitrary. Whatever thou doest is done because, O Father, it seemeth good in thy sight, and thy judgment is always according to truth. Thou art holy in all thy ways, and righteous in all thy works; and thou art good even in wrath. Thou rememberest mercy, and dost not afflict willingly, nor grieve the children of men.

Therefore it is that we have been this day humbling ourselves in thy presence. For we acknowledge that we have been deeply guilty. Thou hast nourished and brought up children, but we have rebelled against thee. The ox knoweth his owner, and the ass his master's crib; but we have not known, we have not considered. Thou hast multiplied thy blessings, but we have perverted them. Because of swearing, the land has mourned. Pride has compassed us about as a chain. Discontent has rebelled against thine appointment. How has the love of money, which is the root of all evil, abounded among us! How have thy Sabbaths been profaned, and thine ordinances disregarded! How has the gospel been undervalued, neglected, despised! And all our transgressions have been more aggravated than those of any other people, because thou hast favored us unspeakably more than all the families of the earth.

Therefore thou couldst easily and justly have destroyed us; but thou hast not stirred up all thy wrath. In all that is come upon us for our evil deeds, thou hast punished us less than our iniquities deserve. Yet thou hast testined thy displeasure; and visited us with thy judgments; so that, when we looked for light and peace, we have seen darkness and trouble.

Oh let us not be inattentive to the design of thy dealings, or insensible under thy rebukes. Thou hast said, Is any afflicted? let him pray. Call upon me in the day of trouble, and I will deliver thee, and thou shalt glorify me. Fulfill the word unto thy servants, upon which thou hast caused us to hope. And oh let not the calamity be removed only, but, above all, sanctified; let it appear that we have felt the rod, and him that appointed it; and may we be able to say, It is good for us that we have been afflicted.

For which purpose, bless, we beseech thee, the word of thy grace which has been spoken, and grant that the professed humiliation of the day may be real; for thou lookest to the heart. And let it also be universal: may it extend from the highest to the lowest; may it pervade the city and the country; may it enter every church and every family; let none of us lose sight of ourselves in the public calamity. May each individual retire and ask, What have I done? and what wilt thou have me to do?

Regard favorably the government under which we live. Bless the representatives of the people and the magistracy of the land; may all be wise in council, exemplary in conduct, and faithful to their trusts.

And thus may we be reformed and not destroyed. Thus may we be a holy that we may be a happy people, whose God is the Lord. Return, O Lord, how long? and let it repent thee concerning thy servants. Make us glad according to the days wherein thou hast afflicted us, and the years wherein we have seen evil. And let the beauty of the Lord our God be upon us, and establish thou the work of our hands upon us; yea, the work of our hands establish thou it.

Finally, blessed Lord, leave us not, nor forsake us, while we are continued in this vale of tears. Let thy whole will be done in us and by us, until we shall be delivered from all the effects of sin and death. And to the Father, the Son, and the Holy Spirit, be rendered the kingdom, power, and glory, forever and ever. *Amen.*

GENERAL HUMILIATION, PRAYER, AND THANKSGIVING

Scripture Lesson
(PSALM 46 or 55)

MERCIFUL God, our Father in Christ, who hast promised that thou wilt regard the prayers of the destitute, and not despise their supplications: make thyself known everywhere as the Father of all men, whom thy Son has purchased with his precious blood. Remember in mercy those to whom the light of thy Gospel hath not penetrated, and let it shine upon all the earth. Graciously remember all who profess to be disciples of thy Son, and grant that they may be Christians, not in name only, but in deed. Destroy superstition, and overthrow the strongholds of unbelief. Let thy Zion be the object of thine especial care, and grant that all who profess to belong to her may experience in their hearts the power of evangelical doctrine, unto the salvation of their souls.

We commend unto thee all the rulers of the earth. Grant unto them a truly Christian spirit, and cause thy fear to be before their eyes and in their hearts. We entreat thee, for Christ's sake, to be especially mindful of our land; and as thou hast in times past made thyself known unto this people as their God, we pray thee, in times to come, to show thy favor unto them. Praise be to thee for the liberty that we enjoy; forbid that it should ever degenerate into licentiousness. Let thine eye be ever open towards this thy people. To this end, inspire the President of the United States, and all others in authority, with the spirit of wisdom and of thy fear. Grant that, through their exertions, peace and unity may be preserved and diffused throughout this republic, and that they may have the honor of thy name and the extension of the kingdom of thy Son at heart. Grant that the several confederated States may remain perpetually united together by the bond of love and peace, that their union may endure to the end of time. We commend unto thine especial favor the State in which we dwell. Direct our government by thy Spirit, that the effect of all its laws may be the welfare of the citizens. Grant that equity and justice may be administered by our magistrates without respect to persons. Purify our land from vice, and grant that the peaceable fruits of righteousness may abound on every hand.

Have mercy upon our beloved congregation; may peace and brotherly love be preserved and increased in our midst; bless the officers of the church; bless parents and children, and especially our Sabbath-schools. Graciously afford thy powerful protection unto all mothers, widows, and orphans. Grant help to all that are in distress or danger, and have mercy upon all who cry unto thee. Graciously preserve us from national calamities; from war, scarcity, and famine; from the rage of fire and of overflowing floods; from pestilence and other plagues, and from all the calamities which our sins have deserved. Grant favorable seasons, that our store-houses may be replenished with the fruits of the earth. Bless the labors of the husbandman, and all pursuits by sea and land that are approved in thy sight.

Thou holy God! preserve us from all sin and wickedness, and assist us by thy good Spirit, that we may not forfeit thy blessings by transgression, nor bring upon us thy righteous chastisements. To this end, enable us to make thy love our chief delight; to seek the gifts of thy Holy Spirit as our highest good; to esteem it our greatest honor to be regarded as thy children and to be like unto thee; and to prize the robes of the Savior's righteousness as our chief ornament. Preserve us, especially in the hour of death, from all assaults of the adversary, and increase our faith in thy Son Jesus, that we may overcome all the terrors of death. And when our tongue can no longer speak, then let thy Spirit make intercession for us with groanings that cannot be uttered, and teach everyone to say in his heart, Abba! Father! into thy hands I commend my spirit. We beseech thee earnestly, our faithful God, that we may live, in thy fear, and die in thy grace, and go hence in thy peace, and rest in the grave under thy protection, and be raised up by thy power, and in the end inherit eternal life, through Jesus Christ, thy dear Son, unto whom, with thee and the Holy Spirit, be adoration and praise, honor and glory, now and forever. *Amen.*

THANKSGIVING DAY MORNING

Scripture Lesson
(PSALM 107)

[To be used on the second or third Thursday of November, or on such other day as shall be appointed by the civil authority.]

MOST gracious God, by whose unspeakable mercy we are again permitted to present the annual tribute of our thanks and praise, we bless thee for the continual manifestations of thy goodness to us and to all the children of men. By thy wisdom, O Lord, thou hast founded the earth; by understanding thou hast established the heavens; by thy knowledge the depths are broken up, and the clouds drop down the dew. We bless thee for the return of seed-time and harvest, and for crowning the year with the bounties of thy providence. We praise thee for all thy gracious dealings towards us, and we beseech thee, of thy great goodness, to receive the thank-offerings with which we come before thee this day.

We acknowledge, heavenly Father, the imperfection of our best services. We confess that we are sinners before thee, and altogether unworthy of thy mercies. But we know that thou art kind, even to the unthankful and the evil. Thou makest thy sun to rise on the evil and on the good, and sendest rain on the just and on the unjust. Give us a due sense of thy wonderful condescension and forbearance, that our hearts may be moved to contrition for our past negligence and sin, and excited to new diligence, zeal, and devotion, for the future.

We beseech thee, O Lord, to pour down upon the inhabitants of this land the spirit of unfeigned gratitude for all thy mercies. May they enter thy gates with thanksgiving, and thy courts with praise. May they honor thee with all their substance, and with the first-fruits of all their increase. And grant that they may show forth their devotion to thee not only with their lips, but also in their lives. Preserve them from the unholy rejoicings of the sensual and profane; restrain every sinful and intemperate indulgence; and grant us all grace, heavenly Father, to use thy blessings without abusing them; with zeal for thy glory, submission to thy will, and a faithful adherence to the gospel of thy Son; with moderation and humility, with justice and purity, with charity, forbearance, and brotherly love; that, amidst these and all thy blessings, we may seek thy glory and the increase of thy kingdom.

Fill our hearts, O God, with a spirit of tenderness and compassion for all around us. May we rejoice with those that rejoice, and weep with those that weep. May we be ready to impart of the abundance which thou hast given to us, to the poor and needy, the distressed and the afflicted, the widow and the fatherless; and thus fulfill the law of pure and undefiled religion before God and the Father.

(Occasional Prayers.)

Grant us, heavenly Father, a continuance of all thy mercies, through Jesus Christ our Lord. *Amen.*

THANKSGIVING-DAY EVENING

Scripture Lesson
(PSALM 104)

O LORD, our Governor, how excellent is thy name in all the world, thou that hast set thy glory above the heavens! What is man, that thou art mindful of him, and the son of man, that thou visitest him? Thou makest him to have dominion over the works of thy hands, and thou hast put all things in subjection under his feet. O Lord, our Governor, how excellent is thy name in all the world!

We praise thee, O Lord; for it is good to sing praises unto our God. We thank thee for the dispensation of thy grace through the mediation of thy blessed Son; for the bounties of thy providence; for the plenty with which thou hast crowned the labors of the husbandman; for the preservation of our health; for the reign of peace; and for the enjoyment of our civil and religious liberties. We thank thee for the comforts and privileges of which we have been permitted to partake this day. We acknowledge thy hand in every mercy, and desire to render back to thee the homage of gratitude and love. We acknowledge that every good and perfect gift is from above, and cometh down from the Father of lights, with whom is no variableness, neither shadow of turning. But we confess unto thee, O God, that our souls are burdened with iniquity; that we are frail and erring creatures; that our hearts are corrupt, and that our hands are not clean in thy sight. We lament that we have so often dishonored thee. We acknowledge and bewail our manifold sins and wickedness, which we from time to time most grievously have committed against thy Divine Majesty. We deplore the alienation of our minds from thee, and the corruption of our hearts. We feel that there is no spiritual health in us. O Lord, have mercy upon us, and enter not into judgment with us. Look with pity upon all that we have thought or said or done amiss this day. Be present with us, as we now present our supplications unto thee; and, through the intercession of thy dear

Son, grant unto us the pardon of all our sins. Give thy Holy Spirit to comfort the troubled mind, and soothe the pains and wipe away the stains of guilt. May we retire to rest in perfect charity with all men. May we be enabled, through thy help, to love our enemies, to bless them that curse us, to do good to them that hate us, and to pray for them which despitefully use us and persecute us; that we may be the children of our Father who is in heaven.

(Occasional Prayers.)

We now commit all our concerns to thee, O God, for the year to come. Grant us thy blessings, both temporal and spiritual, for Jesus Christ's sake, to whom, with thee, O Father, and the Holy Ghost, be honor and glory, world without end.

Unto God's gracious mercy and protection we commit ourselves. The Lord bless us and keep us. The Lord make his face to shine upon us, and be gracious unto us. The Lord lift up his countenance upon us, and give us peace, both now and evermore. *Amen.*

SACRAMENT-SABBATH MORNING

Scripture Lesson
(MARK 15:1–39)

O HOLY and gracious Lord God, who wilt by no means clear the guilty, yet sparest those who confess their sins unto thee, look down with compassion upon us, thy servants, who are now humbled before thee, imploring thy fatherly forgiveness. Spare us, good Lord, spare us, for we are miserable sinners! We cannot set all our transgressions in order before thee, nor confess them so truly as we ought to do; yet we desire not to cloak them nor to dissemble before thy face. Be merciful unto us, we most humbly beseech thee; for we put our confidence wholly in thy mercy, and not in any thing that we do. We have destroyed ourselves, but in thee is our help. To whom else should we go? Thou only hast the words of eternal life. Grant unto us, we beseech thee, pardon and peace, that we may be cleansed from all our sins, and may serve thee with a quiet mind.

We praise thee, O God, for the multitude of thy blessings vouchsafed unto us, particularly for the many opportunities which thou affordest us of becoming wise unto salvation.

What shall we render unto thee this day for all the benefits which thou hast done unto us? We will receive the cup of salvation, and call upon the name of the Lord. We will pay our vows in the courts of thy house, and in the presence of all thy people.

We give thee most humble and hearty thanks, O Almighty God, our heavenly Father, that thou hast given thy Son, our Savior Jesus Christ, not only to die for us, but to be our spiritual food and sustenance in the holy sacrament of his body and blood. Enable us by living faith to receive the same in remembrance of his meritorious passion and death, whereby alone we obtain the remission of our sins, and are made partakers of the kingdom of heaven.

Give grace, O heavenly Father, to all thy ministering servants, that they may, both by their life and doctrine, set forth thy true and lively word, and rightly and duly administer thy holy sacraments. And to all thy people give thy heavenly grace, especially to such as shall assemble with us in thy holy temple, and shall come to the holy communion of the body and blood of our Savior, Christ. And may numbers be added to thy church continually, of those who are willing to join themselves unto thee in an everlasting covenant, not to be forgotten.

Pitifully behold the sorrows of those who are filled with groundless fears lest they should eat and drink unworthily. May they hear and receive the comfortable things which Christ our Savior saith unto all who truly turn unto him. May they come unto him laboring and heavy-laden with the burden of their sins, and so find rest unto their souls.

Finally, we beseech thee to have compassion upon those who shall most unthankfully refuse to come to thy table, though so graciously called and bidden. May they take heed lest, by withdrawing themselves from this holy supper of their Lord, they provoke his just indignation against them. May they earnestly consider how little their excuses will avail before thee, and by thy grace be brought to a better mind; seriously remembering that, if they are not by faith made partakers of Christ's atoning sacrifice, they have no life in them, and neither part nor lot in his salvation.

Grant this, O God of mercy, for the sake of Jesus Christ, our only Lord and Savior. *Amen.*

SACRAMENT-SABBATH EVENING

Scripture Lesson
(ROMANS 12)

ALMIGHTY God and Father, who, according to the multitude of thy mercies, dost so put away the sins of those who truly repent that thou rememberest them no more, look in mercy upon us, thy servants, who earnestly desire pardon and forgiveness. Impute not unto us our manifold transgressions, but wash them away in the blood of thy beloved Son. Graciously vouchsafe to receive us to thy favor. Sanctify us and strengthen us by thy Holy Spirit, and at length bring us unto the kingdom of heaven and to everlasting life. We praise thee for thy promises of forgiveness to those who truly turn unto thee.

We bless thee for another day of sacred rest, which thou hast vouchsafed unto us, and for all the blessings of the same. Above all things, we give thee most humble and hearty thanks for the redemption of the world by the death of our Lord and Savior, Jesus Christ. May we always remember the exceeding great love of our Master and only Savior, Jesus Christ, thus dying for us, and the innumerable benefits which by his precious blood-shedding he hath obtained for us, and also his goodness and loving-kindness in instituting and ordaining holy ordinances as pledges of his love, to our great and endless comfort.

Help us to remember the solemn vows which we have this day renewed in thy presence, and in the presence of all thy people; and enable us truly to perform them. May we go forth into the world bearing about us the marks of a crucified Savior. Having enlisted ourselves again under the banner of the Captain of our salvation, may we manfully fight the good fight of faith, and continue his faithful soldiers and servants unto our life's end. Grant that we may have power and strength to achieve victory, and to triumph over the devil, and the world, and the flesh. May we be encouraged in our holy warfare by the ensamples of the glorious company of the apostles, the goodly fellowship of the prophets, the noble army of martyrs, and of all the holy church triumphant, who have been made more than conquerors through him who loved them and bought them with his blood. And when he shall come to be glorified in his saints, and to be admired in all them that believe, may we sit down with Abraham, Isaac, and Jacob, and all thy redeemed people, at the marriage-supper of the Lamb.

Grant, also, O Lord, we beseech thee, that those who have waited on thee this day in thy holy temple, and around thy table, may renew their spiritual strength. May all professing Christians see that they are thy disciples by the love which they have one to another. O God, who hast taught us that all our doings without charity are worth nothing, send thy Holy Ghost, and pour into our hearts that most excellent gift of love, the very bond of peace and of all virtues, without which whosoever liveth is counted dead before thee. Let there be no schism in the body of Christ; but let the members have the same care one of another, knowing that, if any sin against their brother and wound his weak conscience, they sin against Christ.

Convert the hearts of all those who are thrusting away from them thy great mercies; especially of such as have this day neglected thy ordinances, and turned aside from thy holy table.

And if any have there appeared before thee with unclean hands and unsanctified hearts, without the marriage garment required by thee in holy Scripture, not discerning the Lord's body, may they search and examine their conscience, and repent, lest, after the taking of this holy sacrament, Satan enter into them as he entered into Judas, and fill them full of all iniquity, and bring them to destruction both of body and soul.

We ask these blessings in the name of Jesus Christ, our only Lord and Savior. *Amen.*

ANNIVERSARY OF THE REFORMATION

Scripture Lesson
(EZRA 9)

OUR Father in Christ! Thou hast made manifest thy power and faithfulness, and glorified thy name. Thou hast delivered the church of thy Son from the power of darkness. Thou hast broken the degrading chains of her bondage. Thou hast opened anew thy word of life unto the flock of Christ, and gathered together all who thirsted after righteousness, under the banner of the true and saving faith. It was thy work, and not the work of man. Thou didst raise up those faithful servants, who discerned and deeply lamented the corruptions of the church. Thou gavest them light, and madest them partakers of liberty in Christ, that they might bring others to a knowledge of the same. Thou didst make them willing, and arm them with courage, to stand forth in thy strength, as witnesses for thee, to assail the corruption which had found its way into holy places, and not to fear the enmity of the mighty of this world. They deeply felt that, trusting in their own strength, they could accomplish nothing, and would soon be overcome; but they confided in thee as their tower of defense, their trusty shield and weapon. And thou didst not suffer them to be discomfited. We will magnify thy grace, while we have our being, and declare thy truth continually.

Thanks be unto thee, that thou hast since then preserved unto thy church the dearly-purchased heritage, and made us partakers thereof also. We bless thee that we have thy word, free from additions of human invention, in its purity and its power; and that the sacred ordinances instituted by Christ are administered among us as they were established by him.

Thou good and gracious God, continue evermore to be the shield and buckler, the sure abode and salvation, of thy church. Enlighten, sanctify, and bless her through thy word and ordinances. Enable her rightly to value the privileges which thou hast graciously bestowed upon her, that she may hold fast and faithfully administer the treasure committed to her, and suffer none to spoil her of her crown. Purify her from all offenses, and graciously defend her from all schisms and divisions. Vouchsafe at all times to our congregations pious and faithful teachers, who shall proclaim thy word in its purity and integrity, constrained by the deep convictions of the heart; and accompany their preaching with the powerful influences of thy Spirit, that it may bring forth blessed fruit in the hearts and lives of Christians. O Lord! grant that we may dwell in thy regenerated church as thy regenerated children, walking worthily of the blessed gospel, and adorning its doctrines by a holy life. Help us to stand fast in the liberty wherewith Christ hath made us free, and never suffer us to become the slaves of men or of sin. May holiness be the ornament of thy house forever, and to the glory of our God may the light shine from the candlestick of every congregation. Father of all men, have mercy upon all! Bestow the blessings for which we are permitted to praise thee, upon those of our brethren who are still destitute of them. Restrain everywhere the kingdom of darkness upon earth; diffuse the light of thy gospel amongst the nations which sit in darkness and in the shadow of death. Send forth many laborers, who shall be willing to spend and be spent, in testifying the gospel of the grace of God; and enable them to gather many souls into thy kingdom. Hasten thy coming, O Lord; hasten the time when the heathen shall come and worship before thee, and all the earth shall glorify thy name. Convert those who hate thy word, and forgive them, seeing that they know not what they do. Send help unto all that suffer tribulation and oppression and persecution for conscience' sake, and deliver them by thy mighty arm out of all their troubles. Give light to those who have gone astray; give assurance to the doubting, and strength to the weak; and render thy children more and more meet for their eternal and blissful inheritance. And thus bless us and all men, in Christ our Lord, with understanding and wisdom, with faith and love, with peace in life, with hope in death.

Lord God Almighty, hear and answer our supplications. Unto thee, the Father, with the Son and Holy Spirit, be praise, and honor, and adoration, and thanksgiving, in the church which is in Christ Jesus! *Amen.*

Prayers

FOR THE BEGINNING OF THE HURRICANE SEASON—ABOUT 25th JULY

O MOST powerful and glorious Lord God, who dwellest in heaven, but beholdest all things below, at whose command the winds blow and lift up the waves of the sea, and who stillest the rage thereof, be pleased to receive us into thy almighty and most gracious favor and protection; and although for our iniquities we have deserved to be visited with storm and tempest, yet do thou give us true repentance, and so hold the four winds of heaven, that we may dwell safely in our habitations from all fear of evil, and that we and all the inhabitants of our island, and all the other islands, as well as all other places visited by hurricanes, may in peace and quietness serve thee our God, and be kept in safety during this fearful season, to enjoy the blessings of the hour with a thankful remembrance of thy mercies; learning both by thy past chastisements to amend our lives, and for thy clemency to praise and glorify thy name, through Jesus Christ, our Lord and Savior. *Amen.*

BEGINNING OF THE HURRICANE SEASON

O MOST mighty God and merciful Father, who hast compassion upon all men and hatest nothing that thou hast made, nor wouldest the death of a sinner, but rather that he should turn from his sin and be saved,—mercifully forgive us our trespasses, and receive and comfort us who are grieved and wearied with the burden of our sins. Mercy is thy darling attribute; and to thee only it belongeth to forgive iniquity, transgression, and sin. Spare us, therefore, good Lord, from all the stormy threatenings of this peculiar time, spare thy people whom thou hast redeemed; enter not into judgment with thy servants, who are vile earth and miserable sinners. Thou art a merciful God, full of compassion, long-suffering, and of great pity. Thou sparest when we deserve punishment, and in thy wrath thinkest upon mercy. We are thy people, good Lord; spare us at this time, and let not thine heritage be brought to confusion. Hear us, O Lord, and according to the greatness of thy compassion look thou upon us, through the merits and mediation of thy Son Jesus Christ, our Lord. *Amen.*

DURING THE HURRICANE SEASON

O LORD, thou hast been our dwelling-place in all generations. To whom can we go but unto thee, that hast the words of eternal life? Give us nearer access to thee than ever we enjoyed before. From the end of the earth, will we cry unto thee. When our heart is overwhelmed, lead us to the Rock that is higher than we. Oh grant, that we may trust in thee, and feel thee a present help in trouble.

O Lord, being afflicted, we pray; we set our faces to seek thee in this day of trouble. To thee our God belong mercies and forgiveness, though we have rebelled against thee. Lord, thou hast watched upon the danger, and brought it upon us.

Our sins appear like an infinite deluge, or mountains over our heads. As a fountain casteth out her waters, so our heart casteth out its wickedness. Everything in which our heart is concerned is polluted. If thou wert to deal with us according to our sin, thou wouldst sweep us away from the face of the earth. Our flesh trembleth for fear of thee, and we are afraid of thy judgments. Thou turnest man to destruction, and sayest, Return, ye children of men. Why hast thou spared us hitherto, O Lord? We are no better than others. Lord, teach us so to number our days, that we may apply our hearts unto wisdom. We pray that this time of danger may lead us to cleave closer to the Lord Jesus Christ. O thou that art the hiding-place from the wind and a covert from the tempest, like rivers of waters in a dry place, and the shadow of a great rock in a weary land, hide us deeper in thyself. Cause us to hear thy loving-kindness in the morning, for in thee do we trust. Oh grant, in this time of terror, when so many are taken suddenly to their great account, that we may be found in Christ. May the Lord be all our righteousness. May Jesus be our present and eternal all.

May we be willing to be hell-deserving in ourselves, and heaven-deserving in Christ alone. Love us freely; be like the dew upon our souls. May we be kept in perfect peace, our minds being stayed on thee, because we trust in thee. Make us feel that He who holds the winds in the hollow of his hands, is the same who was nailed to the accursed tree for us. Make thy truth our shield and buckler; do not let us be afraid of the terror by night, nor of the storm that howls by day, nor for the swelling waves that walk in darkness, nor for the destruction that wasteth at noonday. Be thou our refuge; then there shall no evil befall us, neither shall any danger come near our dwelling.

We pray that we may improve by this solemn visitation. May afflicting time be quickening time. Lord, increase our faith; Lord, teach us to pray. Cleanse us from secret faults, keep us back from presumptuous sins. Wean us from this world; may our conversation be in heaven. Make us willing to be in quiet, and willing to be exposed to the threatening storm; willing to live, and willing to die; willing to depart and be with Christ, which is far better.

Most merciful Father, we pray for thine own children who are exposed to the terrible dangers of the hurricane now raging, that thou wilt be their defense; watch over them and comfort them in this their day of trial. Give them peace and joy in believing; give them an anchor within the vail. Make them more than conquerors through him that loved them. O God, who hast no pleasure in the death of the wicked, but rather that they should turn and live, spare unconverted souls who are now trembling on the brink of eternity. Lord, turn their hard hearts, turn their dying eyes to Jesus, lifted up to save sinners. Give them to look as the dying thief looked to Jesus, and to cry, Lord, remember me! Have compassion on the bereaved; may they spread their sorrows before Jesus, and be comforted.

And now turn us, O God of our salvation, and cause thine anger towards us to cease. Wilt thou not revive us again, that thy people may rejoice in thee? Give a double portion of thy Spirit to thy ministers at this solemn time, that they may be instant in season and out of season. Quicken thy people in prayer and supplication, and let this time of trial become a time of blessing from on high. Make us more compassionate to the unfortunate and afflicted; make us more laudably alive to the interests of Zion; make us more humble, more holy, more watchful; make us take heed, watch, and pray, seeing we know not when the time is, lest the Master coming suddenly should find us sleeping.

O Lord, hear; O Lord, forgive, and save us, for Christ's sake. *Amen.*

DURING THE HURRICANE SEASON

O LORD our God, thou art the Almighty God. Thou art the God of the ocean as well as of the dry land. The winds and waves are under thy control. The winds cannot blow, nor the waves of the sea lift up themselves on high, but by thy permission and at thy command. When thou willest, the winds blow and the waves rage; and when thou willest, there is a calm. When thou sayest to the infuriated elements, Hither shalt thou come and no farther, instantly thy voice is obeyed.

In thy sovereign providence we are brought into great peril. The threatening winds are howling around us; our soul is melted because of trouble. O Lord, we cry unto thee in our day of trouble! Oh bring us out of our distresses! Save, Lord, or we perish. Command the winds to be still, and they will instantly obey thee. But if any of us should perish, oh let not our souls perish: but through the death of Jesus, who endured the storms of divine wrath, may they be preserved from hell, and may they enter heaven. Thy will be done! Graciously hear our prayer, for Jesus' sake. *Amen.*

END OF THE HURRICANE SEASON

O LORD our God, thou art most mighty and merciful, and thy mercy is over all thy works. We appear before thee, to present our thanksgivings for the great deliverance thou hast wrought for us. If thou hadst dealt with us according to our deserts, we would have been cut off in the midst of our sins, and our souls sent to the lowest hell. In the midst of judgment thou hast remembered mercy. Glory to thy gracious name, that thou hast extended towards us the arm of thy mercy, and not the hand of thy vengeance!

O Lord, we have seen thy wonders, and thou hast manifested the greatness of thy power in raising the storm, and then in commanding the raging tempest to be still. We thank our God and Father that thou hast heard our supplications, and hast preserved our lives and our property. Thou hast not dealt with us according to our sins, neither hast thou rewarded us according to our iniquities. O Lord, we cried unto thee, and thou didst deliver us out of our distress. Thou didst send forth thy commandment, and the stormy wind was turned into a calm. Holy Spirit, enable us to praise our protecting and delivering God for his goodness, and for his wonderful works to us, the children of men. Let our preserved lives be ever devoted unto thee, O Jesus, who hast saved us from impending danger, and laid down thy life to save us from the miseries of hell. May the obedience and holiness of our future lives testify the unfeigned gratitude of our souls; and deeply impress our hearts with a grateful sense of thy goodness towards us, that we may love thee more fervently, serve thee more cheerfully, and trust in thy salvation more assuredly, than we have done hitherto. Suffer us not to become careless, because thou hast lengthened out our unprofitable lives, which must soon terminate; but make us more watchful and diligent, from gratitude for thy mercies vouchsafed to us. O Lord, be to us the God of our salvation.

It is better to trust in thee, O Lord, than to put confidence in man. Thou art our refuge and our God, and we will praise thee. We will give thanks unto thee; for thou art good, and thy mercy endureth forever. *Amen.*

OCCASIONAL
PRAYERS AND THANKSGIVING
FOR THE EXTENSION OF CHRIST'S KINGDOM

ALMIGHTY and eternal God, thou Father of light and of life! We offer thee adoration and praise, that thou hast sent into this world thine only-begotten Son, our Lord Jesus Christ, in order to make thyself known in him among all nations unto their salvation, and to save them, by a great deliverance, from the night of their sins. We render thanks and praise unto thee that by thy holy gospel thou hast called us also from darkness to light, and from the deep shadow of death to the joyful day of life! We rejoice and give praise to thee that unto us the great mystery of godliness is disclosed. God was manifest in the flesh, justified in the Spirit, seen of angels, preached unto the Gentiles, believed on in the world, received up into glory. We now have a God and Father; we know whence to obtain wisdom and strength to overcome sin, and are enabled to pass with safety and joy even through the dark valley of the shadow of death, seeing that we shall walk before God in the light of the living forever!

We entreat thee, our Father in Christ, that in thy tender mercy thou wouldst cause this heavenly light to shine, at all times, within us and among us, that we may more and more know and honor thee, the only true God, and Jesus Christ, whom thou hast sent; and that, as becometh children of the light, we may let our light shine before men to the praise of thy name.

Build up more and more gloriously thy kingdom of light and peace among all who are called after the name of Christ. May that kingdom come in every congregation, in every family, in the hearts of all Christians, with increased demonstration of the Spirit and of power, and with more abundant fullness of its blessings.

We pray especially for the extension of thy kingdom in our land. O Lord, there are yet many places whence the voice of praise and thanksgiving ariseth not to thee, and where the voice of thy word is not heard. Give entrance unto thy light, that this darkness may be dispelled; grant unto thy servants an open door to preach thy gospel, that it may also reach those hearts that are afar off, converting all unto *thee* that have gone astray.

Hear our supplication in behalf of our brethren in the faith. O Lord, forbid that they should anywhere relapse into indifference and forget thee, the God of their fathers. Bestow upon them, through our instrumentality, the means of grace; open thou our hearts, that we may realize that we are debtors to them, and may resolve to pay the debt of love which we owe them. Make us willing to do good, especially to them who are of the household of faith, until in every place of our land, inhabited by our brethren, the bread of life shall be broken and the voice of all unite to praise the beauty of holiness.

To this end pour out thy blessings upon the institutions which are principally subservient to the promotion of human happiness. Bless the church and her ministers. May all the preachers of thy word be men full of faith and of the Holy Ghost; sincere, humble, godly, and persevering, strong to build up the kingdom of truth and of love. Bless the schools and their teachers. Increase their number, until they shall cover the length and breadth of the land; and may they all flourish and prosper, under the government of wise, active, and faithful teachers. Bless the sacred institution of domestic life, and those who minister at its altar. May pure morals and genuine piety dwell in the bosom of our families; may all parents strive to bring up their children in the love and service of their Savior; and may every earthly habitation become a nursery for our Father's house in heaven!

But thou, O Father of men, hast given thy Son for the whole world, and it is thy will that through Jesus Christ all should be brought to the knowledge of thee. Therefore we come boldly unto thy throne of grace, to pray for the world, which knoweth thee not. Send the glad tidings of salvation through Christ unto all the ends of the earth, that the idols of the heathen may be cast down, that the kingdom of sin and pollution may be destroyed through the kingdom of thy grace, and that, from the rising of the sun unto the going down thereof, the hearts of men may bring unto thee, their God, a pure sacrifice of praise.

With gratitude and joy we see that in many places the field is white for the harvest. Lord of the harvest, send laborers into the great harvest, and deign to accept our services also, that we may be co-workers with thee. Grant thy blessing unto us and all our fellow-Christians in this glorious work of faith and love. Pour out upon all congregations the Spirit of prayer, that they may preserve this holy cause pure and uncorrupted; that it may continually advance, until the sympathies of every heart shall respond to its claims.

O God! hear our prayer, for the sake of Jesus Christ. Let the church of Christ spread from land to land, in the strength of this thy promise: "I shall give thee the heathen for thine inheritance, and the uttermost parts of the earth for thy possession;" until the redeemed of the Lord shall unite with the blessed choir of heaven in the song of praise: "The kingdoms of this world are become the kingdoms of our Lord and of his Christ." "Blessing, and glory, and wisdom, and thanksgiving, and honor, and power, and might, be unto our God, forever and ever." *Amen.*

FOR THE SPREAD OF THE GOSPEL

O FATHER of light and giver of all wisdom, bless every society formed for the conversion of Jews or Gentiles, and for the spread and advancement of thy truth, at home or abroad.

Look with favor on all missionaries now among the heathen. Oh prepare thy way in the wilderness. May every valley be exalted, and every hill be made low; may the crooked be made straight, and the rough places plain; and let thy word have free course everywhere and be glorified. May thy doctrine drop as the rain, and distill as the dew, and thy word never return unto thee void, but prosper abundantly, and accomplish all that for which thou dost send it. Give thy servants health and strength, vigor of mind, and devotedness of heart; and may they all be chosen vessels to bear thy name before the Gentiles. May the deadening influence of climate, heathen customs, and loss of means of grace, be more than counteracted by a special supply of thy Holy Spirit. Give them grace to be faithful unto death, and may they receive from the Savior's hands the crown of life and glory. Grant that thousands and tens of thousands may rise up to call thee blessed. May the little leaven leaven the whole lump; and all nations whom thou hast made, fall down and worship before thee, and glorify thy name, through thy dear Son. *Amen.*

TO BE USED ON ENTERING THE CHURCH

BLESSED Lord, impress my mind with a solemn sense of thy presence. May thy Holy Spirit assist me in my devotions; and enable me to hear thy word with profit to my soul, through Jesus Christ my Savior. *Amen.*

WHEN THE SERVICE IS ENDED

O LORD, I thank thee for this opportunity of worshiping thee in thy holy temple; pardon the wanderings of my heart, and accept my prayers and thanksgivings. Let thy word be profitable to my soul, and bless me and all who have waited upon thee, for thy dear Son's sake, Jesus Christ our Lord. *Amen.*

FOR COMMUNION-DAY MORNING

BLESSED Lord, let thy gracious presence be in an especial manner with those of us who shall approach thy table this day. Pour into our hearts humility, and faith, and charity, and all those holy dispositions which should fill the hearts of those who partake of this holy sacrament. May we remember with continued thankfulness the exceeding great love of our only Savior Jesus Christ in dying for us, and the innumerable benefits which, by his precious blood-shedding, he hath obtained for us; and may we, and all who are partakers of this holy communion, be filled with thy grace and heavenly benediction through Thy Son's true body and blood. Make these pledges of thy love the savor of life unto our souls. May we partake of them, not trusting in our own righteousness, but in thy manifold and great mercies; and may we by faith eat the flesh and drink the blood of the Son of God, and be constrained by a sense of his love to yield ourselves up to his service, and to run with enlarged hearts in, the way of his commandments. *Amen.*

BEFORE RECEIVING THE SACRAMENT

ALMIGHTY God, whose blessed Son Jesus Christ, for the forgiveness of our sins, did suffer death upon the cross; prepare us, we beseech thee, by thy grace, for the worthy celebration of that holy sacrament, wherein thy Son's true body and blood are present, which he has pleased to appoint for a continual remembrance of his death, for a pledge of his love, and for a sign and means of grace, to our great and endless comfort. Make us discern the Lord's body, and remember and adore the exceeding love of Christ our Savior in thus dying for us. Give us repentance unto life, not to be repented of. Endue us with a lively faith, a perfect love, and a universal charity; that, so all carnal affections may die in us, and that all things belonging to the Spirit may live and grow; and that, being continually refreshed and strengthened by thy grace, we may persevere in all godliness unto the end of our lives, and finally receive an everlasting recompense, through the merits of Jesus Christ. *Amen.*

ANOTHER BEFORE SACRAMENT

GRANT us grace, O heavenly Father, to prepare our hearts for a due reception of the holy sacrament of the Lord's supper. May we truly and earnestly repent of our sins. May we cherish a spirit of love and charity towards our neighbors. May we resolve, by thy help, to lead a new life, following thy commandments, and walking from henceforth in thy righteous ways. May we wash our hands in innocency; and so may we draw near in faith to thy holy altar, and take the blessed sacrament of the true body and blood of Christ, to our great and endless comfort. *Amen.*

AFTER COMMUNION

ALMIGHTY and everlasting God, we most heartily thank thee for thy great mercy in permitting us, on this day, to receive the spiritual food of thy Son's true body and blood prepared for thy believing people by thy Son, our Savior Jesus Christ, in his holy supper. We thank thee for the comfortable assurance of thy favor and goodness, and for the blessed hope that we are very members incorporate in the mystical body of thy Son, which is the whole company of all faithful people, and are also heirs through grace of thy everlasting kingdom, by the merits of the most precious death and passion of thy dear Son. And we most humbly beseech thee, O heavenly Father, so to assist us with thy grace, that we may continue in that holy fellowship, and do all such good works as thou hast prepared for us to walk in, through Jesus Christ our Lord. *Amen.*

AFTER BAPTISM

GRANT, O Lord, that the *child* this day dedicated to thee, regenerated, and proclaimed a member of thy church by baptism, may be sanctified by the Holy Ghost, delivered from thy wrath and eternal death, and received as a living member of Christ's mystical body, and ever remain in the number of thy faithful children. *Amen.*

BEFORE CONFIRMATION

Which may be added to the Morning or Evening Prayer.

ALMIGHTY and ever-blessed God! while I am at this time called upon to renew my baptismal engagements, and to devote myself to thy service, by a solemn ordinance of thy church, I would humble myself before thee. O Lord, the number of my sins, and my hardness and impenitency of heart, since the time I was first dedicated to thee in baptism, are not hidden from thee. I am ashamed when I look back and consider how grievously I have sinned against thee; but oh cast me not away from thy presence; take not thy Holy Spirit from me. Thou dost invite and encourage me to return unto thee, in the name of that dear Savior who died for sinners. Oh cleanse my guilty soul in the fountain of his blood, and renew my heart by thy Holy Spirit; that I may approach thine altar with a sincere desire of making a willing and cheerful surrender of myself, and of all I have and am, to thee. And strengthen me by the grace of the same Spirit, that I may not hereafter be ashamed to confess the faith of Christ crucified, but may fight manfully under his banner against sin, the world, and the devil, and continue his faithful soldier and servant unto my life's end. O Lord, enlighten my understanding, quicken my desires after thee, and increase within my soul a principle of faith and love towards that blessed Redeemer who loved me and gave himself for me. Grant that all carnal affections may die in me, and that all things belonging to the Spirit may live and grow in me; and make me faithful unto death, that at last, for thy mercies' sake, and through the merits of my blessed Savior, I may be admitted into thy kingdom and glory. Hear me for the sake of thy dear Son Jesus Christ, my only Mediator and Redeemer. *Amen.*

AFTER CONFIRMATION

WE commend to thy mercy and grace, heavenly Father, all those thy servants who have this day, in their own persons, renewed the promises and vows which they made, or which were made for them by their sureties, in baptism, and who have been confirmed by the laying-on of hands. Direct, sanctify, and govern their hearts and bodies in the ways of thy laws and in the works of thy commandments; and defend them, O Lord, with thy heavenly grace, that they may continue thine forever, and daily increase in the Holy Spirit more and more, until they come unto thy heavenly kingdom. *Amen.*

FOR A NEW-MARRIED PARTY

BLESS those who have just entered a state honorable in all. May they remember the vows they have made at the altar, and in the discharge of their personal and relative duties may they make thy word their rule, that mercy and peace may be upon them. May the husband love his wife even as himself; and may the wife see that she reverence her husband, and both walk together as heirs of the grace of life, that their prayers be not hindered.

Preserve them from the evils which destroy or diminish the welfare and comfort of the condition in which thou hast placed them; and may they enjoy all the happiness resulting from prudence, temper, accommodation, real godliness, and the divine blessing.

May they expect to discern infirmities in one another, but may they be always most deeply conscious of their own. And let them not look for unattainable, by looking for unmingled, bliss on earth, but remember that this is not our rest; and be prepared for difficulties, trials, changes, and final separation. Hear and grant our prayers, through Christ our Lord. *Amen.*

HUSBAND FOR HIS WIFE

GREAT God! thy wisdom hath declared it not good for the man to be alone, and thou hast set the solitary in families. I thank thee for the helpmeet thou hast provided and given to me. Let her life be precious in thy sight, and the gifts of thy great mercy plenteously vouchsafed unto her. May I never forget the solemn covenant which unites us. May our union be blessed, and made a lasting joy and honor to us both. Give me grace to deserve the fond love of her whom I have chosen. Enable me to correct what is wrong in my dispositions, and to be kind, sympathizing, confiding, affectionate, and good, that we may ever delight in each other as those whom thou hast joined together. Let no unquietness, discontent, evil temper, or impatience, mar the sweet peace that should reign between us. Help us to live together in holiness and love; and, having borne the chance and change of time together, may we at length have our perfect bliss and everlasting home in heaven, through our Lord Jesus Christ. *Amen.*

WIFE FOR HER HUSBAND

Lord! bless and preserve that dear person whom thou hast chosen to be my husband. Let his life be long and useful, comfortable and holy; and let me also become a great blessing and a comfort unto him, a sharer in all his sorrows, a meet-helper in all the accidents and changes in the world. Make me amiable forever in his eyes, and forever dear unto him. Unite his heart to me in the dearest love and holiness, and mine to him in all sweetness, charity, and compliance. Keep me from all ungentleness, all discontentedness, and unreasonableness of passion and humor; and make me humble and obedient, useful and observant, that we may delight in each other according to thy blessed word, and both of us rejoice in thee, having our portion in the love and service of our God in Christ Jesus, forever. *Amen.*

UNDER FAMILY AFFLICTION

ALMIGHTY God, the Father of mercies and the God of all consolation, our only help in time of need, we flee unto thee for succor in this season of tribulation and distress. Out of the deeps we call unto thee, O Lord. Lord, hear our voice. Oh let thine ears consider well the voice of our complaint.

Thou art gracious and merciful, full of compassion, and of great goodness. Thou hast not dealt with us according to our sins, nor rewarded us according to our iniquities. Blessed be thy name, that thou not only hast opened unto us a way of escape from the wrath to come, but hast mercifully ordained the sufferings of the present life to work together for good to them that love thee.

Thy wise providence ordereth all things, both in heaven and earth. Not a sparrow falleth to the ground without thy knowledge and appointment; and the very hairs of our head are all numbered. Thou assurest us that thou dost not willingly afflict or grieve the children of men, but for their profit, that they may be partakers of thy holiness. Whom thou lovest, thou chastenest; and scourgest every son whom thou receivest.

Thou afflictest us to humble us, and to prove us, and to know what is in our hearts; and whether we will love thee, and keep thy commandments or no.

Give us grace therefore to consider, in this day of our adversity, wherefore thou contendest with us, and art wroth. Let us not despise thy chastening, nor faint when we are rebuked of thee, nor be weary of thy correction. But let us be still, and know that thou art God. In patience enable us to possess our souls. Grant that our tribulation may work patience, and patience experience, and experience hope, and let not our hope make ashamed, but let thy love be shed abroad in our hearts, through the Holy Ghost given unto us. Let us not cast away our confidence, which hath great recompense of reward. Though troubled on every side, let us not be distressed; though perplexed, let us not be in despair; though cast down, let us not be destroyed. And be pleased to cause our light afflictions, which are but for a moment, to work out for us a far more exceeding and eternal weight of glory. Though no chastening for the present seemeth to be joyous, but grievous, yet afterwards let it yield the peaceable fruit of righteousness unto us who are now exercised thereby. Grant that we may find it good to be afflicted, and see that thou, of very faithfulness, hast caused us to be in trouble.

We beseech thee, also, O Lord, to have compassion on our brethren and companions in tribulation.

Have mercy upon all sick persons, and make all their bed in their sickness. Eternal God, be thou their refuge, and place underneath them thy everlasting arms. Look graciously upon them, O Lord; and the more the outward man decayeth, strengthen them, we beseech thee, so much the more continually, by thy grace and Holy Spirit in the inward man. Give them unfeigned repentance for all the sins of their past lives, and steadfast faith in thy Son Jesus; that their sins may be done away by thy mercy, and their pardon sealed in heaven, before they go hence and are seen no more.

May it please thee, likewise, to defend and provide for the fatherless children, and widows, and all that are desolate and oppressed.

We commend to thy fatherly goodness all those who are any ways afflicted or distressed in mind, body, or estate. May it please thee to comfort and relieve them according to their several necessities, giving them patience under their sufferings, and a happy issue out of all their afflictions. *Amen.*

UNDER AFFLICTION

O MERCIFUL God and heavenly Father, who hast taught us in thy holy word that thou dost not willingly afflict or grieve the children of men, look with pity, we beseech thee, upon us in our present sorrows. In thy wisdom thou hast seen fit to visit us with trouble, and to bring distress upon us. Remember us, O Lord, in mercy; sanctify thy fatherly correction to us; endue our souls with patience under our affliction, and with resignation to thy blessed will; comfort us with a sense of thy goodness; lift up thy countenance upon us, and give us peace, through Jesus Christ our Lord. *Amen.*

IN BEHALF OF A SICK PERSON

ALMIGHTY God, who art the giver and the preserver of life and health, we humbly entreat thee to hear us in behalf of thy servant, for whom we now desire especially to pray. We look up unto thee, O thou compassionate Savior, who wast thyself a man of sorrows and acquainted with grief. O thou, who didst weep at the tomb of Lazarus, and art still touched with the feeling of our infirmities, mercifully behold the sorrows of our hearts, and graciously look upon our afflictions. O thou, who of old didst cure all manner of sickness and all manner of disease among the people, be gracious unto us. Let not this sickness be unto death, but for the glory of thy name. Speak the word only, and thy servant shall be healed. Have mercy upon *him*, O Lord, have mercy upon *him*; and not on *him* only, but on us also, lest we should have sorrow upon sorrow. If it be possible, let this cup pass away from us, without our drinking all its bitterness; but if not, thy will be done. Only be pleased to sanctify this thy fatherly correction to *him*, that the sense of *his* weakness may add strength to *his* faith and efficacy to *his* repentance; that, if it should be thy good pleasure to restore *him* to *his* former health, *he* may lead the residue of *his* life in thy fear and to thy glory; or else give *him* grace so to take thy visitation, that after this painful life is ended, *he* may dwell with thee in life everlasting.

And this we beg for Jesus Christ's sake. *Amen.*

IN BEHALF OF ONE SICK

O LORD GOD, our heavenly Father, we fly to thee for succor in behalf of this thy sick servant, in this day of *his* tribulation and danger. We know, O God, that all things are possible with thee. We know that thy arm is not shortened that it cannot save, nor thy ear heavy that it cannot hear. We know that thou canst, if it be thy gracious will, speak the word only, and this thy servant shall be healed. And we beseech thee, merciful God, thus to interpose thy hand. Take away from us this cup of bitterness; and, if it seem good to thee, alleviate *his* sufferings, remove *his* complaints, restore *him* to health, and grant *him* a longer continuance among us. But thy will, O Father, and not ours, be done. Enable us to submit with patience and resignation to thy righteous dealing. And grant to this thy servant grace, that *his* repentance may be perfect, *his* faith strong, *his* love fervent, and *his* hope steadfast, so that, after *his* departure hence in peace, *he* may rest with thee forever. Hear and grant our humble petitions, for the sake of thy dear Son, our Lord and Savior. *Amen.*

IN BEHALF OF A YOUNG PERSON DURING SICKNESS

O LORD! thou art a present help in every time of trouble. Thou canst bring low and raise up again. Shouldst thou punish *me* according to the number of *my* sins, *my* misery would be far greater than it is. But thou art very merciful to *me* for thy dear Son's sake, in whom alone *I* can have hope. O Lord, cleanse *my* soul from all sin through the blood of Christ and the grace of thy Holy Spirit, that whether *I* live, or whether *I* die, *I* may be thine forever. Help *me* to bear with patience whatever pains thou seest fit to inflict upon *me*. Oh may *I* remember how *my* blessed Redeemer suffered for *my* sins; and that, as he was tempted in all points like as we are, so he will not suffer his children to be tempted above what he will give them grace to bear. O blessed Lord, help *me* in my weakness; thou knowest whereof *I* am made; thou canst comfort *my* soul with thy salvation. If it be for *my* good and for thy glory, rebuke *my* disorder and heal *me*. But if thou shouldst see fit to call *me* from this world of sin and sorrow, oh prepare *me* for *my* last great change, and give *me* a desire to depart, and to be with Christ, which is far better. O Lord, *I* am in thy hands; save *me*, for thy mercies' sake, *I* am altogether unworthy of the least favor; but hear and answer these *my* prayers, through Jesus Christ, the Lamb of God, who bled and died for *me*, and who is *my* only Savior. *Amen.*

[This Prayer, with the slight alteration of the pronouns from the first person to the third, may be used by *any friend* at the bedside of the young person who is sick.]

IN BEHALF OF A SICK CHILD

ALMIGHTY and most merciful God, thou art the fountain of all good, the refuge of the distressed, the friend and comforter of those who look up to thy throne for help. We would offer up our prayers unto thee in behalf of the child on whom thou hast seen fit to lay thine afflicting hand. We beseech thee, if it be consistent with thy wise and holy will, to bless the means employed for *his* recovery, and to raise *him* up to health and strength. Suffer not the wishes of *his* parents to be disappointed; but in thy great mercy spare *him* to be a comfort and support of their advancing years, and to glorify thy name by obeying thee and becoming useful in the world. But, whatever thou hast determined concerning *him*, thy will, O God, be done! Preserve us from fainting under thy chastisement; and, if thou takest *him* away from the world, vouchsafe to receive *his* soul into that blessed land where sorrow and death are unknown. Into thy hands we commit *him*, ourselves, and all whom we love; and we humbly pray that, by all the dispensations of thy providence, we may be trained up for that state where thou wilt wipe away all tears from the eyes of mourners, and where pious friends and relations shall rejoice with each other forever and ever, through thine unspeakable love, in Christ Jesus our Lord. *Amen.*

IN BEHALF OF A SICK CHILD

O ALMIGHTY God and merciful Father, to whom alone belong the issues of life and death, look down from heaven, we humbly beseech thee, with the eyes of mercy, upon this child, now lying under thy hand in sickness. Visit *him*, O Lord, with thy salvation; deliver *him* in thy good appointed time from *his* bodily disease, and save *his* soul, for thy mercies' sake; that, if it shall be thy pleasure to prolong *his* days here on earth, *he* may live to thee, and be an instrument of thy glory, by serving thee faithfully and doing good in *his* generation: or else receive *him* into those heavenly habitations where the souls of those who sleep in the Lord Jesus enjoy perpetual rest and felicity. Grant this, O Lord, for thy mercies' sake. *Amen.*

FOR A BLESSING ON THE MEANS OF RECOVERY

O ALMIGHTY God, by whose word man lives, and not by any human means alone, prosper, we beseech thee, the means which are used for the recovery of this thy sick servant. Let not *his* confidence in any human means lessen *his* dependence upon thee. Make *him* sensible that every good gift is from above; that it is thou only who givest help in time of need. To thee, gracious God, we fly for succor in the day of our visitation; and may this thy sick servant look to thee for bodily as well as spiritual strength and salvation. Let thine, O God, be the glory, and *his* the comfort, of the means used for *his* recovery. Let *him* own thee as the author of *his* mercies, to thee pay *his* vows and services, and to thy glory devote the remainder of *his* days, through Jesus Christ our Lord. *Amen.*

UPON A BEGINNING OF RECOVERY FROM SICKNESS

GREAT and mighty God, who bringest down to the grave and bringest up again, we bless thy great goodness for having turned our heaviness into joy; and our mourning into gladness, by restoring this thy servant to some degree of *his* former health. Blessed be thy name, that thou didst not forsake *him* in *his* sickness, but didst visit *him* with comforts from above; didst support *him* in patience and submission to thy will; and, at last, didst send *him* seasonable relief. Perfect, we beseech thee, this thy mercy towards *him*; and prosper the means which shall be made use of for *his* cure; that, being restored to health of body, vigor of mind, and cheerfulness of spirit, *he* may be able to go to thine house to offer thee an oblation with great gladness; and to bless thy holy name for all thy goodness towards *him*, through Jesus Christ our Savior. *Amen.*

AFTER RECOVERY FROM SICKNESS

BLESS the Lord, O my soul, and all that is within me bless his holy name! Bless the Lord, O my soul, and forget not all his benefits! Thou hast been very merciful to me, O my God, in my late illness; thou hast eased my pain; thou hast healed my disease; thou art renewing my strength. O Lord, my sins have been many, and I deserved to be cut down as a cumberer of the ground; but, blessed be thy name, thou hast spared me in the midst of danger, and hast given me a longer time for repentance. Enable me, O Lord, sincerely to repent of my sins, and let the life which is now renewed be a life of faith upon the Son of God. May his name be dearer to me than before, and his cross be my only dependence; and may his love be shed abroad in my heart; that I may, more than ever, flee from sinful desires which war against the soul; that I may die unto sin and live unto righteousness, and walk in humility, integrity, and heavenly-mindedness. And though I am now restored to health, may my late illness teach me the uncertainty of life and the vanity of earthly things. Oh take off my heart from perishing comforts, and let my affections surely there be fixed where true joys are to be found, through Jesus Christ my Lord and Savior, to whom, with thee and the Holy Ghost, be all honor and glory. *Amen.*

UPON RECOVERY FROM SICKNESS

O GOD, who art the giver of life, of health, and of safety, we bless thy name, that thou hast been pleased to deliver from *his* bodily sickness *this* thy servant, who is now enabled to unite with us in returning thanks unto thee for this thy great mercy. Blessed be thy name, that though thou hast chastened *him,* thou hast not delivered *him* over unto death. Gracious art thou, O Lord, and full of compassion to the children of men. May *his* heart be duly impressed with a sense of thy merciful goodness, and may *he* devote the residue of *his* days to an humble, holy, and obedient walking before thee, through Jesus Christ our Lord. *Amen.*

FOR ONE ABOUT TO DIE

O ALMIGHTY God, with whom do live the spirits of just men made perfect, after they are delivered from their earthly prisons, we humbly commend the soul of this thy servant into thy hands, most humbly beseeching thee that it may be precious in thy sight. Wash it, we pray thee, in the blood of that Immaculate Lamb that was slain to take away the sins of the world; that whatsoever defilements it may have contracted in the midst of this miserable and sinful world, being purged and done away, it may be presented pure and without spot before thee. And teach us who survive, in this and every other spectacle of mortality, to see how frail and uncertain our own condition is; and so to number our days that we may seriously apply our hearts to that holy and heavenly wisdom, whilst we live here, which may in the end bring us to life everlasting, through the merits of Jesus Christ, thine only Son, our Lord. *Amen.*

AFTER A FUNERAL

O GOD, whose days are without end, and whose mercies cannot be numbered, grant that the solemn services of this day may make us deeply sensible of the shortness and uncertainty of human life, and of the transitory nature of all earthly things. Sanctify to us, and to all the friends and relatives of the deceased, this afflictive dispensation of thy providence. May the lively sense of the bereavement which we have sustained lead us to cleave more closely to thee our God. In all our troubles, may our whole trust and confidence be placed in thy mercy. Awakened by this visitation to a realizing sense of our own danger, may we resolve to seek supremely those things which are above; to resign ourselves and all our concerns to thy disposal; and in the fullness of resignation to say, with holy Job, "The Lord gave, and the Lord hath taken away, blessed be the name of the Lord." *Amen.*

ABOUT TO GO UPON A JOURNEY

O LORD, thou art the same God in all places, and no where can we go but thou art there. Both at home and abroad, on our way and at the end, thou art ever with us, by the universal presence of thy grace and thy good Spirit, to conduct and guide us continually; to protect and save us from all dangers and mischiefs; and to make our way prosperous and all our affairs successful. Oh let the blessing of the Lord follow us and rest upon us; and preserve our going out and our coming in; and never leave us nor forsake us, O Lord, but be our God and guide this day, in all this journey, and all our life long, which is but a pilgrimage and passage through this world, in which we are continually hastening home to the period of all our travels, to the place where we must take up our abode and dwell forever. *Amen.*

IN BEHALF OF ONE ABSENT AT SEA

O ETERNAL God, who alone spreadest out the heavens, and rulest the raging of the sea, we commend to thy Almighty protection thy servant, for whose preservation on the great deep we offer up our humble supplications. Guard *him*, we beseech thee, from the dangers of the sea, from pestilence and sickness, from the violence of enemies, and from every evil to which *he* may be exposed. Conduct *him* in safety to *his* place of destination, and in thy good time restore *him* in health and peace to *his* home, *his* family, and *his* friends; and above all, give *him* a grateful sense of all thy mercies, through Jesus Christ our Lord. *Amen.*

IN BEHALF OF ONE ABSENT ON A JOURNEY

O FATHER Almighty, whose mercy is over all thy works, we commend to thy protection and care thy servant, now absent from *his* home and family. Preserve *him,* we beseech thee, in all *his* journeyings; guard *him* in every danger and calamity; keep *him* in health and safety; and in thy good time restore *him* again to the joys and comforts of *his* household, that *he* may praise thee for all thy mercies, and love and serve thee faithfully all *his* days, through Jesus Christ our Lord. *Amen.*

UPON A SAFE RETURN FROM A JOURNEY

MERCIFUL Father, we render unto thee our united and hearty thanks for thy great goodness and abundant mercies, and we desire now to bless thee especially for thy providential care in protecting this thy servant in *his* late absence from *his* home and family. We thank thee for *his* preservation in *his* journeyings; for *his* exemption from danger, and sickness, and death; and for *his* safe return to the joys and comforts of *his* household. May the remembrance of the care thou hast taken of *him* during *his* absence, inspire *him* with a lively confidence of thy power and protection. May *he* ever praise thee for all thy mercies, and love and serve thee faithfully all *his* days, through Jesus Christ our Lord. *Amen.*

IN BEHALF OF A YOUTH GOING FROM HOME

(*If with a view to Business*)

O GOD, thou appointest the bounds of our habitation, and arrangest all our individual concerns; and it is thy pleasure not only that we should part at death, but often separate in life. When absent from each other in body, may we be present in spirit; and may our natural affection be strengthened and sanctified by inquiry, and correspondence, and divine remembrance at the throne of grace.

Regard the member of our family who is now leaving the parental roof. In all his ways may he acknowledge thee; and be thou the guide and the guard of his youth. Secure him from the paths of the destroyer and the evils of the world. May uprightness preserve him. In the situation he will be called to fill, may he be dutiful, and obliging, and diligent, and faithful: may he always remember that the eye of God is upon him; and be not only amiable, but pious; and in favor with God as well as man. Hear our prayer, O Lord, we beseech thee. *Amen.*

(If with a view to School)

O THOU God of providence and grace, we commend to thy care the dear child about to leave our abode for a season, in order to receive needful instruction. Let his (*or her*) life be precious in thy sight. May he redeem his time, and acquire the improvement that will fit him for usefulness in his day and generation. And oh let him be made wise unto salvation; and let the beauty of the Lord our God be upon him, that he may be a useful and ornamental member in thy church below, and hereafter a pillar in thy temple above, never more to go out. Grant our prayer, merciful Father, for Christ's sake. *Amen.*

IN TIME OF POPULAR COMMOTION

ALMIGHTY and everlasting God, who art the Sovereign of the universe, and rulest the children of men as seemeth good in thy sight, look down, we beseech thee, in mercy upon the world that lieth in wickedness. Restrain the inordinate passions of restless and ambitious men; incline them to peace and good-will. Suffer not the wicked to accomplish their ungodly purposes; defeat the designs and machinations of those who would invade the equal rights or abridge the just privileges of the people. Arrest also all tendencies to degeneracy, licentiousness, and anarchy. May law and order, justice and equity, and the sound principles of thy holy word prevail in our land and in all the nations of the earth. Our trust is in thee; thou livest and reignest on high: oh come down and live and reign also among the people, and overrule their agitations to thine own glory and the furtherance of thy purposes of wisdom and mercy. Cause the wrath of man to praise thee, and the remainder of wrath do thou restrain. May peace and harmony take the place of discontent and commotion, and may love and good-will animate the hearts of the children of men everywhere, through our Lord Jesus Christ. *Amen.*

IN TIME OF THREATENING WAR

O LORD our God! thou art the God of peace and the Fountain of all love and mercy. Thou rulest in the armies of heaven, and doest whatsoever thou pleasest among the nations of the earth. In thee do we put our trust. We would live in peace and friendship in our own land and with all the earth. We have indeed nationally, as well as personally, deserved thy judgments; and shouldst thou scourge us with war and all its frightful concomitants and consequences, we could not charge thee with injustice. We have been proud and self-sufficient; we have violated thy holy Sabbath and repaid thy numerous blessings with ingratitude. We have taken credit to ourselves, and ascribed to our wisdom and skill what was the result of thy goodness and mercy. O Lord, enter not into judgment, and deal not according to our offenses, but according to thine infinite compassion in Christ Jesus. Put an end to the agitations of unruly men; turn away from us the wrath we have merited: may both people and the government be influenced by thy good Spirit to peace and quiet. In thy good providence remove all the causes of reasonable discontent; give us not over to the consequences of reckless passion; and suffer no wrong principles, no erroneous policy, no false views of honor, and no unholy ambition to control the legislature of the States or of the Federal Government. Save us, we beseech thee,—save us from war and its frightful horrors, and make us a holy, peace-loving, righteous people, whom thou wilt delight to bless, through Jesus Christ, the Prince of peace. *Amen.*

IN TIME OF WAR

WE adore thee, O God, as the Lord of hosts. Great and mighty are thy armies, by which thou canst lay waste the guilty nations of the earth. We come unto thee in time of public calamity. We would mourn, O Lord, over the pride, and ambition, and envy, and revenge which agitate the bosoms of earthly rulers, and make them rush into wars, and thus hazard the property, the comfort, the blood, and the life of the children of men. In thy mercy, O Lord, remove the causes which lead to such great evils; subdue and change the wicked passions and designs of all ungodly men who rashly and corruptly exercise their influence and authority. Oh put to naught the counsels of those who delight in war and bloodshed, and will adopt no method to adjust disputes but that of leading thousands into the field of battle, and ushering multitudes unprepared into the presence of an offended and awful God.

O Lord, hear our prayers for peace. Teach rulers and people to cultivate harmony and love; make an end of tumult and bloodshed. Let all false ideas of dignity and glory be buried in the dust; and may all in authority see that it is their greatest glory to legislate and govern in the fear of the Lord and for the peace and quiet of the nation.

Oh look in pity on those who are in the tented field, the fort, the ship of war, and the very arena of strife: have thy eye upon them for good; let them not forget that a day of judgment is nigh at hand; and, above all things, preserve their souls; prepare them and us all for the peaceful abodes of heaven; forgive our sins, and save us through Jesus Christ our Lord. *Amen.*

THANKSGIVING FOR PEACE

GOD of salvation, with joyful hearts we would present the sacrifice of thanksgiving and praise for the return of peace. Blessed be thy name for hushing the storm of war and putting an end to the effusion of blood. It is the Lord who breaketh the bow, and cutteth the spear asunder, and burneth the chariot in fire. To thy most holy name be all the glory. As thou hast made peace in our borders, and canst bring good out of evil, we pray that thou wilt overrule the late war to thy glory and the good of the nation. May the eyes of all be opened to behold the great guilt of those who occasion war, and by their evil passions and false views lead to the wanton and wholesale destruction of human life and property.

We lament the evils of war, both natural and moral; and confess with shame that ever since man became an apostate from thee, he has been an enemy to his brother; and that from the death of Abel, our earth has been a field of blood. Oh let thy word be speedily accomplished. Let the nations learn war no more, but beat their swords into ploughshares and their spears into pruning-hooks; and only emulate each other in husbandry, and commerce, and science, and religion.

We pray for the universal extension of the holy, wise, and benign principles of the gospel of Christ. May these blessed principles enter into the legislatures, the cabinets, and councils of all countries. Then shall wars cease to the ends of the earth, and peace and righteousness flourish among the nations. O Lord, God of heaven and earth! we pray most earnestly for the universal reign of Jesus Christ, the Prince of peace; hasten the day when he shall rule among nations as he does in the hearts of his faithful followers. Teach us all to cultivate peace in our own bosom, and in our family and our neighborhood, and make us heirs of the peaceful joys of heaven and immortality, for the Redeemer's sake. *Amen.*

IN TIME OF PESTILENCE

O LORD God, the giver of our health, it is only of thy mercy that we have so much health continued after the manner in which we have lived. And oh how just were it with thee utterly to take away that health from us which we have so greatly abused, to a forgetfulness of thee and wantonness against thee! How justly mightest thou smite us with sharp and noisome diseases, which our nature most abhorreth; to hurry us out of the land of the living, and put a sorrowful end to our wretched days! But, O thou Hope of Israel, the Savior thereof in time of trouble! regard not our ill-deserts; but remember thy own tender mercies and gracious promises; and take pity on us, and turn away this plague from us. Put a stop to the raging pestilence, and say to the destroying angel, "It is enough;" that we may not be afraid of the terror by night, nor for the arrow that flies by day; nor for the pestilence that walketh in darkness, nor for the destruction that wasteth at noonday: but, with calmness in our minds and gladness in our hearts, may serve thee faithfully and cheerfully all our days, and devote our spared lives, which we have begged at thy hands, and our health and every mercy, to thy honor and glory, through the strength and the righteousness of thy dear Son, our most compassionate and prevailing Mediator, Jesus Christ. *Amen.*

ANOTHER, IN TIME OF PESTILENCE

O ALMIGHTY God, the Lord of life and death, of sickness and health! regard our supplications, we humbly beseech thee; and, as thou hast thought fit to visit us for our sins with great sickness and mortality, in the midst of thy judgment, O Lord, remember mercy. Have pity upon us miserable sinners, and withdraw from us the grievous sickness with which we are afflicted. May this thy fatherly correction have its due influence upon us, by leading us to consider the frailty and uncertainty of our life, that we may apply our hearts unto that heavenly wisdom which in the end will bring us to everlasting life, through Jesus Christ our Lord. *Amen.*

IN TIME OF DEARTH AND FAMINE

O GOD, heavenly Father, whose gift it is that the rain doth fall and the earth bring forth her increase, behold, we beseech thee, the afflictions of thy people; increase the fruits of the earth by thy heavenly benediction; and grant that the scarcity and dearth which we now most justly suffer for our sins may, through thy goodness, be mercifully turned into plenty, for the love of Jesus Christ our Lord. *Amen.*

AFTER A RESTORATION OF PLENTY

O MOST merciful Father, who of thy gracious goodness hast heard our prayers and supplications, and turned our dearth and scarcity into plenty, we give thee humble thanks for this thy special bounty; beseeching thee to continue thy loving-kindness unto us, that our land may yield us her fruits of increase, to thy glory and our comfort, through Jesus Christ our Lord. *Amen.*

FOR RAIN

WE confess, O Lord, that we have so greatly abused the comforts of thy good creatures, that thou mightest justly withdraw them from us, and make the heavens over us as brass, and the rain of our land dust, and the land itself to mourn, and all that grows upon it to wither. But, O thou Father of mercies, who in judgment rememberest mercy, consult not now our demerits, but thy own mercies, how to use us. Thou that hast the treasures of heaven at thy command, be pleased now to open the windows of heaven, and cause the rain to come down in its sea son, making grass to grow for the cattle, and herbs and fruits of the earth for the service of men. And however thou art pleased to deal with us, oh suppress all our repinings at any of thy dealings; and let them all amend and better us, and make us a people prepared to receive the mercies which we want, and wait and beg for at thy gracious hands, upon the account of Jesus Christ. *Amen.*

FOR FAIR WEATHER

How numberless are our wants and dangers! Our hopes are destroyed, not only by the deficiency but the excess of our supplies. May the overflowing showers cease which damp the joy of the harvest; cause thy sun not only to rise, but to shine—give us the clear shining after rain, that the earth may yield her increase in maturity, and opportunity be afforded for the wholesome ingathering of grass for the cattle and grain for the use of man: that there may be no complaining in the land, but that we may eat in plenty and be satisfied, and praise the Lord.

And oh let us not forget our souls in our mindfulness of the body, nor expend all our concerns upon the meat that perisheth—but be, above all things, anxious to secure that meat which endureth unto everlasting life, and which the Son of man will give; for him hath God the Father sealed. Hear and grant our prayer, for Christ's sake. *Amen.*

AFTER HARVEST

ALMIGHTY God! in thy hands are the fruits of the earth; and thou who art infinitely good hast again opened thy hand to satisfy the desire of every living thing. Thy protecting power hath blessed the seed of the husbandman, that the mower might fill his hand, and he that bindeth sheaves his bosom. Thou hast crowned the year with thy goodness; thou hast brought forth food out of the earth, and hast permitted thy gifts to be gathered in safety and in peace.

Lord, we are utterly unworthy of all this compassion. Thy favored children we all are, but all are not thy grateful children. Alas! our hearts are not as faithful as our lands. Unto us belongeth shame in thy sight and in our own. And yet thy compassions fail not, thy mercy is new every morning; great is thy faithfulness.

Holy Father! give us thy Spirit, that we may duly acknowledge the riches of thy goodness, patience, and long-suffering, and be suitably affected by them.

Every harvest is a new miracle of thine all-preserving power and love, a new memorial of thy kind care and faithfulness, a new proof that thou hast thoughts of peace towards the children of men. And oh that each returning harvest may bring anew to our remembrance the declaration of thy word: Knowest thou not that the goodness of God leadeth thee to repentance? Enable us to consider this in the exercise of true faith, that we may receive thy gifts with thanksgiving, and use them according to thy will. Preserve us from that levity that makes light of thy word and despises thy commandments; from that pride which exalts itself before thee; from that envy which is grieved when thou art good to others; from all intemperance which abuses thy gifts, and from that avarice which buries thy talents in the earth. Give us a wise and contented heart, a meek and humble spirit, that we may be satisfied with such things as thou shalt see fit to bestow; that we may improve them wisely, and with believing hearts put our whole confidence in thee. Mightily influence us all, as disciples of Christ, not to grow weary of well-doing, knowing that in due season we shall reap if we faint not.

O God, our Father! continue, in days to come, to extend unto us thy goodness, and let thine eyes be upon our whole land, that scarcity, famine, and other plagues may not visit us. Fill our rulers with that wisdom which is not of this world, and all the citizens of the land with reverence for thy laws; grant them obedient hearts and the spirit of harmony, that righteousness and faith may exalt our nation and thy blessing be its chief good. To this end let the word of Christ dwell richly in all churches, schools, and families, and the fruit of the Spirit be everywhere manifest, which is in all goodness, righteousness, and truth. Especially incline the hearts of our children unto thee, that they may early receive, and willingly admit, and faithfully preserve, the good seed of thy word, and be one day found as trees of righteousness and planting of the Lord, that he may be glorified. Dispose the hearts of the rich that they may do good, and not forget to communicate, thus exercising pure religion and undefiled before thee our Father. Make those who are poor in this world rich in faith, that they may reap a harvest of blessings in the world to come. All who are afflicted revive by the heavenly dew of thy grace, and refresh the dying with that living water that springeth up unto everlasting life. O God and Father of us all, who art rich to all that call upon thee! grant, according to thy great goodness, that we, who here sow in tears, may hereafter reap in joy, and on the great harvest-day of thy second advent may come again with rejoicing, bringing our sheaves with us; yea, may be ourselves gathered as blessed sheaves into thy garner, through the merits of thy dear Son, our Lord Jesus Christ. *Amen.*

SPRING

THOU art the fountain of life; in thee we live, move, and have our being; and the prerogative of that being is, that we are able to contemplate thy perfections and rise from thy works to thyself.

Thou sendest forth thy Spirit and renewest the face of the earth, and from apparent death all nature starts into reanimated vigor and joy. In what myriads of productions art thou displaying afresh the wonders of thy wisdom, power, and goodness!—the whole earth is full of thy riches.

While we partake of the general sympathy and delight, may we join with all thy works to praise thee. And, O thou God of all grace, bless us with the renewing of the Holy Ghost in all the powers of our souls. May old things pass away, and all become new in Christ; may the beauty of the Lord be upon us, and the joy of the Lord be our strength.

May the young remember that they are now in the spring of life, and that *this* spring, once gone, returns no more. May they, therefore, eagerly seize and zealously improve the short but all-important season, for the cultivation of their minds, the formation of their habits, the correction of their tempers, their preparation for future usefulness, and their gaining that good part which shall not be taken away from them. *Amen.*

SUMMER

WE hail thee in the varying aspects of the year, and bless thee for all their appropriate influences and advantages. Oh let us not view them and enjoy them as men only, but as Christians also, and ever connect with them the better blessings of thy grace.

How wise, and useful, and necessary are these intermingled rains and sunbeams! May Jesus, as the Sun of Righteousness, arise upon us with healing under his wings, and may he come down as rain upon the mown grass, and as showers that water the earth.

When we walk by the cooling brook, may we think of that river the streams whereof make glad the city of God.

When we retire from the scorching warmth of the day into the inviting shade, may we be thankful for a rest at noon, a shelter from the heat, the shadow of a rock in a weary land.

May thy servants behold the moral fields that are already white unto harvest, and be all anxiety to save the multitudes that are perishing for lack of knowledge.

The harvest truly is great, but the laborers are few; we therefore pray that thou wilt send forth laborers into thy harvest.

He that gathereth in summer is a wise son; he that sleepeth in harvest is a son that causeth shame. Now is our accepted time, now is our day of salvation. Oh let us not waste our precious privileges, and in a dying hour exclaim, The harvest is past, the summer is ended, and we are not saved! Hear these our prayers for ourselves and others; and do for us abundantly above all that we can ask or think, for the merits of our Lord and Savior Jesus Christ, to whom we would ascribe all glory and praise now and forever. *Amen.*

AUTUMN

HOW fleeting as well as varying are the seasons of the year! How insensibly have the months of spring and summer vanished! and nature has no sooner attained its maturities, than we behold its declension and decay. The fields are now shorn of their produce; the beauties of the garden are withered; the woods are changing their verdure, and the trees shedding their foliage—we also never continue in one state. Many of our connections and comforts have already dropped away from us, and the remaining are holden by a slender tenure; while we ourselves do all fade as a leaf, and in a little time our place will know us no more.

Blessed be the God and Father of our Lord Jesus Christ for the announcement of an inheritance that fadeth not away. Oh for a hope full of immortality! for a possession of that good part which shall not be taken away from us! *Amen.*

WINTER

O THOU God of nature and providence, manifold are thy works; in wisdom thou hast made them all; and all are full of thy goodness. The welfare of thy creatures requires the severity of winter as well as the pleasures of spring. We adore thy hand in all. Thou givest snow like wool; thou scatterest the hoar-frost like ashes; thou sendest abroad thine ice like morsels: who can stand before thy cold?

But we bless thee for a house to shelter us, for raiment to cover us, for fuel to warm us, and all the accommodations that render life, even at this inclement season, not only tolerable, but full of comfort.

May we be grateful, and may we be pitiful. May we reflect on the condition of those who are the victims of every kind of privation and distress; and waste nothing, hoard nothing, but hasten to be ministers of mercy, and the disciples of Him who went abroad doing good.

Oh let the rich *now* deservedly prize their wealth, and use it as the instrument of usefulness. May they be willing to communicate and ready to distribute, and enjoy the blessing of him that is ready to perish, and make the widow's heart to sing for joy. *Amen.*

FOR RELIGIOUS AND BENEVOLENT INSTITUTIONS

WE thank thee, O Lord, for Bible, Missionary, Tract, and other kindred Societies, which contemplate the diffusion of evangelic truth, the enlargement of thy kingdom, and the salvation of immortal souls. We greatly rejoice that these free, voluntary associations have been preserved so long, and been made the means of so much good to the children of men. Glory to God, that through their instrumentality, accompanied by his smiles, so many portions of the earth, in the darkness of pagan idolatry, now enjoy the life-giving and sanctifying light of the gospel. Blessed be thy name, that many have already cast their idols to the moles and bats, and now acknowledge Jehovah as the only object of their worship, and Jesus Christ as the only Savior of a perishing world. O Lord our God! we pray that all these Societies may be controlled by thy gracious influences, and that they may grow in efficiency, purity, and zeal, until the world shall be filled with the glory of God, and not one vestige of false religion shall remain among the children of men. Have mercy, we pray thee, on all nations; and may the promised season soon arrive when the heathen shall be given to Jesus for his inheritance, and the utmost ends of the earth for his possession. O Lord Jesus, thou King of glory! take unto thyself thy great power, and reign thou King of nations as thou dost already King of saints. Say to the north, "Give up; and to the south, Keep thou not back; bring my sons from far and my daughters from the ends of the earth." Soon may it be said in every land, The Lord God omnipotent reigneth! We ask it for Jesus' sake. *Amen.*

FOR AN AFFLICTED MINISTER

O LORD, we present our humble and earnest prayers in behalf of thy servant, our beloved minister, whom thou hast laid upon a bed of affliction. We pray that he may be speedily delivered from this visitation, and be restored to usefulness in his holy calling. Give him patience and confidence in thee during his illness, and sanctify this sore trial to him and to us, so that we may all have cause to kiss the rod and bless the hand that afflicts us. We thank thee that in our appeals we are permitted to use arguments. For the honor of thy name, and for the furtherance of thy gospel, mercifully restore our minister to health. For the conversion of sinners, and for the edification and comfort of saints, add many years to his life, that many more souls may be added as seals of his ministry. Prepare him and prepare us all for thy holy will. If he live, may it be for Christ; if he die, may it be gain, everlasting gain, to himself. May he shine in the heavenly world as the brightness of the firmament, forever and ever. Hear us, we entreat thee; forgive our sins, and save us for Jesus' sake. *Amen.*

FOR A WOMAN APPROACHING THE TIME OF TRAVAIL

MERCIFULLY regard thine handmaid, O Lord, who is looking forward to an important hour. Be not thou far from me when trouble is near. May my mind be kept in perfect peace, being stayed upon the God of my salvation. Bring to the birth, and give me strength to bring forth. Soften the pains of labor, as well as command deliverance; and in due time may I remember no more my anguish, for joy that a child is born into the world. And may the root and the branch abide under the shade of the Almighty. Into thy hands I commend myself, O Lord my God. Forsake me not in the hour of trial, but vouchsafe a speedy and safe deliverance; and I will praise and magnify thy name, now and forever. *Amen.*

FOR A WOMAN AFTER SAFE DELIVERY

I LOVE the Lord, because he hath heard my voice and my supplication. Consider, O my soul, how greatly thou art indebted to the divine goodness. Look back and reflect on thy former fears and anxieties; look up and bless God that they are gone, and that their cause is removed. I found trouble and sorrow; then called I upon the name of the Lord, and said, O Lord, I beseech thee, deliver my soul. Gracious is the Lord and righteous; yea, our God is merciful. I was brought low, and he helped me. Return unto thy rest, O my soul, for the Lord hath dealt bountifully with thee.

O my God, I sincerely thank thee for thy great goodness to me and mine. By supporting me in the hour of pain, by granting me proper assistance, by blessing the means which thy providence afforded me, by making me the living mother of a living child, by strengthening me thus far, and by giving me the prospect of a speedy recovery and confirmed health, thou hast dissipated our fears, calmed our minds, gladdened our hearts, and made a family happy. Thou hast exchanged our face of care for a bosom full of joy, and turned our earnest cries into hymns of ardent praise. Bless the Lord, O my soul, and forget not all his benefits; who forgiveth all thine iniquities; who healeth all thy diseases; who redeemeth thy life from destruction; who crowneth thee with loving-kindness and tender mercies.

What shall I render unto the Lord for all his benefits towards me? I will take the cup of salvation, and call upon the name of the Lord.

I will cheerfully devote myself, and all I have, unto the God of my life. Oh! never may I forget the mercies I have received. Never may I be unthankful for them. May a lively sense of them dwell on my mind, and be ever visible in my actions; may it be my daily care to pay unto God those vows which I made when my soul was in trouble.

To thee I owe myself, and every blessing I possess. To thee I dedicate this infant. Lord, take it for thine own. On the soul of this dear child draw thine holy image, and keep it forever from the pollutions of this wicked world. Give me and its father grace to set it a constant good example, and may we bring it up in the nurture and admonition of the Lord. While we pray that its life may be spared, we also pray for entire resignation to thy blessed will; but shouldst thou, as we hope, be pleased to allot to it the years of man, we earnestly beseech thee to make it a pillar in thy church, a blessing to the world, and a lasting comfort to its parents. To thee, O Father, and the Holy Spirit, I desire to ascribe everlasting praises. *Amen.*

PRAYERS AT TABLE

BEFORE MEAT

ALMIGHTY God! the eyes of all wait upon thee, and thou givest them their meat in due season. Bless, we beseech thee, the provisions of thine earthly bounty, which are now before us; and let them nourish and strengthen our frail bodies, that we may the better serve thee, through Jesus Christ. *Amen.*

OR THUS:

LET thy blessing, Almighty God, descend on this portion of thy bounty, and on us, thy unworthy servants, through Jesus Christ, our Lord. *Amen*

OR THUS:

ALMIGHTY God, we beseech thee to pardon our sins: to bless the refreshment now before us to our use, and us to thy service, through Jesus Christ. *Amen.*

OR THUS:

FATHER of lights, from whom cometh down every good and perfect gift, enable us to receive these fruits of thy bounty with humility and gratitude, and give us grace, that whether we eat or drink, or whatever we do, we may do all to thy glory, and be accepted through the great Redeemer. *Amen.*

OR THUS:

BOUNTEOUS God, we acknowledge our dependence on thee, and our unworthiness of thy benefits. We pray thee to forgive our sins; to bless us in the reception of this food, and enable us to improve the strength we may derive from it to thy glory, for Christ's sake. *Amen.*

OR THUS:

SANCTIFY, O Lord, we beseech thee, these thy productions to our use, and us to thy service, through Jesus Christ, our Lord. *Amen.*

OR THUS:

WE bless thee, O God, for covering our table with plenty, and for the present opportunity of partaking of thy bounties. Nourish our bodies with these provisions of thy hand, and our souls with the bread of life, for the sake of Jesus Christ, our Lord. *Amen.*

OR THUS:

WE thank thee, heavenly Father, for this portion of thy bounty. Thou dost daily supply our returning wants, notwithstanding our ungratefulness. Oh help us to be deeply sensible of thy goodness and mercy. Bless the provision now before us to our use, forgive our sins, and in the end save us through Christ, our Lord. *Amen.*

OR THUS:

FATHER of mercies, we praise thee for permitting us again to sit down and partake of the provisions of thine earthly bounty. Do thou feed our souls with the bread of life. Pardon our numerous offenses, and own us at last in heaven for Christ's sake. *Amen.*

OR THUS:

BOUNTIFUL giver of all good and perfect gifts! thou art never weary of supplying our returning wants: grant, we pray thee, that the food of which we are about to partake, may contribute to the comfort and support of our bodies, and enable us to engage with more zeal in thy service, which we ask, for Jesus Christ's sake. *Amen.*

AFTER MEAT

WHAT shall we render to thee, O God, for all thy benefits? Every day of our lives we are receiving fresh tokens of thy favor. Oh, let thy goodness lead us to repentance. And if we can do no more than express our gratitude, help us to do that in the sincerity of our souls, and thine shall be the glory, forever, through Jesus Christ. *Amen.*

OR THUS:

ACCEPT, heavenly Father, our humble thanks for this and for all thy blessings, through Jesus Christ. *Amen.*

OR THUS:

WE praise thee, O Lord, for the provisions of thy providence and grace, and in particular for this renewed token of thy favor. May we feel our increased obligations to be thine, and be fitted at length to eat bread in thy heavenly kingdom, through our Lord Jesus Christ. *Amen.*

OR THUS:

WE bless thee, O Lord, for this kind refreshment. Be pleased to continue thy favors, and feed us with the bread of life. Supply the wants of the needy; and enable us, while we live on thy bounty, to live to thy glory, for Christ's sake. *Amen.*

OR THUS:

WE would praise and magnify thy holy name, O Lord, for this and all other blessings bestowed upon us, through Jesus Christ our Lord. *Amen.*

OR THUS:

O GOD, for all thy mercies, for the food that supports our bodies and the grace that sustains our souls, we bless and praise thy holy name, through Jesus Christ our Lord. *Amen.*

PRAYERS FOR CHILDREN

SUNDAY MORNING

O LORD, my heavenly Father, who hast safely brought me to the beginning of this holy day, defend me with thy mighty power, and grant that I may fall into no sin, neither run into any kind of danger. May I remember the Sabbath-day to keep it holy. May I delight in the duties of thy house, and worship thee with a sincere and thankful heart. Help me in my feeble efforts to do thy will and to keep thy commandments; and may I never forget that thou, O God, seest me at all times.

O LORD, bless my parents and all my dear relatives and friends. Bless my beloved minister, my Sunday-school teacher, and all my Sunday-school mates. Oh may we all so improve the privileges which we enjoy, that we may at last enter into that rest which remains for the people of God. Pardon all my sins, O Lord, and hear my prayer, for the sake of thy Son, Jesus Christ, my most blessed and precious Savior. *Amen.*

SUNDAY EVENING

O LORD, my God, hear my prayer at the close of this sacred day, and accept my thanks for all thy mercies.

Forgive me every wicked thought, every wicked word, and every wrong thing that I have done. Pardon all my sins, for Christ's sake, and help me to serve thee better in time to come. May I remember the good things I have heard and learned this day. May I love thy holy day more and more. And when all my days are ended, and I can no more go to thy house of prayer, oh may I be among the saints and angels that forever worship around thy throne.

I thank thee, O Lord, for all thy goodness to me this day. All that I have is from thee; oh give me a grateful heart for every blessing. May thy mercies lead me to thyself, and may I show forth thy praise in doing thy commandments. Be always near me, O Lord; protect me from all harm, help me to shun evil, and at last save me in heaven, for the love of thy only Son, my Savior, Jesus Christ. *Amen.*

ALMIGHTY and most merciful Father, I come before thee to thank thee for thy goodness and mercy, and to ask for thy blessing upon me this day. Direct me in all my ways, and be graciously pleased to take me, and all who are near and dear to me, under thy kind care and protection. Help me, O Lord, to give up all my sinful desires and wicked habits, to believe in Christ my Savior with all my heart, and obediently to keep his holy will and commandments, and walk in the same all the days of my life. May I be truly a member of Christ, a child of God, and an inheritor of the kingdom of heaven. May I love thee more and more; and when all my days on earth have passed away, oh receive me unto thyself in glory everlasting, for Jesus' sake. *Amen.*

O GOD, I bless thee for thy constant care over me. Wilt thou continue to keep me from all danger? Pardon my sins, O Lord, and give me grace to do thy will. Create in me a new and contrite heart, and help me to become like the holy child Jesus. Give me thy Holy Spirit, that I may love to do what is right, and fear and hate everything that is wrong. May I trust in the Savior for the forgiveness of my sins, and try every day to follow his blessed example. Bless my dear parents, and make me thankful to thee for such kind friends; and finally make us all a happy family in thy heavenly kingdom, for the sake of Jesus Christ, my precious Redeemer. *Amen.*

ALMIGHTY God, the Maker of everything in heaven and earth. I thank thee that thou hast taken care of me to the present time. Keep me, O Lord, from everything that would do me harm, and give me every good thing that is needful and proper for my body and for my soul. Help me, by thy Holy Spirit, to do what thou hast commanded, and make me always afraid to offend thee. Pardon my sins for the sake of thy beloved Son, who died for sinners, and now lives in heaven to pray for them and to save them. Bless and take care of all poor and orphan children. Be pleased, O Lord, to hear my prayers, for Jesus Christ's sake. *Amen.*

O GOD, the Father of heaven, how gracious art thou to permit me, a sinful creature, to pray to thee! I come now to implore thy protection. Defend me from all dangers and mischiefs, and from the fear of them. Make me ever mindful of the time when I shall lie down in the dust, and grant me grace always to live in such a state that I may never be afraid to die. I thank thee for the many mercies and benefits I have enjoyed, and pray that thy goodness may lead me to repentance for all my sins. I ask thy blessing upon my father and mother, [brothers and sisters,] and all my dear friends, and pray thee to make us thine here and forever, for Christ's sake. *Amen.*

O LORD, accept my sincere thanks for taking care of me to the present time. Guard me this day from every evil. May I feel that thy all-seeing eye is always upon me, and let me not sin against thee. May I not waste my precious time, but try to improve every hour. Bless me in my studies and in my plays; and make me obedient to my parents and teachers, and kind and affectionate to [my brothers and sisters, and] all my companions. May I remember thee, my Creator, in the days of my childhood and youth. May I love the Savior, who died for me, and may the Holy Ghost ever dwell in my heart. Guide me, O Lord, this day and all my life by thy counsel, and afterwards receive me to glory, for Christ's sake. *Amen.*

SATURDAY EVENING

MY Father and my God, I thank thee for having brought me safely to the end of another day and another week. I pray thee to forgive me all that I have done that is wrong, and grant me thy grace, that I may avoid everything that is sinful. Keep me safe this night while I sleep, and permit me to see the light of thy holy day. May the close of the day and the week remind me that the time will soon come when I shall lie down to sleep in the grave; and wilt thou help me so to number my days, that I may apply my heart unto wisdom. Oh, when time with me shall be no more, may I enter that kingdom which Jesus has gone to prepare for all that love thee. Bless my dear friends, and make us all thy friends here, that we may enjoy thee forever. Bless all children that are poor and needy, and make me thankful for every comfort, for Christ's sake. *Amen.*

PRAYERS FOR LITTLE CHILDREN

MORNING OR EVENING

O LORD, I come to thee, confessing that I am a sinful child, and pray thee to pardon me. I have done many things I ought not to have done, and have broken thy holy laws. May I remember that thine eye is always watching over me, and that thou knowest all my thoughts and words and actions. Wilt thou help me to love, honor, and obey my father and mother, to respect and mind my teachers, and in all things to do thy will. May I never give way to angry feelings or an evil temper, but delight in being gentle, kind, and dutiful. Hear my prayer, I beseech thee, for Christ's sake. *Amen.*

MORNING OR EVENING

O LORD, thou hast made me and all the world; teach me to love thee and to praise thee with my whole heart. Bless [my father and mother, &c., and] all my dear friends. May I love them and obey them. Forgive me, for my Savior's sake, every thing that I have done wrong; and when I die, may I go to heaven, to be with thee forever. Hear me, for the sake of Jesus Christ, my only Savior. *Amen.*

MORNING PRAYERS

FOR THE SABBATH MORNING.

OH let me be glad, heavenly Father, that the Sabbath has come; let me love thy holy day, and think of thee, and love to talk about thee. Jesus my Savior said, "Suffer little children to come unto me;" oh bring me to Jesus, that I may learn of him to be good, and that he may make me good, and take my soul to heaven when my body dies. Heavenly Father, grant my prayer, for his sake. *Amen.*

FOR THE SABBATH MORNING.

O HEAVENLY Father, bless the Sabbath-day, and make my heart love it better than any other day, because I can go to church and to Sunday-school, and learn about thee, my kind creator God, and about Jesus, the good Savior, who loves to bless little children, and to take them to heaven when they die. Oh let me love thee, Lord, this day and forever. *Amen.*

O LORD, I thank thee for taking care of me all last night, when I was asleep. I thank thee for the pleasant sleep I have enjoyed, and that I am alive and well this morning. Keep me from all danger this day. May I not do any thing that is wrong, but try to please thee and my dear parents by doing right; and may we all at last go to heaven, and be happy forever, for Jesus' sake. *Amen.*

ALMIGHTY God, my heavenly Father, the night and the day are alike to thee, for thou hast made them both. I should not be safe in the day, nor in the night, without thy kind care. I thank thee for thy care of me last night, and pray to thee to take care of me this day, and make me good, that I may please thee, and then I shall have a happy day. Oh hear my prayer, for Jesus Christ's sake. *Amen.*

HEAVENLY Father, I am glad to see the morning light. I thank thee for keeping me from harm all the night. Oh, please to take care of me all the day long, and make me to be one of those good children whom the kind Savior Jesus calls his lambs. *Amen.*

HEAVENLY Father, I thank thee for taking care of me all the night; please to take care of me all this day, and love me, and make me a very good child, and when I die take me to thyself in heaven, for my dear Savior's sake. *Amen.*

O GOD, my heavenly Father, bless me to-day, and make me a good child. May I always remember that the eye of God is upon me, and be afraid to do any thing wrong. Bless my father and mother, and sisters and brothers, and everybody, for the sake of Jesus Christ. *Amen.*

> I THANK thee, Lord, for quiet rest,
>   And for thy care of me;
> Oh! let me through this day be blest,
>   And kept from harm by thee.
>
> Oh, let me love thee! kind thou art
>   To children such as I;
> Give me a gentle, holy heart,
>   Be thoū my friend on high!
>
> Help me to please my parents dear,
>   And do whate'er they tell;
> Bless all my friends, both far and near,
>   And keep them safe and well. *Amen.*

EVENING PRAYERS

O LORD, I thank thee for thy care over me this day; and I pray thee to keep me safe this night. If I have done anything that is wrong, forgive me, for Jesus' sake, and may I do so no more. Bless my dear father and mother, and all my friends, and make us all happy, here and forever. *Amen.*

O GOD, my heavenly Father, bless me; forgive me all I have done wrong this day. Oh take care of me, and my father, and mother, and sisters, and brothers, this night; love us all, for the sake of Jesus Christ. *Amen.*

HEAVENLY Father, before I go to sleep, I pray thee to forgive me for having done some naughty things this day. Take care of me this night, holy Father, and let me awake in the morning well. Make me a better child than I ever have been. Bless all my relations and friends, and may the blessed Jesus be our Savior. *Amen.*

Jesus, heavenly Shepherd, hear me:
    Bless thy little lamb to-night;
Through the darkness be thou near me,
    Watch my sleep till morning light.

All this day thy hand has led me,
    And I thank thee for thy care;
Thou hast warm'd, and fed, and clothed me,—
    Listen to my evening prayer.

May my sins be all forgiven;
    Bless the friends I love so well;
When I die, take me to heaven,
    Happy there with thee to dwell. *Amen.*

THE LORD'S PRAYER

OUR Father God, who art in heaven,
To thy great name be reverence given;
Thy peaceful kingdom wide extend,
And reign, O Lord, till time shall end.

Thy sacred will on earth be done,
As 'tis by angels round the throne;
And let us every day be fed
With earthly, and with heavenly bread.

Our sins forgive, and teach us thus
To pardon those who injure us;
Our shield in all temptations prove,
And every evil far remove.

Thine is the kingdom to control,
And thine the power to save the soul;
Great be the glory of thy name,
Let every creature say—*Amen.*

LORD, look upon a little child,
By nature sinful, rude, and wild;
Oh! let thy grace descend on me,
And make me all I ought to be!

Make me thy child, a child of God,
Washed in the Savior's precious blood,
And my whole heart from sin set free—
A little vessel full of thee.

Dear Savior, take me to thy breast,
And bless me that I may be blest;
Both when I wake, and when I sleep,
Thy little lamb in safety keep. *Amen.*

THOU from whom we never part,
    Thou whose love is everywhere,
Thou who seest every heart,
    Listen to our evening prayer.

Father! fill our souls with love,
    Love unfailing, full, and free,
Love no injuries can move,
    Love that ever rests on thee.

Heavenly Father! through the night
    Keep us safe from every ill;
Cheerful as the morning light,
    May we wake to do thy will. *Amen.*

Now I lay me down to sleep,
I pray the Lord my soul to keep;
If I should die before I wake,
I pray the Lord my soul to take. *Amen.*

IMPROVED VERSION.

Now when I lay me down to sleep
I give my soul to Christ to keep;
Wake I at morn, or wake I never,
I give my soul to Christ forever. *Amen.*

THANKS to thee, thou God of love!
For all thy blessings from above;
Pardon my sins, for Jesus' sake;
My all into thy keeping take. *Amen.*

JESUS, Savior, dearest Lord!
Wash me in thy precious blood
I thy little lamb would be;
Help me, Lord, to look to thee. *Amen.*

MY Savior, who art meek and mild,
Look down and see a little child
Obedient at thy footstool stay,
And help me by thy grace to pray.

Teach me to understand thy word,
And wash me in thy precious blood.
Thy faithful lamb I fain would be;
Assist me, Lord, to look to thee. *Amen.*

Lord, prepare me for my end;
To my heart thy Spirit send;
Help me, Jesus, thee to love;
Take my soul to heaven above. *Amen.*

FOR SABBATH-SCHOOLS

GRANT, O Lord, thy heavenly grace to the Sunday-schools and other institutions for the religious instruction of the children and youth of thy flock. Make the teachers of these children duly sensible of the great charge committed to their trust. Endue them plenteously with thy heavenly gifts, and make them faithful in training up the young in thy fear and service, that they may from the heart believe in thee, the Lord their God, and worship and serve thee, their Creator, Redeemer, and Sanctifier; that they may renounce the devil and all his works, the pomps and vanities of this wicked world, and all the sinful desires of the flesh, and keep thy holy will and commandments, and walk in the same all the days of their life. Graft in their hearts the love of thy name; increase in them true religion; nourish them with all goodness; and by thy great mercy keep them in the same, that so, in the end, they may obtain everlasting life, through Jesus Christ our only Redeemer. *Amen.*

FOR SABBATH-SCHOOLS

OUR heavenly Father, we humbly implore thy blessing on all teachers and scholars of Sabbath-schools. Enlighten by the Holy Spirit all teachers, that they may truly understand thy word. Make them the true friends of Jesus Christ. May they be endowed with his spirit of self-denial, patience, humility, and prayer. May they evermore copy the example of Him who, when on earth, said, Suffer little children, and forbid them not to come unto me. While engaged in instructing the rising generation, in leading others to the cross of Christ, may they themselves be interested in thy promises, and sanctified by all their efforts to promote thy glory. And grant, O gracious God, that their labors may be attended with thy blessing. Do thou send down thy Spirit on all Sunday-schools, that the rising generation may grow up in the knowledge of Jesus Christ, and in preparation for great usefulness in the church and in the State. May schools be established in all the destitute places of our land, and all the means used to enlarge and perpetuate these blessings be crowned with success. Never suffer the zeal of thy people to languish in this cause, or thy ministers to forget their obligations to use every influence in their power to promote the religious training of the rising generation. Hear and answer the prayers which this day may have been offered in behalf of Sunday-schools, excite in all thy people a spirit of benevolence, and fill the earth with thy glory. Hear us, we beseech thee, and grant our prayer, for Christ's sake. *Amen.*

FORM

FOR THE USE OF SUNDAY-SCHOOLS

Before Prayer, a portion selected from the Bible may be read, and a suitable Hymn sung by the children. The Superintendent or Teacher may then read this exhortation:

MY dear children, before you enter upon your Sunday-school exercises, it is your duty to implore the blessing of Almighty God, your Maker and your Judge. Remember that his all-seeing eye beholds all your thoughts, as well as your actions, and abhors the outward worship of the lips, in which the heart is not engaged. Let this consideration cause you to look up for the influence of the Holy Spirit, that your hearts may be filled with reverence and godly fear, and that you may be enabled, through the mediation of Jesus Christ our Savior, to worship the great God, who is a Spirit, in spirit and in truth.

Superintendent. Lift up your hearts.*

Children. We lift them up unto the Lord.

S. Oh come, let us worship and bow down; let us kneel before the Lord our Maker. Ps. 95:6.

C. For thou, Lord, art good, and ready to forgive, and plenteous in mercy unto all them that call upon thee. Ps. 86:5.

S. So teach us to number our days, that we may apply our hearts unto wisdom. Ps. 90:12.

C. Oh satisfy us early with thy mercy, that we may rejoice and be glad all our days. Ps. 90:14.

S. The wicked shall be turned into hell, and all the nations that forget God. Ps. 9:17.

C. Create in me a clean heart, O God, and renew a right spirit within me. Ps. 51:10.

S. This is the day which the Lord hath made; we will rejoice and be glad in it. Ps. 118:24.

C. We will go into his tabernacle; we will worship at his footstool. Ps. 132:7.

S. How amiable are thy tabernacles, O Lord of hosts! Ps. 84:1.

C. For a day in thy courts is better than a thousand: I had rather be a door-keeper in the house of God, than to dwell in the tents of wickedness. Ps. 84:10.

S. Glory be to the Father, and to the Son, and to the Holy Ghost.

C. As it was in the beginning, is now, and ever shall be, world without end. *Amen.*

S. Let us pray. (*All shall kneel down.*)

O Lord, our most merciful Redeemer, who didst take up little children in thine arms, and didst bless them, look down graciously on us, and bless us also. We confess that we are miserable sinners; from the youngest to the eldest of us, we have erred and strayed from thee like lost sheep. But, O Lord, have mercy on us; turn us, and so shall we be turned; and wash away all our guilt in the blood of Jesus Christ, our only Mediator and Advocate. O thou, who out of the mouths of babes and sucklings hast ordained praise, fill our hearts, we beseech thee, with love and our lips with thanksgiving. To thy goodness we owe every blessing we enjoy. While other children are suffering hunger, and disease, and cold, thou art doing us good by day and by night, and giving us food, and health, and raiment. We bless thee for these thy mercies towards us; but, above all, we bless thee for the redeeming love of Christ, for all the means of grace, and for the hope of glory. O God, the Creator and Preserver of all mankind, we beseech thee for all sorts and conditions of men. Bless the country and all the officers of government; bless thy church, and give her speedy victory over all her enemies; bless all Sunday-schools, with their officers and teachers, and make them more and more useful. Let thy blessing descend also upon the ministers of thy gospel; and may thy kingdom be established in the hearts of all people. Look down in mercy on our relations and friends, and teach them to value thy favor above life itself. Finally, we beseech thee to bless us, even us also; help us to improve the hours we spend within these walls; as scholars, make us obedient to our teachers and affectionate to our companions.

Especially bless us on this holy day. May thy presence dwell with us in thy house of prayer; enable us to worship thee in spirit and in truth, and prevent us from being drowsy or forgetful hearers of thy word.

Open our understandings to understand the holy Scriptures. Endue our souls with every holy disposition, and preserve us from the corruptions and evils which are in the world. We ask every blessing, for the sake of Jesus Christ, our Savior. *Amen.*

THE grace of our Lord Jesus Christ, and the love of God, and the fellowship of the Holy Ghost, be with us all, evermore. *Amen.*

www.ingramcontent.com/pod-product-compliance
Lightning Source LLC
Chambersburg PA
CBHW051814090426
42736CB00011B/1479